Matthias Bosse

Using TurboCAD® in technica

Matthias Bosse

Using TurboCAD® in technical professions

For draftsmen, technicians, and engineers

1st Edition

Matthias Bosse completed an apprenticeship as a draftsman and then a bachelor's and master's degree at the Cologne University of Applied Sciences in the field of process and supply engineering. During his training and later professional career, he gained experience with various CAD software (including SolidWorks®, AutoCAD®, MagiCAD®, MicroStation®) and subsequently got to know the different working methods and program designs. As a mechanical engineer in shipbuilding in Hamburg, he came in contact with the software TurboCAD®. He quickly familiarized himself with it through training and the almost daily use of the software. He currently works as an independent design engineer under the name of CryoCAD Consulting & Engineering (www.cryocad.com) and offers design services in the areas of mechanical engineering and plant design as well as offering TurboCAD® training.

Bibliographic information of the German National Library: The German National Library lists this publication in the German National Bibliography, detailed bibliographic data are available on the Internet at http://dnb.dnb.de.

ISBN: 9783746098708

1st Edition (July 2018)

Production and publishing: BoD – Books on Demand, Norderstedt, Germany

Foreword

A word from the author:

When choosing the listed TurboCAD® tools, I followed my own way of working. Often there are different ways to get the same results. This is particularly evident in the tasks of the "Getting started" chapter. For example, just because I decide not to use some features due to having bad experiences with them, this doesn't mean that other users don't find them useful for their particular working practices.

Suggestions for improvement are welcome and can be directed to info@cryocad.com. As with many CAD programs, you always discover new ways to get the desired result. This book is not intended as a substitute for the official software help, which can be viewed in the program under "Help" online and offline.

Acknowledgments:

My thanks go to Bob Mayer, Josh Horsman, Sivoney Rodríguez Núñez, Darryl Impey and Wolfgang Sagroll.

1 TABLE OF CONTENTS

PREFACE

This book aims to help companies, the self-employed, and individuals looking for cost-effective CAD software that provides the basic and necessary tools for computer-aided design in 2D and 3D without having to pay tens of thousands of Dollars for a single user license. Also, users who are already working with TurboCAD® will receive important tips on how to use the software in order to improve their previous working methods and to familiarize themselves with unknown features.

The book contains a detailed program description and shows the first steps in dealing with TurboCAD®. In addition, it contains tips and tricks for two and three-dimensional drawing, which are specifically designed to make working in technical professions more efficient, so as to save time and money.

The possibilities and limits of TurboCAD® are shown, so that the reader can decide whether the available tools meet their own requirements.

The cost of a full version license of TurboCAD® Pro Platinum, the high-end product of the TurboCAD® series, costs substantially less than other professional CAD software available on the market. The 2D version is already under a hundred Dollars to purchase. The high price spike to established CAD software such as SolidWorks® or AutoCAD® is not always justified for a company with its own design department, due to the fact that TurboCAD® also provides useful tools for creating technical drawings and usually offers solutions for basic requirements of drawing production.

When implemented in the enterprise, TurboCAD® offers the ability to use centrally stored standard templates and symbol libraries, making design standards easy to develop and maintain. It supports the import of all popular CAD exchange formats and thus proves to be an all-round interface for converting drawings.

It offers a versatile layer structure and allows history-based modeling to be undertaken. Section and detail views can be derived from 3D models and generated BOMs. Large drawings can be split by using external block references.

The US-based company IMSI Design with its TurboCAD® software does not appeal to a clear target group, even though a trend towards architecture and furniture construction is recognizable. Big names like SolidWorks®, Catia®, NX®

or AutoCAD® have managed to establish themselves in certain sectors. However, TurboCAD® remains, probably due to its comparatively smaller distribution in the market, not pinned down to a specific target group and more flexible and broad to the user. Although the program contains many architectural features, it also offers features suitable for mechanical engineering purposes like standard parts libraries, a hole wizard, sheet metal bending tools and commands for inserting symbols for welds, surface roughness and shape and position tolerances.

With years of software development, the ever-expanding range of tools, through annual program updates, TurboCAD® now has a considerable number of commands, tools, and capabilities to create even the most challenging 3D models. An editing history makes it possible to see, intervene in and change previous work steps.

Many tools added in recent years are increasingly closing the gap between TurboCAD® and other established high-end CAD programs.

However, this jungle of tools, which by default are not intuitively arranged and named, makes it much harder to get the full potential out of the program. On the other hand, self-study is not adequately supported by the superficial and non-industry-specific online tutorials. Although the program's almost 2500-page program help guide explains the software right up to the smallest detail, it does not have the user at heart when getting to know and starting to use the program. Therefore, program training is often indispensable to use the software professionally. This book also addresses this problem and guides the user through the core areas of 2D drawing, 3D construction and drawing derivation using a practice-oriented example in a "step by step" tutorial. Based on this basic understanding of the structure and operation of TurboCAD®, the user can widen their knowledge as the book progresses, before being able to fully apply the software professionally.

For use in technical professions, the program can be redesigned with a few simple steps so that quick access to the necessary commands for creating CAD parts, assemblies and drawing derivations is possible. Which tools are specifically designed for this, and how the program can be tailored to their own needs, is shown in this book.

Comparison of Versions

TurboCAD® is available in different versions for both PC and MAC®. These versions are compared below for PC. All commands, tools, and procedures presented in this book refer to the TurboCAD® 2017 "Pro Platinum" version. However, many of the commands shown are already included in cheaper software packages such as the "Expert" version.

TurboCAD® Designer

The most affordable "Designer" package allows you to easily draw, modify, and dimension floor plans, engineering drawings, maps, and flowcharts in 2D using a variety of drawing tools. Compatible with over 20 industry-standard file formats, such as DWG, DXF or PDF, data exchange with the most popular CAD programs is possible.

TurboCAD® Deluxe

The "Deluxe" variant represents a hybrid of 2D and 3D CAD system. However, equipped with all 2D tools of the 2D variant, the tool palette is extended by some 3D features, allowing the conceptual modeling of simple 3D geometries.

TurboCAD® Expert

TurboCAD® Expert comes with an AutoCAD®-like 2D drafting Interface option, a more extended tool palette and greater interoperability.

TurboCAD® Pro Platinum

The flagship "Pro Platinum" offers the full range of professional CAD tools for integrated design, editing, presentation and documentation. Architectural and design tools provide flexibility and control.

Comparison of versions

The following table lists the most important features and shows the similarities and differences between the four program versions. Further product features and decision support, which version would be suitable for your own requirements, can be found on the website www.turbocad.com.

Table 1 TurboCAD® Versions in direct comparison

Version:	Pro Platinum	Expert	Deluxe	Designer
UI & PERFORMANCE				
Windows 64-bit and 32-bit Compatible	✓	✓	✓	✓
Design Director - for object property management	✓	✓	✓	
Layer Management	✓	✓	✓	✓
Easy, Handle-Based Editing	✓	✓	✓	✓
Conceptual Selector	✓	✓		
Fully Customizable User Interface and Preferences	✓	✓	✓	✓
ePack with New Intelligent File Send	✓			
Layer Filters	✓	✓	✓	
Command Line with Dynamic Input Cursor	✓	✓		
2D DRAFTING & EDITING				
2D Geometric and Dimension Constraints	✓			
2D Drawing, Editing and Modifying	✓	✓	✓	✓
Advanced Drawing Tools (Gear, Surface Tolerance, Text along Curve)	✓			
Arrow tools	✓	✓		
Auto Tools (for Scaling, Sizing, Positioning, Rotating, and Movement)	✓	✓	✓	✓
Bezier and Fair Curves	✓	✓		
Drafting and Detailing Palette - create associative sections and cut planes	✓			
Hatch Pattern Creator & Gradient Fills	✓	✓		
PDF Underlay Tool	✓	✓		
Purge Tool	✓			
Smart and Quick Dimension Tools	✓	✓	✓	✓
3D DRAWING, MODELING, & EDITING				
Assembly Tools	✓	✓	✓	
3D Booleans - Add, Subtract, Intersection	✓	✓	✓	
3D Helix	✓	✓	✓	
3D Patterns from Compound Profiles	✓			
3D Splines and Polylines	✓	✓	✓	
3D Surface Primitives	✓	✓	✓	
Extrude (simple)	✓	✓	✓	
Part Tree/History Tree	✓			
Sweep	✓	✓	✓	

Comparison of versions

Revolve	✓	✓	✓	
ACIS® Solid Modeling	✓			
Sheet Metal Tools	✓			
Mirror Copy Tool for 3D Objects	✓	✓	✓	
Advanced Blending Functionality	✓			
3D Slice by Facet	✓			
Slot Tools	✓	✓	✓	
DATABASE AND PROGRAMMATIC SUPPORT; CONTENT				
Blocks, Block Editor and Xref Support	✓	✓	✓	✓
Internal Database and Custom Data; External Database Connectivity	✓	✓		
Parametric Parts Editor for 2D and 3D parts creation and management	✓			
Symbols, Part Library	✓	✓	✓	✓
INTEROPERABILITY				
Adobe 3D PDF (.U3D and .PRC) Export	✓	U3D only		
3D Printer Support via .STL Import and Export	✓	✓	✓	
Import and Open File Formats	41	25	22	15
Export of Coordinate Data	✓	✓		
Export, Save As, and Publish File Formats	34	27	23	16
Network License Support	✓	✓	✓	

1 GETTING STARTED

The chapter "Getting Started" includes exercises whose goal is to provide the user with a fast but sound and practical introduction to the TurboCAD® software. It covers the CAD core areas of 2D drawing, 3D design and drawing derivation. The user is guided through the tasks step by step and gets to know the structure of the user interface as well as the handling of basic drawing and modification commands. The chapter "Getting Started" is to be understood as a self-contained chapter. In addition, cross-chapter references are given, which provide further explanations when needed. The tasks are simultaneously aimed at both CAD beginners and experienced professionals.

The exercises can be performed with the TurboCAD® versions "Deluxe", "Expert" and "Pro Platinum". Given that only basic commands are used, older versions of the program can be adopted. The exercises were created with the TurboCAD® Pro Platinum 2017 version and are based on an unchanged user interface and program setting, straight after installation.

If required, a 30-day demo of the various program versions can be downloaded from the website of TurboCAD®. These offer the full range of tools and are therefore well suited to getting to know the software.

During program installation, the default paths are recommended. Depending on the hardware available, graphical representations and program handling may vary. The system requirements of the manufacturer should be taken into account to ensure proper operation.

If significant graphics problems occur, you can first select "GDI" under "Options/ Setup programs/ Native drawing". A restart is usually required to make the change effective. If the graphics problems persist, the TurboCAD® support service should be contacted.

All questions and suggestions for improvement are welcome and can be directed to info@cryocad.com.

> The subsequent value entries and illustrations usually require a metric unit system. If an English unit system is activated after installing TurboCAD®, you can switch to a metric system under "Options/ Drawing Setup/ Space Units" as shown in Figure 3-16 on page 106.

1.1 GETTING TO KNOW THE USER INTERFACE

In the first part of this task, you will get to know the user interface (UI) of TurboCAD®.

➔ Start your TurboCAD® Version.
➔ Choose the option "New from Scratch" in the "New TurboCAD 2017 Drawing" menu.

If your graphics card is not supported, a message will appear. This must be confirmed with "OK". The exercise can still be done. If TurboCAD® is to be used in the 3D area, a suitable graphics card should be retrofitted in order to use the full potential of the CAD software.

Now a new drawing will be opened. First, familiarize yourself with the user interface. At the top of the screen the standard TurboCAD® menus can be found (File, Edit, View, etc.). Below these menus there is a toolbar with the standard Windows® commands such as "New", "Open" or "Save".

This is followed by a toolbar that controls object properties such as layer, color or line width (hereafter referred to as properties toolbar).

In the middle of the screen is the still empty model space, in which will be drawn later. This is surrounded by other toolbars and palettes. In the lower left corner of the model space are the tabs "Model" and "Paper1". The model space is used to create 2D and 3D objects, and the paper space is the later drawing sheet for the printout.

The inspector and status bars located at the bottom of the screen are used to enter values when executing various drawing and modification tools. The status bar at the bottom of the screen prompts you for certain actions and, further to the right of the screen, information is provided about the current coordinates of the mouse pointer. For more information on the UI layout, see Figure 2-1 on page 69.

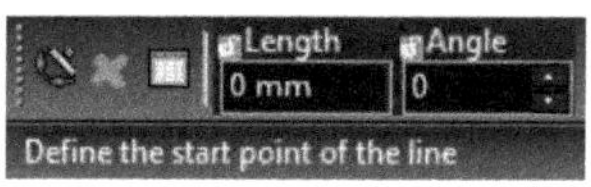

Now you will apply a drawing tool. When a new drawing is opened, the command "Line"  is activated. This is located in the left toolbar. The fact that a command is activated is indicated by the orange framing of the command symbol. Each icon in the toolbar corresponds to a command. If you move the mouse pointer over an icon and leave it there for a short time, the name of the command is automatically displayed. This helps to recognize and retrieve commands because the graphics are not always clear. Since the drawing command "Line" is already activated, the status bar at the bottom of the screen already prompts you to set the first point (starting point) of the line.

➔ Please click[1] anywhere in the model space. This sets the starting point of the line. Now when you move the mouse pointer, you notice that the endpoint of the line sticks to it.

➔ Move the mouse pointer and keep track of the information in the "Inspector Bar" ("Length" and "Angle") as well as the mouse pointer coordinates in the status bar.

➔ Now click anywhere in the model space again.

The line has been drawn. The line command then remains activated and more lines can now be drawn.

The zoom level can be adjusted with the mouse wheel.

➔ Now activate the "Select" tool  in the left toolbar.

One or more objects can be selected with the "Select" tool, for example, to move or query information. Activating the "Select" tool automatically terminates any activated commands.

➔ Click on the line you just created. When using the "Select" tool for the first time, the "Selection Info" palette may appear on the right side of the screen. If so, close the palette. It will be used later.

The line (shown below by way of example) now changes to the color magenta and is surrounded by a bounding rectangle (selector shell) which detects the outer boundaries of the line.

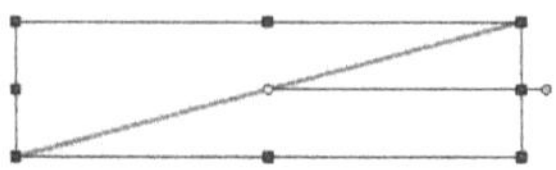

[1] Left mouse button. The use of the right mouse button or mouse wheel is explicitly mentioned.

➔ Make sure that the "Toggle 2D/3D" button, which is located in the Inspector bar, is activated. This means that the 2D mode is activated.

TurboCAD® has a 2D and 3D mode. In the subsequent parts of this exercise, first the 2D mode is used. More information on this topic can be found in chapter 5.3.

Now use the mouse wheel to familiarize yourself with the zoom function. By turning the mouse wheel, you can change the zoom factor and, for example, zoom in on a component. Note that the position of the mouse pointer during zooming controls where to zoom. You can also use the arrow keys on the keyboard or the scroll bars on the edge of the model space to move the view.

If you lose sight of what you are drawing while zooming, use the "Zoom Extents" command . This is located in the upper toolbar. The command increases or decreases the zoom factor to the extent that all objects in the drawing are displayed within the screen.

Now you will move and rotate the line that you have just created.

➔ Move the mouse pointer to the yellow dot (reference point) in the middle of the selector shell.

The mouse pointer changes to a four-arrow symbol.

➔ Click on the reference point.

The line now hangs on your mouse pointer and can be placed in any position, with another click.

➔ Now move the mouse pointer over the green point (rotation point).

The mouse pointer icon shows two circular arrows.

➔ Click on the rotation point and move the mouse pointer.

The drawn line can thus be rotated around the reference point. The rotation angle is displayed in the "Inspector Bar".

➔ Click the model space again to drop the line.
➔ Press the delete key.

This deletes the line.

This gives you a first impression of the structure of the user interface and the use of drawing commands in TurboCAD®.

The first task "Crane hook 2D" follows.

1.2 Crane hook 2D

In this task, you create a 2D drawing of a crane hook, as shown below.

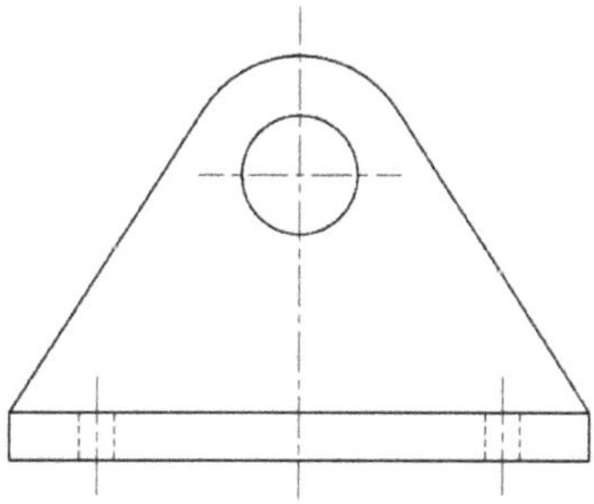

It covers the following topics:

- Simple line tools ("Line", "Parallel", "Circle center and point", "Tangent to Arc or Curve", "Bisector")
- Snap options ("Vertex", "Middle Point", "Center", "Quadrant Point")
- Layer structure (Create, edit and use layers)
- Moving objects
- Modification tools ("Mirror Copy", "Object Trim", "Offset", using the "Inspector Bar" and the "Selection Info" palette)

1. Before you start drawing, layers are first applied which control line properties such as color and thickness. With a layer structure, drawings can be built on several levels. These layers can contain objects, hatches, or dimensions. Each layer can then be shown or hidden individually without deleting the drawing objects on it. More information about "Layers" can be found in chapter 2.7.

   ➔ Use the "Layers" command in the properties toolbar to open the Layer menu.

   ➔ Add three more layers in succession to the existing layer using the "New Layer" command . Name these layers "Contour", "Hidden" and "Centerline".

   Apply the line style and pen width settings as shown in the following figure.

   ➔ To do this, click on the corresponding fields and select from the given line styles or pen widths.

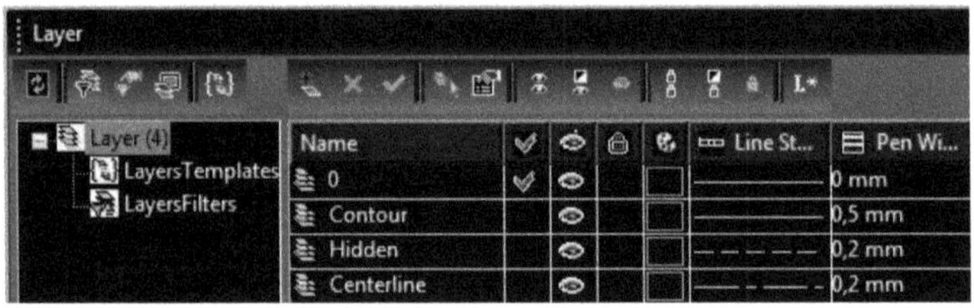

   ➔ Close the menu.

2. You will now start by drawing the base plate of the crane hook, which is created from four individual lines.

   ➔ Activate the drawing command "Line" again.

   ➔ Then, in the properties toolbar, change the layer to "Contour" as shown below, and change the other values to "By Layer" for the next three fields (Color, Line Style, and Pen Width). In the color menu, the selection "By Layer" is made by using the following icon: .

The aforementioned object properties are now controlled via the adjusted layer. If you change the layer of an object, it automatically adopts the properties that were stored in the Layer menu. Further information on the object properties and the layer structure can be found in chapters 2.7 und 2.8.

3. The "Line" command should still be activated (indicated by the orange symbol frame ).
   ➔ If this is not the case, activate it now.

Instead of randomly setting the starting point of the first line as previously shown in chapter 1.1, it is now set to the origin point with the coordinates X=0, Y=0. The "TAB" key can be used to change to the input fields of the inspector and status bar. This technique is often easier than marking the input fields with the mouse pointer.

➔ Press the "TAB" key three times in succession.

You will see how the input fields are selected from left to right one after the other. If you have pressed the "TAB" button too many times, keep pressing it until you reach the desired input field again.

➔ If the selection remains in the X coordinate field at the bottom right of the screen (indicated by the blue background color), enter the value "0".
➔ Press the "TAB" key again.
➔ Also enter the value "0" in the now selected Y coordinate field.
➔ Press the "ENTER" key.

This sets the starting point of the line in the coordinates X = 0, Y = 0.

If you move the mouse pointer over the model area, the endpoint hangs on the mouse pointer again. Instead of setting the endpoint with a mouse click, the line can be defined by its length and angle or, as before at the start point, by entering the coordinates.
➔ Use the "TAB" key again to jump to the "Length" field and enter the value "100".

Units do not have to be specified.

➔ Do not press the "ENTER" key, but jump to the next field "Angle" with the "TAB" key.
➔ Enter the value "0" there.

➔ Confirm the line command with "ENTER".

The line has been created.

4. Click the "Zoom Extents" command . The 100 mm long horizontal line is now displayed in the center of the screen.

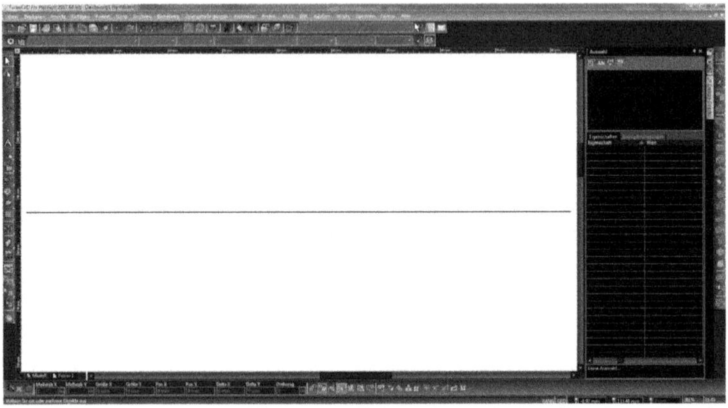

5. In the next step, a second line parallel to the existing line is created. For this the command "Parallel"  is used.

➔ Click on the "Line" command  on the left hand side of the screen again except this time hold the mouse button down.

This opens a drop-down menu that contains other line commands. Drop-down menus are indicated by a small white triangle at the bottom right of the icon.

➔ Now select the command "Parallel"  from the second row.

If the menu closes again, the last used command of the drop-down menu is displayed. If the "Parallel" command  is activated, the line must first be selected by clicking on which parallel line is to be created.

➔ Click on the line.

Now the offset between the two lines must be specified.

➔ Use the "TAB" key to jump to the "Offset" field and enter the value "8".

➔ Confirm the entry with the "ENTER" key.

A new line has been created, which is parallel and with a distance of 8 mm to the first one. This is above the first line. If you enter a positive value in the "Offset" field, the parallel line will move horizontally upwards, and if it's a vertical one, it will jump to the right. With a negative value it will move downwards or to the left.

6. Use the mouse wheel to familiarize yourself with the zoom function. By turning the mouse wheel, you can change the zoom factor and, zoom in on a component. Note that the position of the mouse pointer during zooming controls where to zoom. You can also use the arrow keys on the keyboard to move the view. Even with the horizontal and vertical slide bars at the edge of the model area, the view can be moved. If you lose sight of the drawn image while zooming, use the command "Zoom Extents" .
   When holding down the mouse wheel and simultaneously moving the mouse, the drawing view might be rotated three-dimensionally. Lines are then displayed at an angle. The "World Plan" command  in the top toolbar returns you to the planar 2D view.
   ➔ Zoom in and move to adjust the view as shown below.

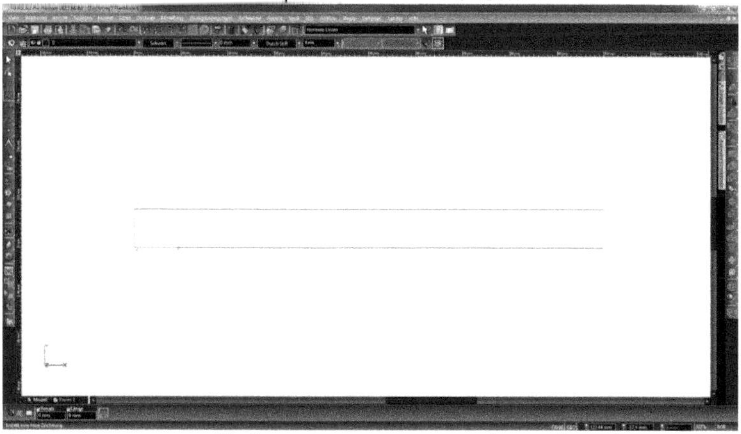

7. In the next step you will close the two open ends, each with a single line, using the snap options. Snap options allow precise placement of certain

object points, such as the ends or middle points of lines. In order to use these, some settings must first be made.

➔ Open the menu "Tools/ Customize".
➔ Switch to the tab "Toolbars".

This manages pre-set and custom toolbars.

➔ Activate the toolbar "Snap Modes".
➔ Close the "Customize" menu.

Now a toolbar has been added containing the most important snap options. These can be switched on and off individually here.

➔ Set the snap options according to the figure below. The snap options "Vertex", "Middle Point", "Center", "Intersection" and "Show Magnetic Point" must be activated.

Toolbars can be moved by clicking on the row of dots on the left edge of the bar with the mouse button held down and they can be pinned to the edge of the screen.

➔ Click with the right mouse button on the "SNAP" icon in the right area of the status bar.

The "Drawing Aids" menu opens. This contains further setting options for the snap options. On the right-hand side you will see the column "Priority". Here you can specify which snap options you would like to be offered.

➔ Set all snap options to 1.

As a result, all snap options are initially offered, and the user can then decide which one to choose.

➔ If checked, remove the checkmark in the "Grid" line.

Further information on the grid snap can be found in chapter 4.8.

➔ Close the menu with "OK".
➔ Make sure that the "SNAP" button is activated.

It can be switched on and off by clicking on the button. When turned off (shown by appearing in grey), no snap options are available.

- ➔ Select the "Line" command  again from the drop-down menu in the left toolbar.
- ➔ Move the mouse pointer slowly over the four endpoints of the already drawn lines.

You will see a small magenta diamond symbol at the end of the line. This signals that a snap option is available here. In addition, a symbol appears next to the mouse pointer, which is similar to the command symbol of the "Vertex"  snap option. The symbol shown next to the mouse pointer always tells you which snap option is offered. If these two indicators (diamond and symbol) are visible on the mouse pointer, a new line start point can be set exactly to the end of the existing line by a simple click.

- ➔ Click on the upper right end of the line.
- ➔ Move the mouse pointer over the underlying right endpoint of the bottom line.
- ➔ Click on it as soon as the "Vertex" snap option is offered.

Zoom in to make sure both points are accurately placed and there are no gaps between the vertical and horizontal lines. Catch options can also be selected and used with a right mouse click in the menu item "Local Snap" while the drawing command is activated. If a snap option is selected in this way, it will be the only one offered. Other snap options are ignored.

- ➔ Draw a second vertical line using the same procedure.

You have now created a rectangle measuring 100 x 8 mm from four individual lines.

8. You will now draw the crane eye and the upper curve of the crane hook.

- ➔ Activate the "Circle Center and Point" command  in the left toolbar.
- ➔ Make sure the properties toolbar is set as shown below.

- ➔ With the "Circle Center and Point" command  activated, move the mouse pointer over the middle of the upper horizontal line.

The snap option "Middle Point" should be available. If not, check the “Snap Modes” toolbar, which you have already added and set in step 7.

- ➔ Set the center of the circle in the middle of the upper horizontal line by clicking.
- ➔ Enter the value "20" in the "Diameter" field.
- ➔ Confirm the command by using the “ENTER” key.
- ➔ Place a second 40 mm diameter circle in the same position.

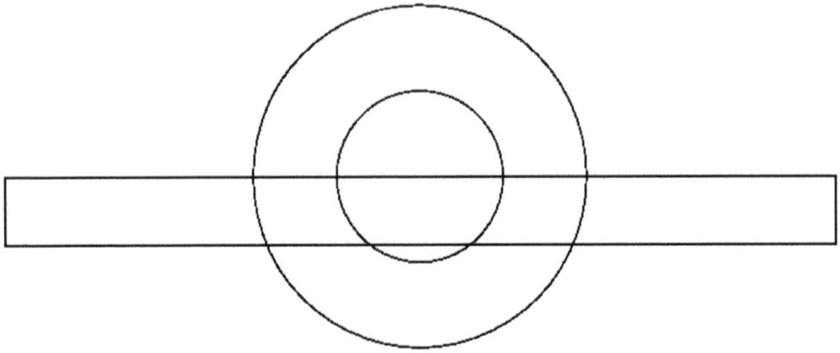

9. The two circles are now being moved. These must first be selected.

- ➔ Switch to the “Select” tool .

Multiple objects can either be selected by using a selection rectangle or individually added to the current selection by holding down the “Shift” key. When dragging a selection rectangle from left to right, only the objects that are completely within the purple shaded rectangle are selected. If you draw the selection rectangle from right to left, all objects are selected which come into contact with the now green shaded rectangle.

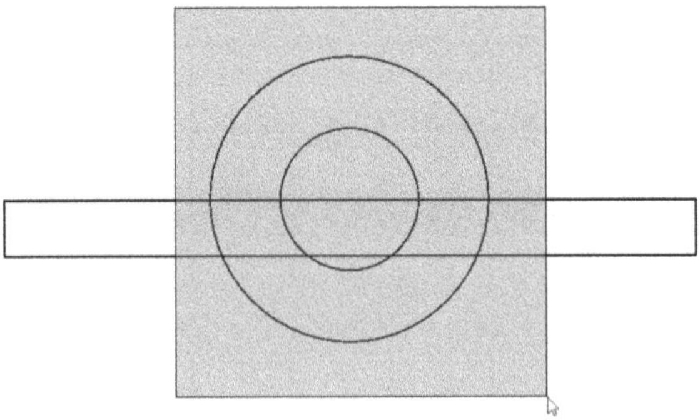

- ➔ Select the two circles.
- ➔ If the two circles are marked, they are shown in magenta.
- ➔ Enter 40 in the "Delta Y" field.
- ➔ Confirm with "ENTER".

The circles are now shifted in the Y direction by 40 mm. If necessary, use the "Zoom Extents" command  again to display the entire drawing in full screen.

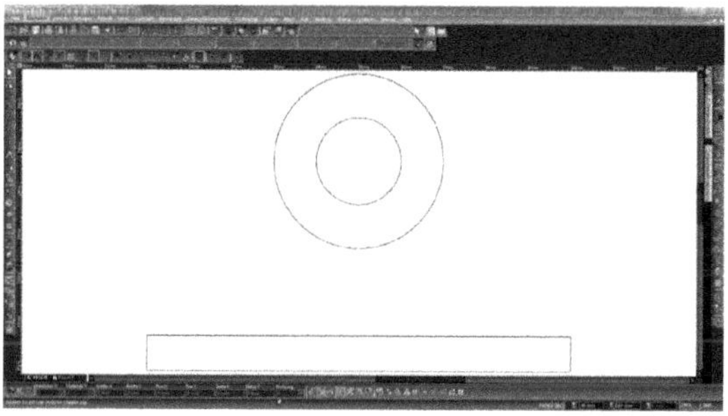

10. Now use the "Tangent from Arc or Curve" command to draw a line connecting the rectangle to the outer circle. The command is in the same drop-down menu as the previously used line commands.

- ➔ Activate the "Tangent from Arc or Curve" command .
- ➔ Click on the outer circle.

If you move the mouse pointer freely over the model space, you will see that the line is always tangent to the circle.

- ➔ Create both connection lines between the circle and the end points of the upper horizontal line as shown in the following figure.

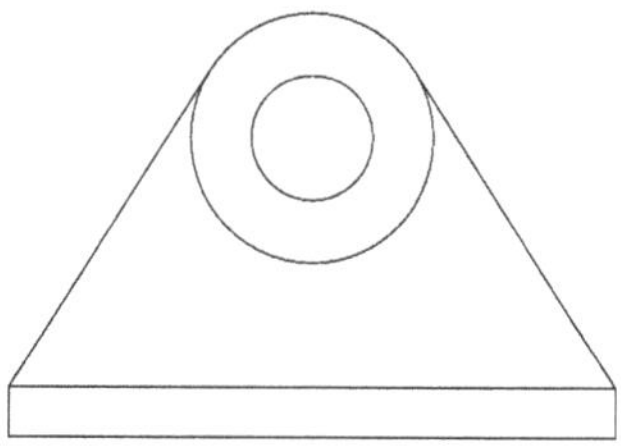

11. The lower part of the outer circle must now be trimmed.

- ➔ Activate the "Object Trim" command .

This is <u>inside</u> the second drop-down menu in the right toolbar.

➔ First select the two diagonal lines one after the other while holding down the "Shift" key.

These are displayed in magenta.

➔ Release the "Shift" key and click on the inner circle segment of the outer circle.

This is trimmed at the diagonal outlines.

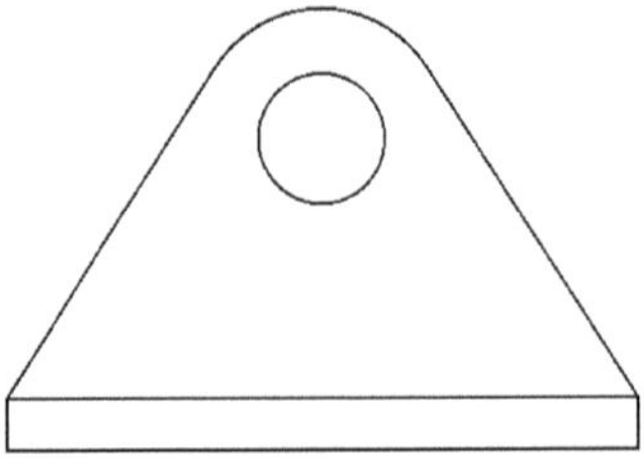

The visible edges of the 2D view of the crane hook are now drawn.

12. In the next steps, the holes in the base plate are represented by hidden lines and the entire drawing is provided with symmetry axes.
    ➔ Zoom in on the left area of the crane hook.

    ➔ Use the "Parallel" command  to create a line at 20 mm from the left vertical line.

    This will represent the centerline of the hole.

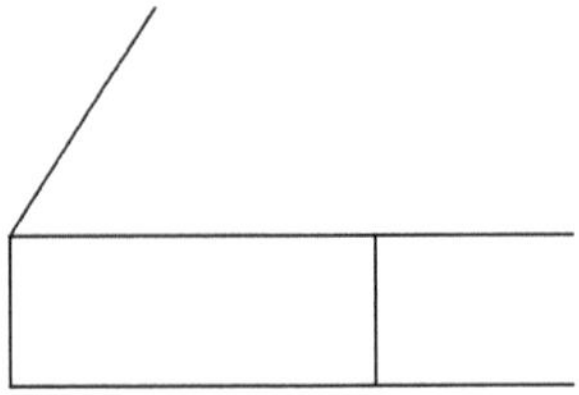

13. The "Offset" command  now creates two lines parallel from the hole's centerline, each spaced 3 mm apart. The "Offset" command in this

application is similar in function to the "Parallel" command, but it can also be used with bent or compound profiles[1].

➔ Activate the "Offset" command  in the first drop-down menu of the right-hand toolbar.
➔ Click on the centerline created in step 12.
➔ Enter an offset distance of 3 mm with a copy count ("Sets") of 2 and a "ZOffset" of 0 mm.

The position of the next click in the model area determines whether the offset line is created to the left or right of the centerline.

➔ Click to the left of the centerline.
➔ Run the command again.
➔ Click to the right of the centerline.

You have now drawn the edges of the hole.

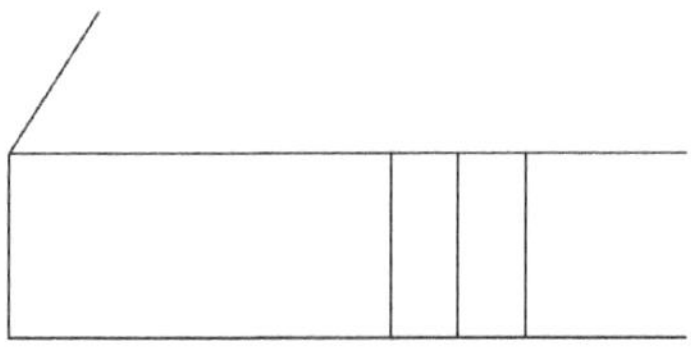

14. The three lines, which are to represent a hole in the base plate, lie on the "Contour" layer, due to the fact that they were derived from the outer contour lines by the command "Parallel" or "Offset".

    ➔ Mark the center line with the "Select" tool .
    ➔ Select the "Centerline" layer in the properties toolbar.
    ➔ Mark the two outer lines of the hole.
    ➔ In the properties toolbar, select the "Hidden" layer.

15. The centerline of the hole will now be resized to extend beyond the two horizontal lines.

    ➔ Mark the centerline.

    The panel should now show the following values:

[1] A compound profile is an open or closed chain of connected curves or lines

➔ Change the value in the "Size Y" box to 15 mm.

This extends the line from the yellow reference point from 8 to 15 mm.

16. You might notice that the line patterns defined in step 1 are not perfectly recognizable. The lines may still be shown as a solid line, although other line patterns have been selected in the "Layer" menu.

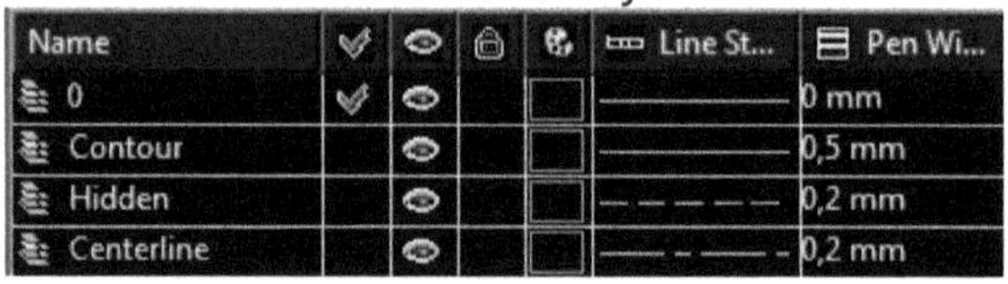

This is because the line scale that controls the lengths and spacing of the line patterns is too large for the drawn lines.

➔ Mark all three lines.

Use a selection rectangle as described in step 9.

➔ Click on the "Properties" button  in the "Inspector Bar".

The object properties now open. Entries automatically refer to all three marked lines at the same time.

➔ Navigate to the "Pen" menu.
➔ Enter a "Dash Scale" of 0,5 as shown below
➔ Check "Alignment".

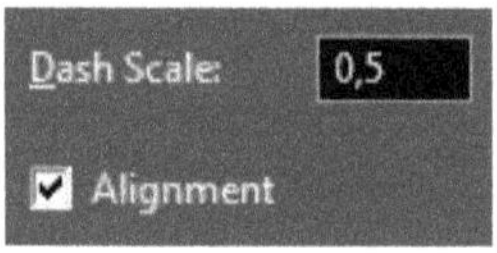

➔ Confirm with "OK".

Now the different bar patterns should be easily recognizable. If necessary, press the "F5" key to update the drawing.

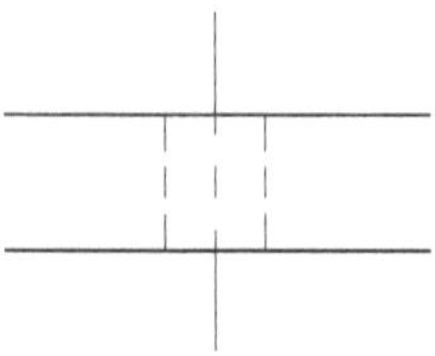

17. In the next step, the hole is also mirrored on the other side of the component.

- ➔ Run the "Zoom Extents" command  to show the entire drawing.
- ➔ Select the three lines of the hole.
- ➔ Activate the "Mirror Copy" command  in the first drop-down menu on the right-hand toolbar.

A mirror axis must be defined around which the selected objects are to be mirrored. The mirror axis is defined by a start and end point. Alternatively, a starting point can be set, and the direction of the axis can be defined via the angle in the "Inspector Bar".

- ➔ For the mirror axis, select the circle center with the snap option "Center" as the first reference.
- ➔ Define the mirror axis either by a second point (midpoint of a horizontal line) or by entering the angles 90 ° or 270 °.

The crane hook should now show two holes:

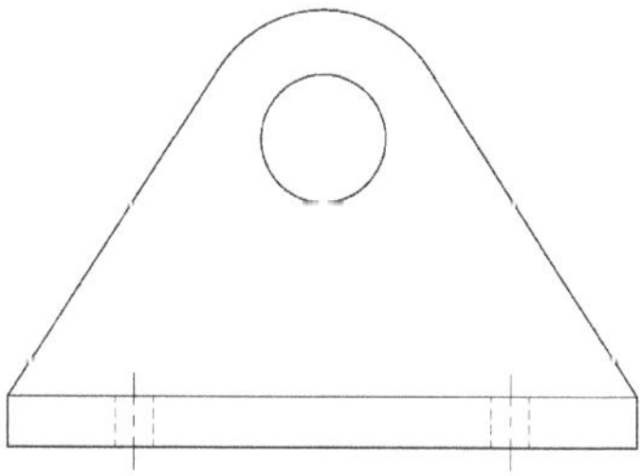

18. In this step, the remaining symmetry axes are added.

- ➔ Disable the snap options by activating the "No Snap" command .

These could become irritating in the following selection of lines.

- ➔ Activate the "Bisector" command .
- ➔ Follow the instructions in the "Status Bar" and select successively the two diagonal outer edges of the crane hook.

➔ Zoom out by turning the mouse wheel or using the "Zoom Out" command  in the top toolbar until you see the highest of the three blue nodes.

This represents the projected intersection of the two diagonal lines. Starting from this, an angle bisector can now be created.

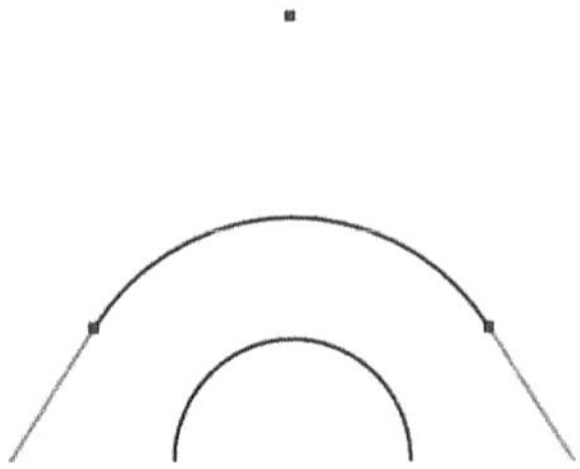

➔ Click once in the model space.

The length of the angle bisector can be determined by manually settling or by entering the length in the "Inspector Bar". The position of the mouse pointer also determines the direction. In this example, it should point downwards from the projected intersection point.

➔ Move the mouse to a position so that the bisector in the preview is facing down.
➔ Use the "TAB" key to jump to the "Length" box in the "Inspector Bar".
➔ Enter a value of "100".
➔ Confirm with ENTER.

19. The missing symmetry axis, horizontally through the crane eye, is now added.

➔ Activate the snap options by switching off the "No Snap"  command.
➔ With the "Line" command  and the "Quadrant Point"  snap option, you can now draw a horizontal line connecting the right and left quadrant points of the circle.
➔ Select this new line.
➔ Change the "Size X" box in the "Inspector Bar" to 30 mm.

20. With the “Format Painter” tool located in the top toolbar, formatting settings can be transferred from one object to another.

➔ Activate the “Format Painter” tool .
➔ Click on the centerline of one of the holes.
➔ Click on the newly created symmetry axes one after the other.
➔ Press the “ESC” tab.
➔ Activate the “Zoom Extents” command .

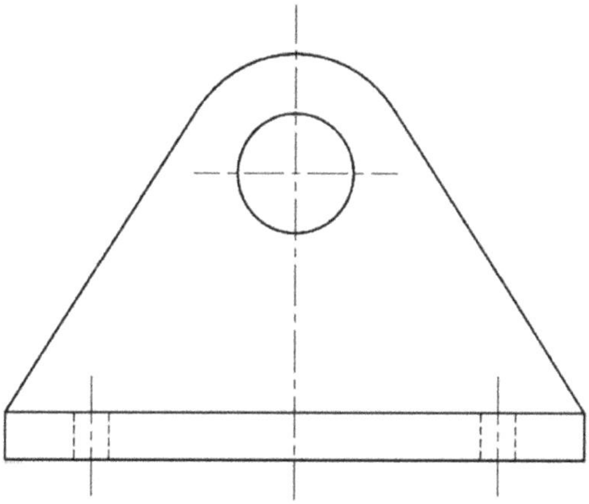

21. This concludes the task "Crane Hook 2D". In theory, a drawing derivation could already be created from this 2D view. The steps to create a drawing derivation in section 1.4 could be applied.
➔ Save the drawing on your desktop or a folder of your choice ("File/ Save As ...").
➔ Confirm the "Summary Info" menu with "OK".

The drawing will be needed to process the following task, "Crane hook 3D".

1.3 CRANE HOOK 3D

In this part of the "Getting Started" chapter, you will learn how to create a 3D model of the crane hook using the 2D drawing from the previous task.

It covers the following topics:

- 3D mode
- Creating a 3D body by extrusion
- Standard views and rendering modes
- Hole tool

1. The previously created 2D drawing is used in this task to create a 3D model of the crane hook by extrusion.
   ➔ Open the drawing from the task "Crane Hook 2D".
   ➔ Activate the "Select" tool .
   ➔ Switch to 3D mode with the "Toggle 2D/3D" command . The command is located in the "Inspector Bar".

   If the command symbol is <u>not</u> surrounded by an orange frame, the 3D mode is active. In addition to the X and Y coordinates, Z coordinates should also be listed in the "Inspector Bar".

2. To get a better orientation in 3D space, you will now activate a coordinate system. In addition, this part of the task shows the use of the selection list. This is especially important in 3D, as it simplifies the selection of objects.
   ➔ Open the menu "Options/ Program Setup/ Preferences".
   ➔ Check "Show world CS" and "Use Choice if several Entities in Aperture while selection".
   ➔ Confirm with "OK".

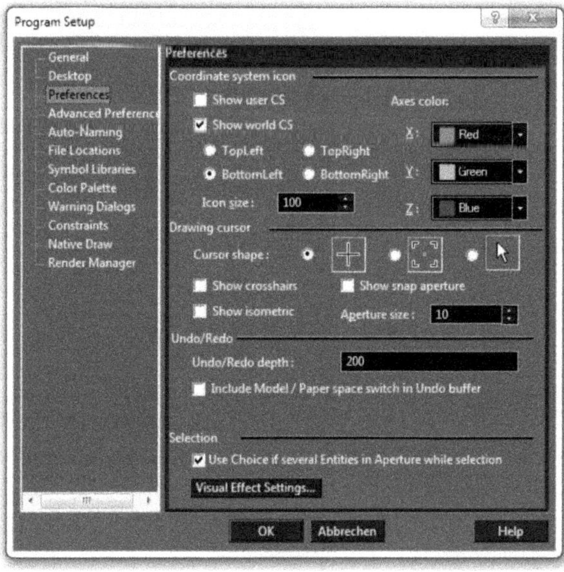

You will now see a coordinate system in the lower left corner of the model space. This coordinate system is oriented so that the x-axis points to the right, the y-axis to the top, and the z-axis to you.

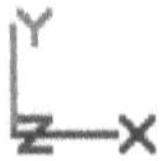

This is called the plan view. This view can be activated with the command "World Plan". The default views are located in the top toolbar in a drop-down menu, which is hidden behind the "World Plan" command. Click through the different views (Left, Front, and so on). As soon as you get to the "Isometric_SE"  view you will notice that the created 2D-drawing of the crane hook is not optimally aligned to start the 3D-modeling. The suffix "SE" stands for the direction southeast. The crane hook is not upright but lies horizontal. The Z axis should always be the height in a 3D model to use the default views of TurboCAD®.

➔ Switch to the "Isometric_SE" view .

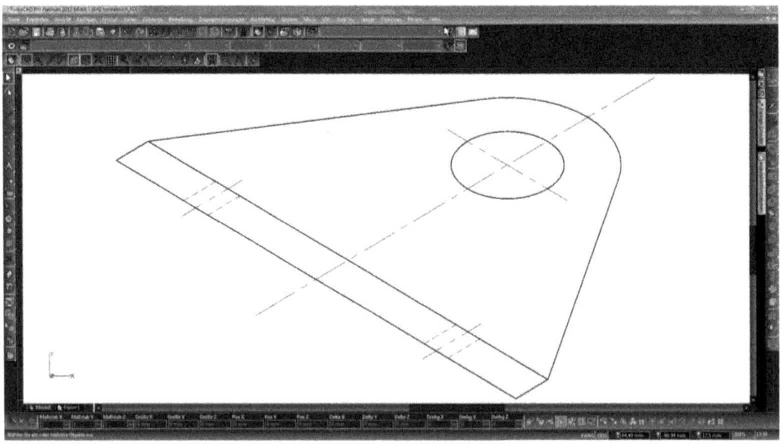

➔ Right-click anywhere in the model space and open the "Selector 3D Properties…" menu.
➔ Make sure that there is <u>no</u> check mark under "Selector 3D/ Configuration/ Use Conceptual".

More information about the conceptual selection tool can be found in chapter 5.9.

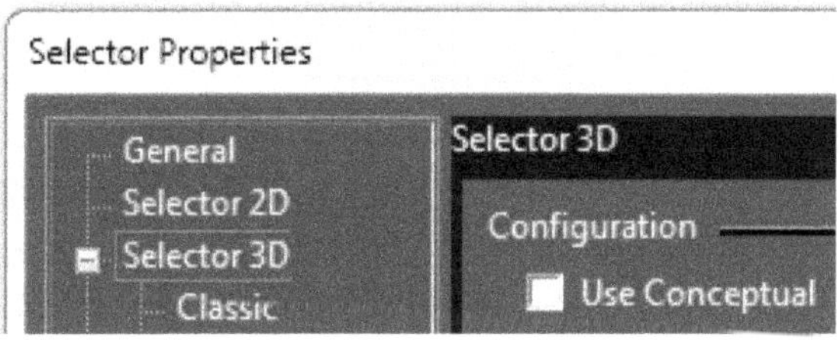

3. You will now rotate the 2D drawing, which will help you in the next steps to create the 3D model, by 90 °, thus raising the crane hook.
   ➔ Mark the <u>entire</u> drawing with a selection frame that captures all drawing objects or use the key combination "CTRL + A". [1]

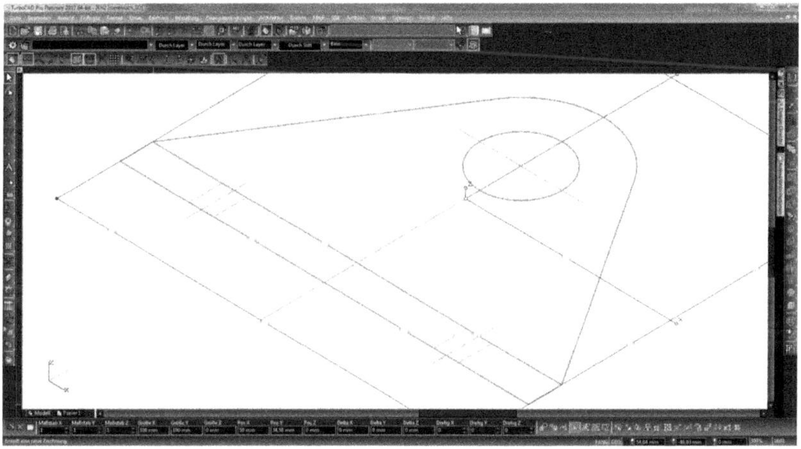

In the middle of the selection frame, which now covers the entire drawing, you will see a second coordinate system. At the origin, a yellow reference point is displayed, to which the position coordinates in the "Inspector Bar" refer. Furthermore, at the ends of the three axes, green rotation points are shown where the model can be rotated around the reference point. To raise the crane hook, in other words to turn it 90° around the lower

[1] The key combination "CTRL + A" selects all drawing objects that are in the model space

edge of the base plate, you must first move the reference point, and automatically with it the axis of rotation.

This technique of moving the reference point to realign objects is essential for working in TurboCAD® in both the 2D and 3D realm. Reference points and rotation points can be selected and moved while holding down the "CTRL" key.

➔ Press and hold down the "CTRL" key.
➔ Move the mouse pointer over the reference point.

The mouse pointer now has the shape of a hand.

➔ Click on the reference point ("CTRL" key still pressed).
➔ Release the "CTRL" key.

The reference point together with the coordinate system is now attached to the mouse pointer and can be placed anywhere.

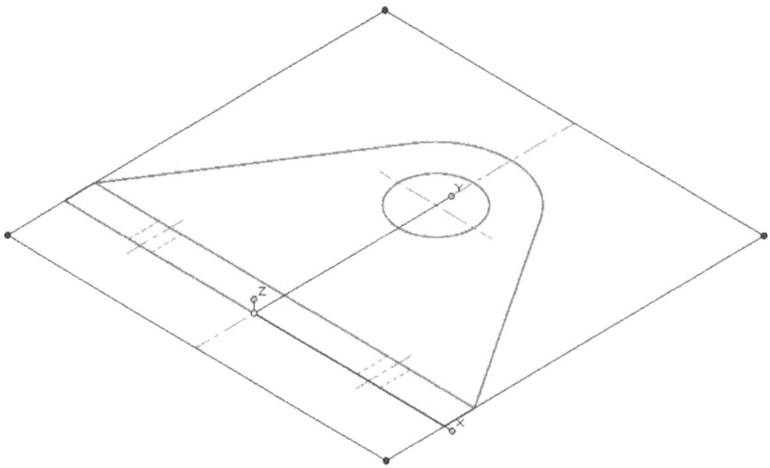

After the reference point is set, a system notification may appear.

➔ Place the yellow reference point as shown above, centered on the lower edge of the crane hook. You can specifically select the "Intercept" snap option while sticking the coordinate system to the mouse pointer by right-clicking the mouse and selecting the snap option from the "Local Snap" pop-up menu.
➔ Tick the box next to "Don't show this message again" and confirm the message by pressing "Yes".

4. You have now moved the reference point and can start turning the crane hook.
   - ➔ Click on the green Y-rotation point and move the mouse pointer. You can see that the whole model is spinning around the X-axis. It should be noted that with more distance between the mouse pointer and the reference point, the rotation can be performed smoother and more controlled.
   - ➔ Now enter the value "90" in the "Inspector Bar" box "Rot X". You can use the "TAB" key or the mouse to do this.
   - ➔ Confirm the entry with "ENTER".

   You have successfully rotated the drawing 90 ° around the X axis, aligning the crane hook to create the 3D model.

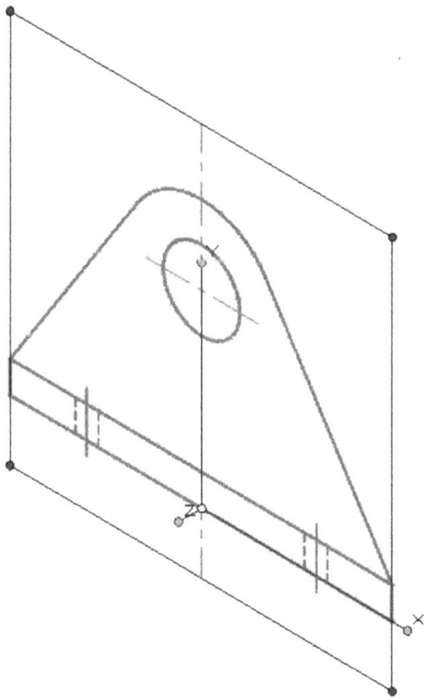

- ➔ Press the "ESC" key to deselect.
- ➔ Press the command "Isometric_SE" .

5. Create another layer named "3D-Object", as already shown in Step 1 of the "Crane hook 2D" exercise.

   ➔ Open the "Layer" menu with the "Layers" command in the properties toolbar.

   ➔ Click the "New Layer" button .
   ➔ Enter the name "3D-Object" and confirm with "OK".
   ➔ For this layer, set the default color to "Gray" as shown below. Line style and pen width remain unchanged.

Name	✓	👁	🔒	Color	Line St...	Pen Wi...
0		👁			————	0 mm
Contour	✓	👁			————	0,5 mm
Hidden		👁			– – – – –	0,2 mm
Centerline		👁			—— - —— -	0,2 mm
3D-Object		👁			————	0 mm

   ➔ Close the menu.
6. In the next step, a 3D body is created by extruding a 2D sketch (for example the extrusion of a circle to create a cylinder).

   ➔ Select the command "Simple Extrude" from the left toolbar.
   ➔ In the properties toolbar, choose the new layer "3D-Object" and set all parameters to the option "By Layer". In the color menu, select "By Layer" using the following icon: .

The "Simple Extrude" command on the "Inspector Bar" contains the "Height" field, which indicates to what extend the 2D profile is extruded, and the three command options, which are located to the right of the input field.

   ➔ Activate the option "Use Compound Profile" and "Two sided extrude" as shown below.

Now you have to select a profile to create the extrusion.

   ➔ Disable the snap options by activating the "No snap" command .

These could hinder you in choosing the 2D profile, as they tend to catch other nearby objects.

➔ First select one of the short side edges of the base plate.

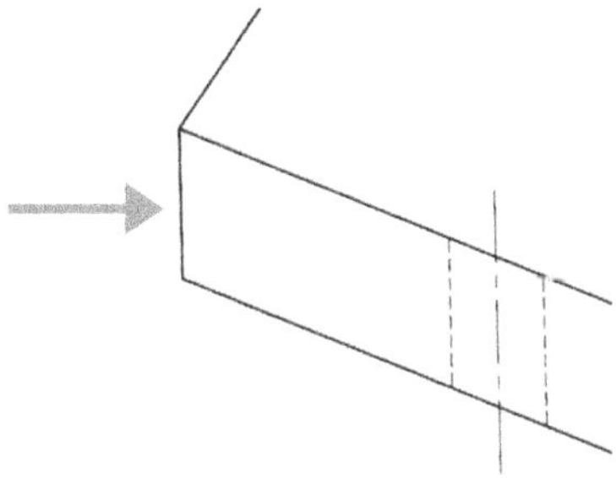

Not only this line, but also the lower edge and the opposite side are automatically included in the selection. If the command option "Use Compound Profile" is activated, contiguous line objects are automatically detected and selected.

➔ With the next click you add the line parallel to the lower edge of the selection. The selection should now include the lines as shown in the screenshot below.

If you now move the mouse in the model space, you will notice that the selected 2D profile will be extruded on both sides. You can define the extent of this extrusion by clicking the mouse, or by entering a height value.

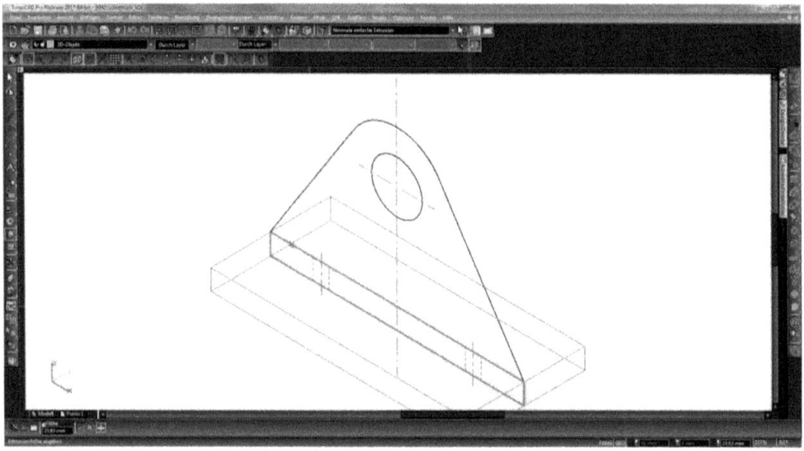

- ➔ Enter the value “20” in the “Height” field.
- ➔ Confirm the command with “ENTER”.

The selected 2D profile has now been expanded outwards on both sides by 20 mm each.

- ➔ Click again on the view “Isometric_SE” .

7. Next, the upper part of the crane hook with the crane eye is extruded and combined with the already created base plate on to a single 3D-body.

   - ➔ Activate the “Simple Extrude” command  again. This would have to have the same command options as in the last application. If not, set the above-mentioned options again (Layer to “3D-Object”, “Use Compound Profile” and “Two sided extrude”).
   - ➔ Click on one of the sloping side edges.

   Again, an automatic selection of further lines takes place.

   - ➔ To create a closed profile [1] for extrusion, with the next click, select the horizontal edge that joins the beveled outer edges.

[1] If an open profile is extruded, surfaces are created

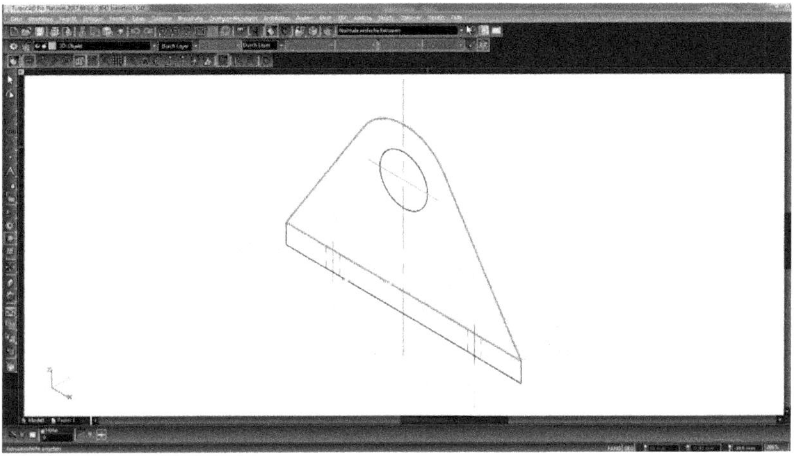

This profile could have already been turned into a solid. However, with TurboCAD® you have the opportunity to cut away nested profiles (compound profiles within each other). You can now use this option to map the eyelet. This would otherwise have to be removed from the model in a later step.

➔ Press the "Shift" key and move the mouse pointer over the circle.

A "±" sign appears next to the mouse pointer.

➔ Click on the circle.

This will be added to the existing selection. In the preview, you will see that where the circle is, a hole is created in the 3D rendering.

➔ Enter the value "4" in the "Height" box of the "Inspector Bar".
➔ Confirm with "ENTER".

➔ Switch the render mode "Hidden Line" .

This is located in a drop-down menu to the right of the "Properties Toolbar". If this rendering mode is selected, edges that would not actually be visible when viewing the 3D model, are shown in dashed lines. Depending on the existing hardware, the graphical representation may deviate from the figures shown in this task.

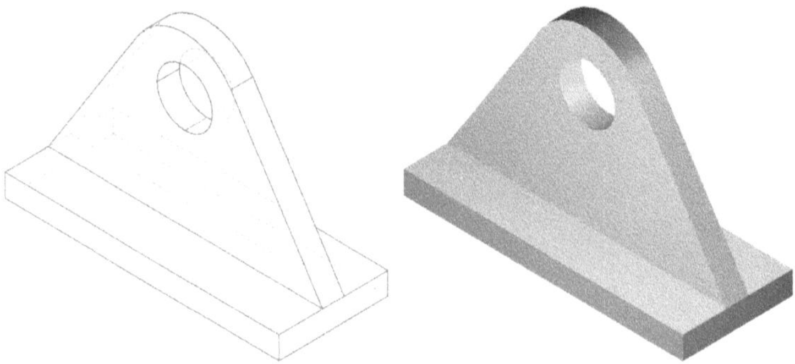

- ➔ Now switch to the mode "Draft". Since there are no light sources in the drawing, you will first be asked if you want to set default light sources.
- ➔ Confirm with "YES".

If the selected color appears too bright, a darker layer color can be selected as described in Step 5.

The render mode "Draft" provides a realistic view of 3D objects, as surfaces are filled in and shaded. The render modes "Quality" and "Advanced" are designed to create photorealistic renderings. Creating renderings to visualize 3D models is covered in chapter 5.13.

- ➔ Hold down the mouse wheel and move the mouse pointer.
- ➔ Now hold down the "Shift" key and move the mouse pointer over the model area while holding down the mouse wheel.

You dynamically pan around the 3D object. Take your time to look at the crane hook from all sides. If you have a 3D mouse, you can use it as well.

- ➔ Click on the standard view "Isometric_SE".
- ➔ Keep the render mode "Draft" activated for the next step.

8. Interesting values can be taken from selected objects via the "Inspector Bar".
   - ➔ Click on the base plate of the crane hook with the "Select" tool.

This is now surrounded by a selection box, which has blue dots on all corners. In the spatial center of this box, which has the exact size of the marked 3D object, is the reference point. In addition, the 2D profile is displayed in blue, which was used for the extrusion of the creation of the 3D body.

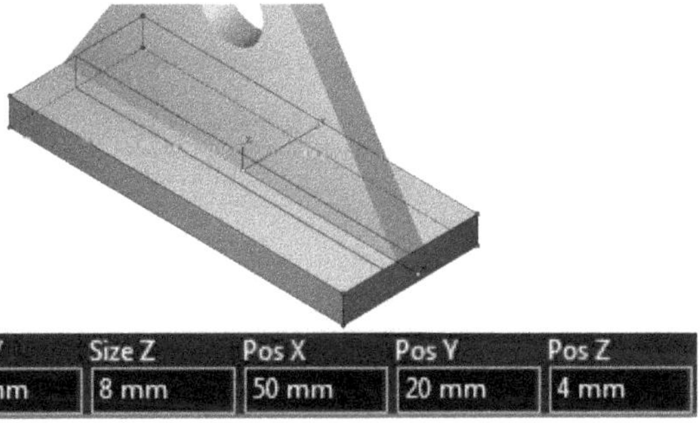

Since the selection frame in this case corresponds to the exact size of the base plate, its size can be read off from the values displayed in the "Inspector Bar". The size is 100x40x8 mm.

➔ Add the upper part of the crane hook to the selection by holding down the "Shift" key and clicking on it.

➔ Look at the selection box and the values in the "Inspector Bar".

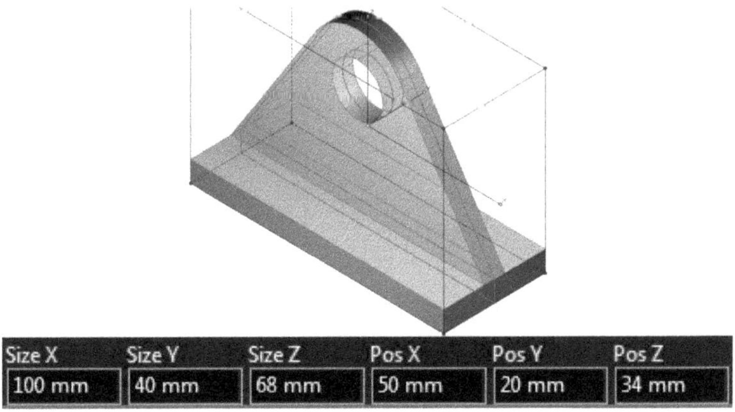

The overall dimensions of the crane hook are 100x40x68 mm.

9. More information about the created part can be found in the "Selection Info" palette.

➔ Keep the object selection.

➔ If the "Selection Info" menu isn't open on the right edge of the screen, open it under "Tools/ Palettes/ Selection Info ...".

The "Selection Info" palette now appears on the right side of the screen. Palettes automatically close after a certain time, if they are not used.

➔ In the open palette in the upper right corner, press the small pin icon.

If the needle is vertical, the palette is firmly attached to the edge of the screen and remains open.

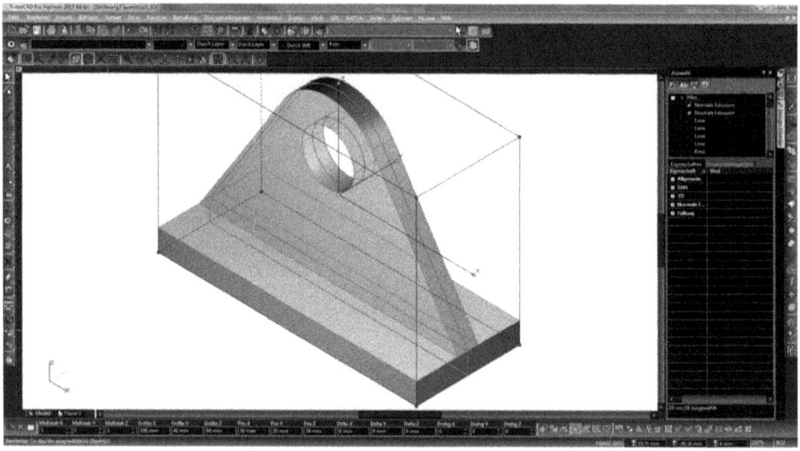

In the upper window of this menu all selected objects are listed. Look at this window. It lists the two extrusions.

10. You have already created a nice 3D model of the crane hook.

➔ Save the file using the "Save" command .

11. At this time, the 3D model of the crane hook still consists of <u>two</u> separate volumes, namely the base plate and the upright plate with the crane eye. With the command "3D Add" in the right toolbar, these two objects can now be merged into one body. When using this command for the first time, you will be asked if you want to deactivate the editing history ("Part

Tree"). The editing history is absolutely necessary for history based modeling and must therefore be activated.

- ➔ Now activate the command "3D Add" .
- ➔ Click on the 3D bodies one after the other. The order does not matter.
- ➔ In the above system note, press the "No" button.

The two bodies were now merged into one body. Once the 3D union has been performed, nothing changes in the graphical representation of the crane hook.

- ➔ Select the now merged 3D body and take another look at the "Selection Info" palette.

There is now a "PartTree" entry.

- ➔ Expand it with the plus sign.

The parts structure shows the chronological course of the processing steps of a part. At a later date, changes to the geometries are possible here. In the following exercise "Crane hook drawing derivation" this technique is exemplarily applied.

- ➔ Leave the "Selection Info" palette open.

In some cases, the "Selection Info" palette does not list a "PartTree" but an "ACIS Solid". This indicates that no editing history has been created (more information on the "PartTree" can be found in chapter 5.7).

If so, follow these steps:

- ➔ Undo the 3D union .
- ➔ Open the menu "Options/ Drawing Setup / ACIS" and check the box "Create Editing History (Part Tree)".
- ➔ Close the menu with "OK".
- ➔ Perform the command "3D Add" again as described above.

12. The base plate of the crane hook is now provided with four holes. To do this, use the "Add Holes" command later in this task. This can be used to create different types of holes (such as Counter Sink), but also to create bosses such as guiding pins. The "Add Holes" tool requires a 2D point for the exact position of the hole as well as a flat surface on which the drill hits vertically. To place the 2D point on top of the baseplate, you must first move the work plane. By default, the work plane is on the XY plane of the "World coordinate system", which was displayed in step 2 of this task.

➔ Activate the command "Show/ Hide WorkPlane" .

This command makes the current work plane visible. This is represented by a dashed red frame. However, this red frame does not represent a limitation of the work plane. It extends infinitely far.

➔ Disable the "Show/Hide WorkPlane" 

2D objects can only be drawn on the work plane. Instead of placing the 2D points on the current work plane and then moving them in the Z direction, in this exercise you move the work plane to the top of the base plate and place the 2D points directly on it.

➔ Switch to the render mode "Hidden Line" .

➔ Click with the right mouse button on the cup symbol shown.

The "Camera Properties" menu opens.

➔ Make sure that in the menu area "Hidden Line" a checkmark is set for the option "Nonrenderable objects".

This setting not only displays 3D objects but also 2D objects in the "Hidden Line" mode.

➔ Close the menu with "OK".

➔ If not currently set, activate the view "Isometric_SE" .

➔ End the selection with the "ESC" key.

The model should look something like the following:

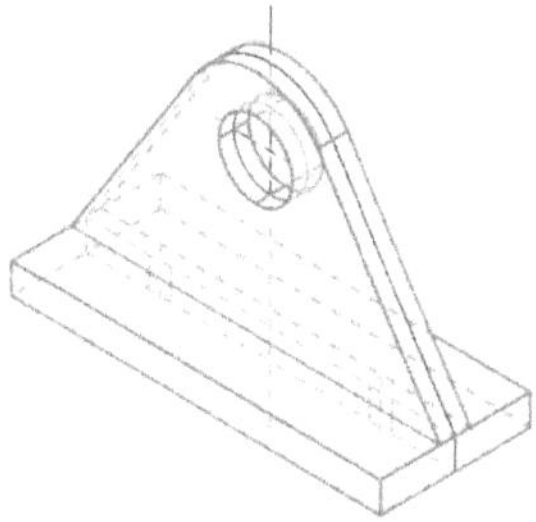

➔ Select the "By Facet" command  from the top toolbar.

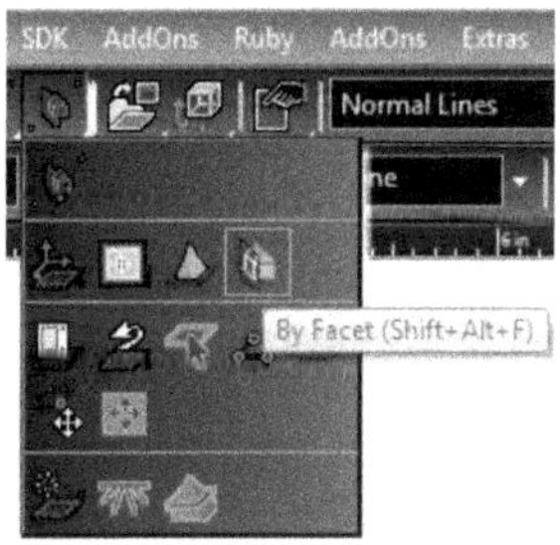

With this command, you can lay the work plane on a specific surface of a 3D body. If you hover over an area of the model, it will be highlighted in color. This signals that the work plane can be "stored" here.

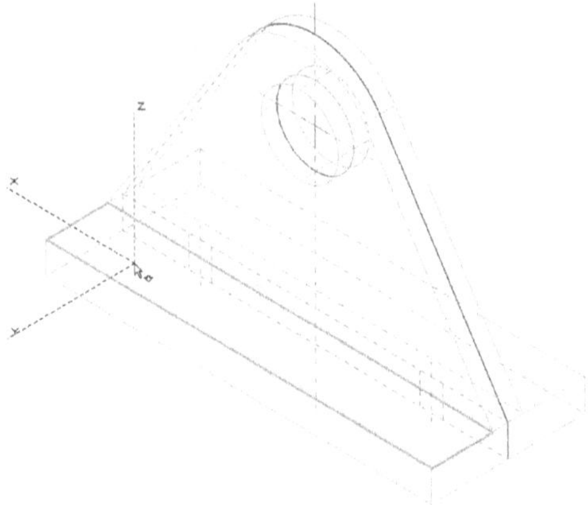

➔ Select the displayed area and click on it.

The work plane is now congruent with the selected surface. You can control this by showing or hiding the work plane with the command "Show/Hide WorkPlane" 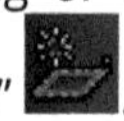.

13. In the next step, you will put so-called 2D points, which are needed to create the holes with the "Add Holes" command, on the work plane that you have just specified.

    ➔ Activate the command "Circle"  in the pop-up menu shown below.

    ➔ Place a 2D point exactly on the corner of the base plate as shown below using the snap options.

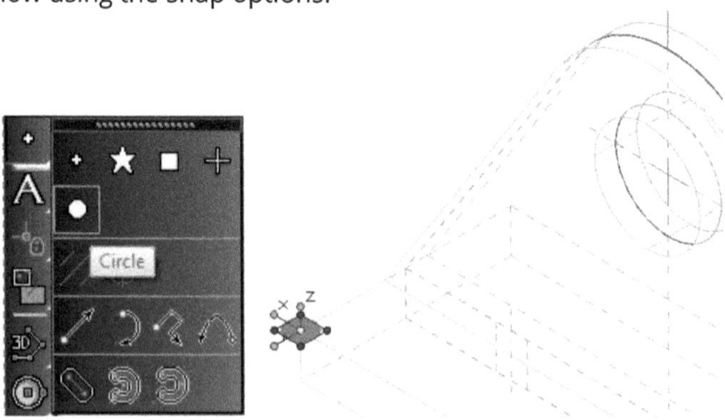

➔ Execute the command "Plane by World" . This is located in the same pop-up toolbar as the previously used command "By Facet" .

This returns the work plane to the default setting.

14. In this step, you will move the added 2D point inwards by 7.5 mm from the long edge and 20 mm from the short edge inward as shown in the figure below.

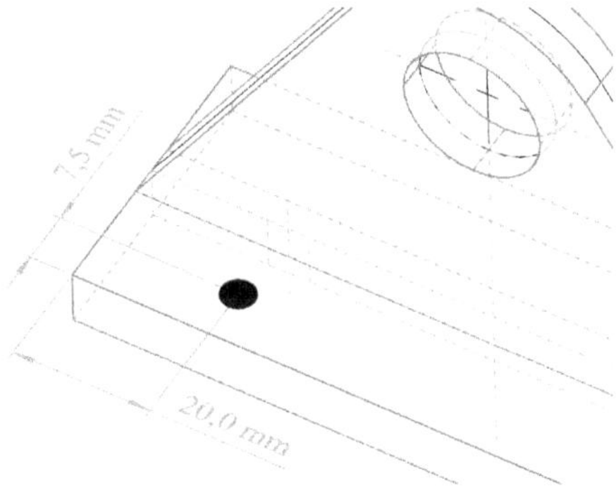

➔ Select the point and move it by entering values in the "Delta X" and "Delta Y" fields by 20 mm in the X direction and 7.5 mm in the Y direction.

Please note that the entries in the "Inspector Bar" refer to the coordinate system on the 2D point. If this is aligned differently than shown, adjust the input values accordingly. By setting a negative value, you can reverse the direction if necessary.

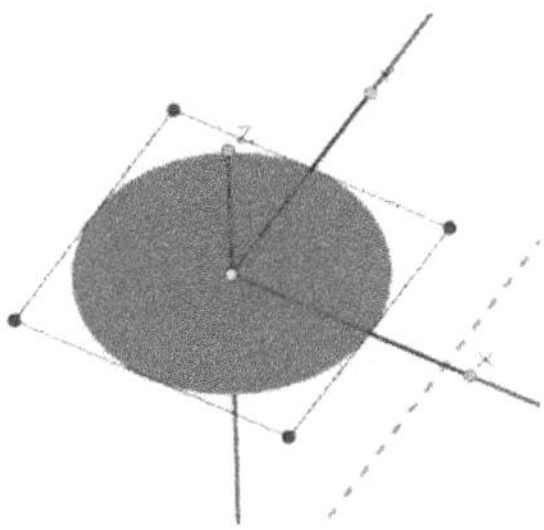

15. The set 2D point is now multiplied by the command "Mirror Copy". Use the mirror axes shown below. When using sample and mirror tools in 3D space, special attention must be paid to the selection of the correct snap points. Here, the selection of a specific snap option via the right-click menu selection is to be preferred, as otherwise other snap points may hinder the selection. Hold down the "Shift" key to add more items to a selection.

    ➔ Use the "Select" tool to select the existing 2D point.
    ➔ Activate the command "Mirror Copy" in the right toolbar.
    ➔ First define the left mirror axis as indicated below by defining the start and end point of the axis with two mouse clicks. The mirror axes <u>must be centered</u> so that the 2D points are mirrored exactly and all four points are the same distance from the outer edge of the base plate.
    ➔ Now select both 2D points while holding down the Shift key.
    ➔ Finally mirror them around the mirror axis shown on the right.

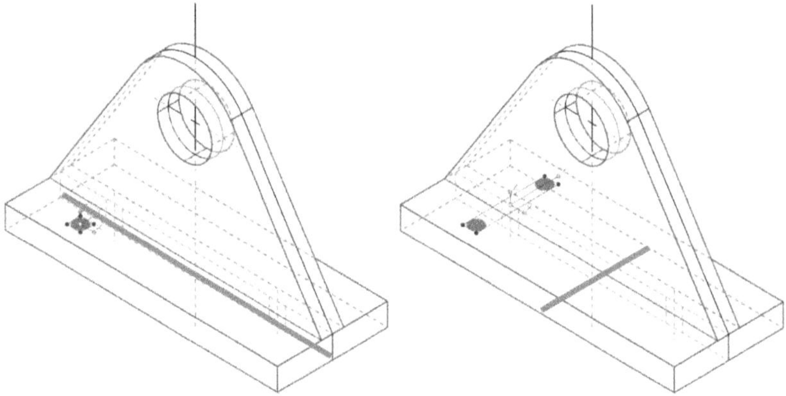

16. Once the four points have been set, the holes can be created.
    ➔ First deactivate the snap options by activating the command "No Snap". These are not needed.
    ➔ Execute the "Add Holes" command.

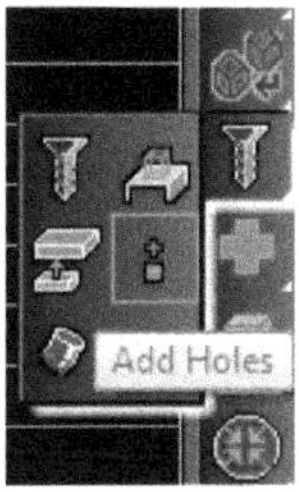

If this command is activated, the drilling surface must first be selected.

- ➔ Select the top of the base plate. This is highlighted in color.
- ➔ Then select all four 2D points one after the other whilst holding down on the "Shift" key.
- ➔ With the four points in the selection, set the hole properties in the "Selection Info" palette according to the following figure.

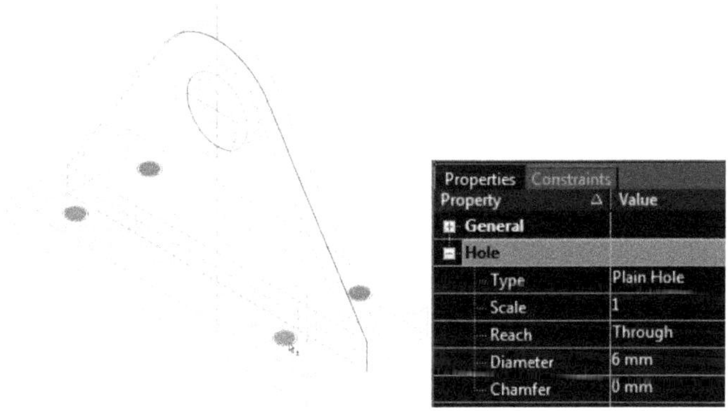

- ➔ Press the "Finish"  command in the "Inspector Bar". The holes are now added.

17. You have created the 3D model of the crane hook.

- ➔ Switch to render mode "Draft" .
- ➔ If necessary, disable the display of the 2D objects in the camera properties to get a better view of 3D model of the crane hook.

This completes the Step "Crane hook 3D".

- ➔ Save the drawing. This is needed to do the following task "Crane hook drawing derivation".

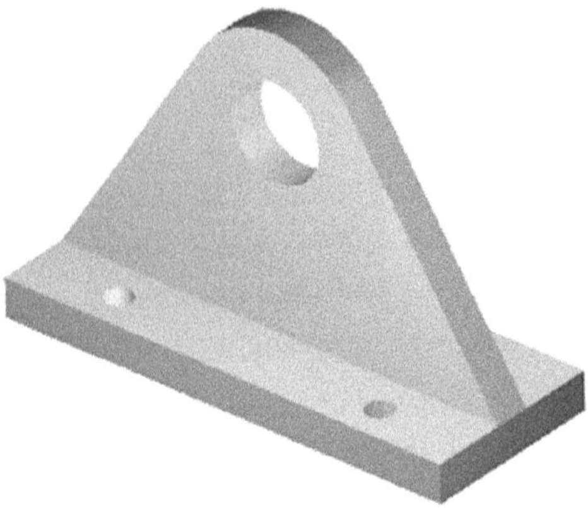

1.4 CRANE HOOK DRAWING DERIVATION

In this part of the tutorial you will create a drawing derivation of the crane hook in the paper space of TurboCAD®. You will create viewports that bring defined object views to the drawing sheet, which are provided with associative dimensions. At the end, you will intervene in the editing history of the crane hook and thus slightly change the 3D model.

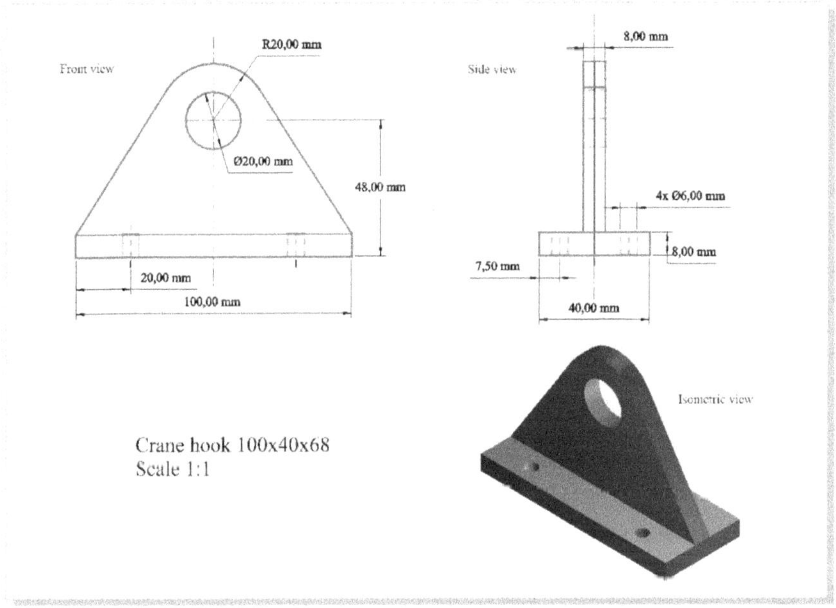

The following topics are covered:

- Viewports
- Dimensions and text notes
- Associativity between drawing objects and dimensions
- Editing history (Part Tree)

First of all, from different views of the crane hook, you will create so-called viewports, which enable the transfer of the draft or 3D model from the model space to the paper space.

- ➔ Open the previously created crane hook model from the exercise task "Crane hook 3D".
- ➔ Switch to the standard view "Front" .

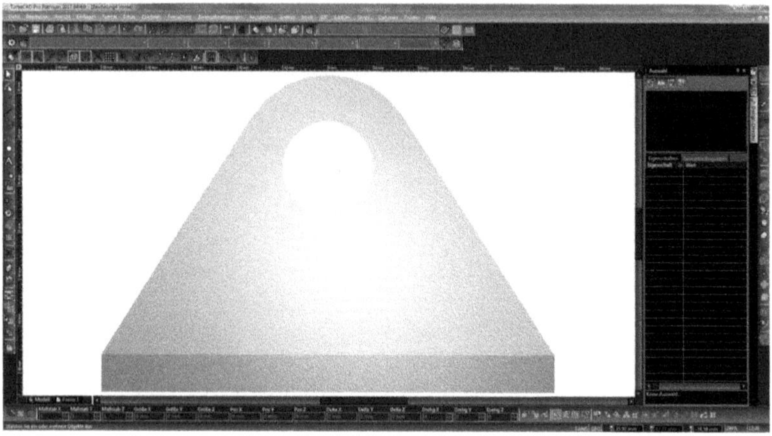

- ➔ Activate the command "Create View" in the left toolbar .
- ➔ Draw a selection frame around the entire crane hook.
- ➔ In the menu "Create Named View" type in the name "Front View".
- ➔ Press "OK".
- ➔ Switch to the standard view "Right" .
- ➔ Create a viewport named "Side View".
- ➔ Switch to the standard view "Isometric_SE" .
- ➔ Create a viewport named "Isometric View".

1. You have now created the views that are to be transferred to the paper space.
   ➔ Now open the menu window "View" with the command "Named view" . This lists all named drawing views. It should now look like this:

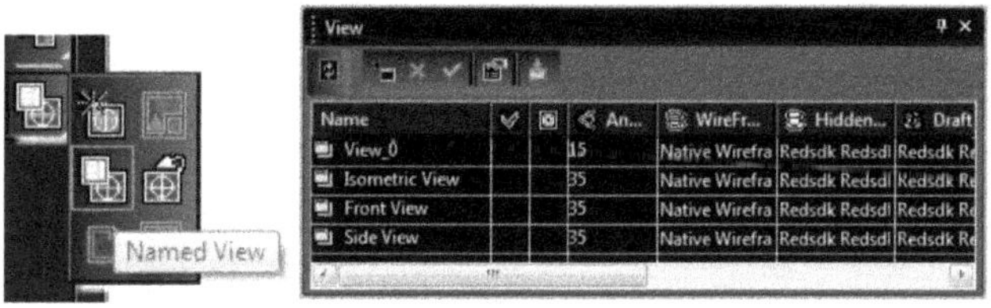

2. Now you will leave the model space in which the crane hook was modelled.
   ➔ Switch to the paper space by clicking on the "Paper 1" tab (in the lower left corner of the model space).

   The paper space is used to create drawing derivations. The previously created views are inserted here as viewports, scaled and then dimensioned. The white shaded area represents the drawing sheet. For more information, see chapter 6.

3. In this step, you take a look at the paper and printer properties of the paper space.
   ➔ Click with the right mouse button on the tab "Paper 1" and select "Properties...".
   ➔ In the field “Workspace name:” enter the name "DIN A4” instead of “Paper 1”.
   ➔ Navigate to the next menu item “Page Setup”.
   ➔ Set up a printer with which you will later print the drawing.

   It can also be an installed PDF printer.

   ➔ Set the paper size to A4 landscape for the printer and in the workspace sheet properties.
   ➔ Origin should be set to X=0 and Y=0.
   ➔ Close the menu with “OK”.

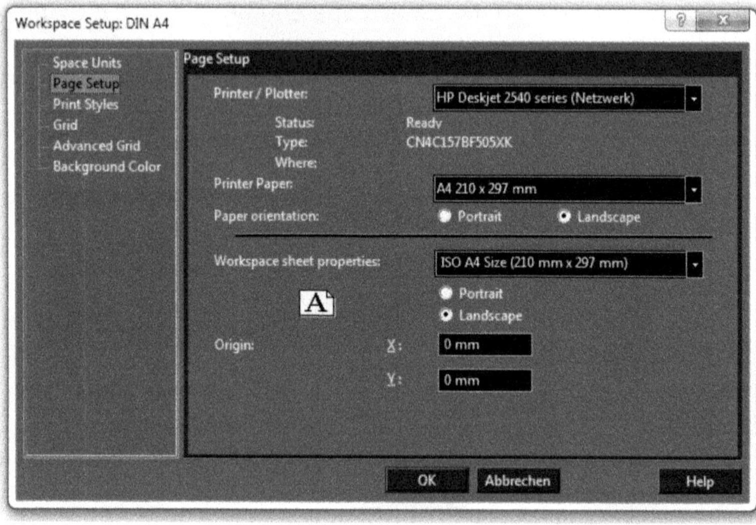

4. The previously created views of the crane hook are now inserted in the drawing sheet.

   ➔ Activate the command “Insert Viewport” .
   ➔ Drag a frame that fills approximately a quarter of the drawing sheet.
   ➔ Select the view “Front View”.
   ➔ Confirm with "Go to".
   ➔ Press “Close”.

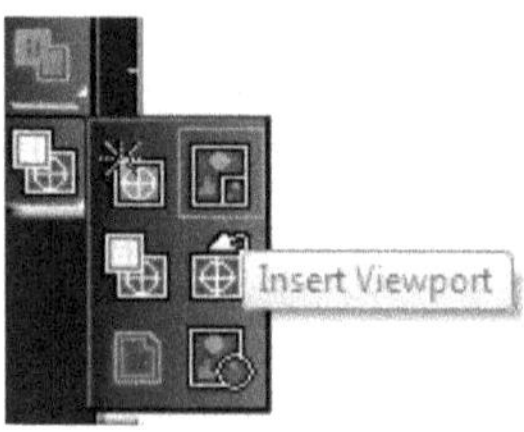

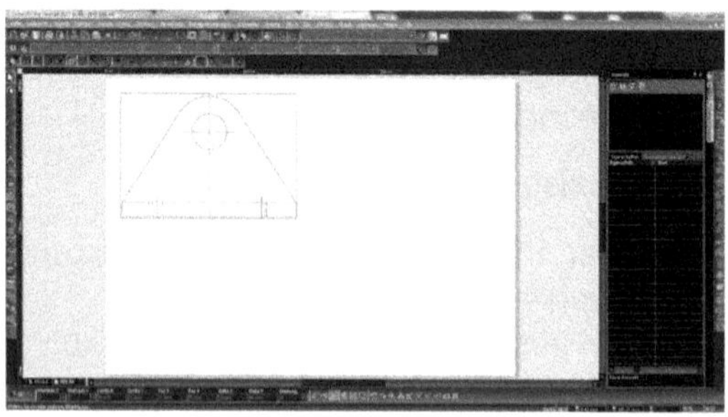

5. If a viewport is inserted, its scale is initially flexible. It adapts to the size of the viewport. You will now set the scale to 1:1. Furthermore, in the properties of the viewport you will change the selected render mode and the frame.

   ➔ Activate the "Select" tool .
   ➔ Double-click on the inserted viewport.
   ➔ In the "Viewport" menu tab in the "Scale" area, check the box "Fixed".
   ➔ Select the scale 1: 1 from the drop-down list.
   ➔ Under "Box" uncheck "Visible Box". This will remove the currently existing frame around the viewport.
   ➔ Activate the "Hidden Line" rendering mode in the left-hand navigation by ticking it.
   ➔ The option "Nonrenderable objects" shown in the right-hand area must be activated.
   ➔ Close the menu with "OK".

6. The rest of the viewports are now placed freehand on the drawing sheet. Use the following screenshot as a template and position the side view in the upper right corner and the isometric view in the lower right corner of the page. Then, the same settings from step 5 and 6 are applied to the new viewports.

   ➔ Insert the two viewports using the "Insert Viewport" command .
   ➔ Also set a 1:1 scale for the two views and remove the visible frame.
   ➔ For the isometric viewport, do not choose the "Hidden Line" mode, but "Draft".

   Viewports can be moved by their reference points, or by clicking on the object shown. After a viewport is selected, you can resize the window by dragging the blue nodes at the boundary frame. If, after setting the fixed scale, the whole of the drawing object isn't completely displayed due to the view window being initially made too small, the size can be adjusted accordingly.

   ➔ Save the file using the "Save" command .

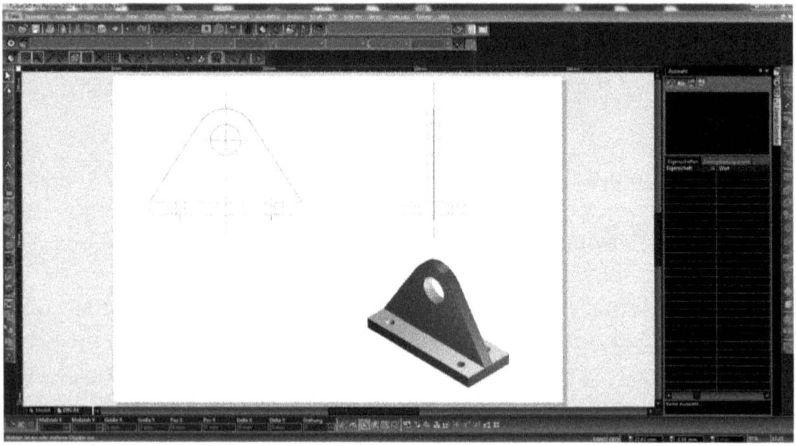

7. Zoom in on the front view, so that it is displayed full screen. Move the mouse pointer to the corresponding viewport and slowly turn the mouse wheel away from you. Alternatively, you can use the "Zoom Window" command .
   ➔ Activate the command and drag a narrow border around the viewport.

   The content of this frame is now displayed full screen.

8. You will now start with the dimensioning. This involves using the frequently used dimensioning options "Orthogonal" , "Smart" , "Radius"  und "Diameter" . The dimension commands are located in the left-hand toolbar in a drop-down menu.

   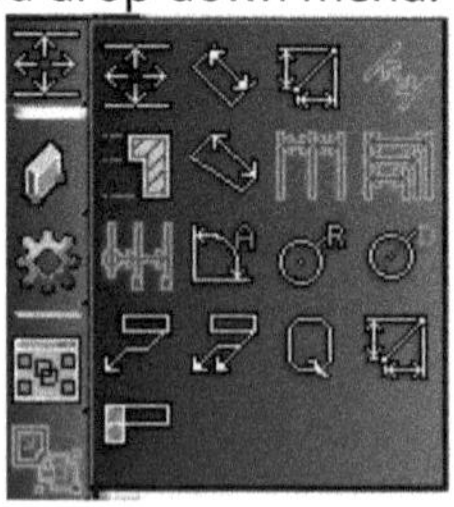

   Alternatively, they can also be selected in the "Dimension" menu in the menu bar at the top of the screen.

➔ Activate the "Orthogonal" command .

➔ Place a dimension between the left outer edge of the base plate and the nearest center hole, as shown below.

To set the dimension, you must define two points between which to do this. If these two points are not vertical or horizontal, the position of the dimension number determines whether the vertical or horizontal distance of the selected reference points is dimensioned. If you have defined two points, move the mouse pointer and set the dimension number as shown below. Always use snap tools to select dimension points within the "Orthogonal" dimension to avoid accidentally drawing a dimension that appears to touch the desired objects, but in truth does not accurately reach them. This can lead to incorrect dimensions and the dimension won't automatically adjust as the geometry changes.

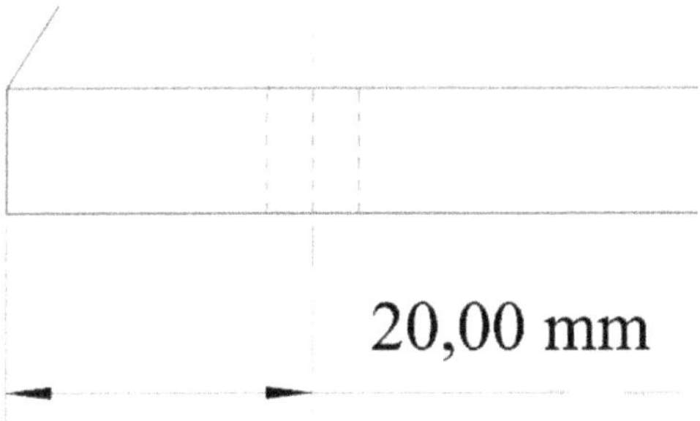

9. You will now measure the length of the base plate of the crane hook.

➔ Activate the "Smart" command " in the menu "Dimension".

➔ Click on the lower edge of the base plate.

It automatically creates a dimension that captures the entire length of the line.

➔ Place the dimension that you have just created below the first dimension with the next click as shown in the following figure.

If necessary, disable the snap options for this command. This will be obvious as there will be too many snap options and the mouse will jump around the screen trying to get them.

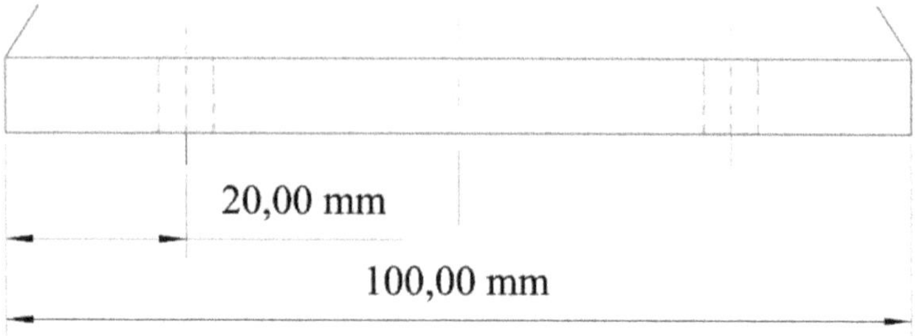

10. Now, the crane eyelet and the upper rounding of the crane hook are going to be dimensioned.

   ➔ Activate the command "Diameter" .
   ➔ Click on the circle of the crane eyelet.
   ➔ Place the dimension as shown below.

   ➔ Use the "Radius" command  to dimension the upper rounding as shown below.

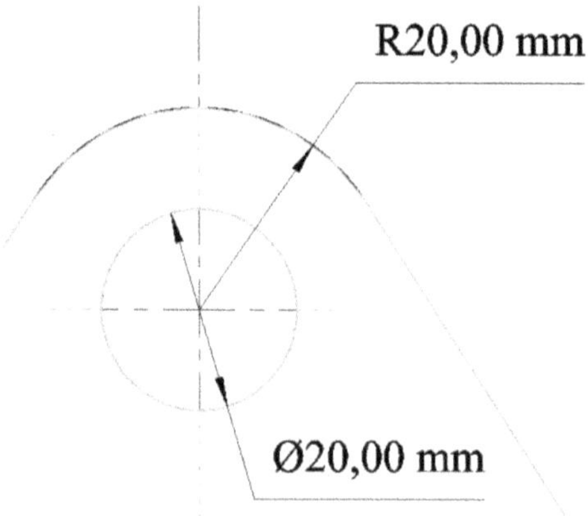

11. In this step, you will set the dimensions of the hole in the side view.
    - ➔ Zoom in on the side view of the crane hook.
    - ➔ Activate the command "Orthogonal" .
    - ➔ Dimension the right hole using snap options.

12. The diameter of the hole is missing the diameter symbol as well as further information.
    - ➔ Select the dimension.
    - ➔ Open the object properties of the dimension via the command "Properties"  in the "Inspector Bar".

    The input window "Attribute" contains the value "<6.00>". The brackets indicate that it is a controlled value that is dependent on the dimensioned object.

    - ➔ Set the additional value "4x Ø" before this value as shown below, since there are four holes with a diameter of 6 mm.

    The entry of a diameter symbol is made via the key combination "ALT" + 0 2 1 6.

    - ➔ Close the menu with "OK".

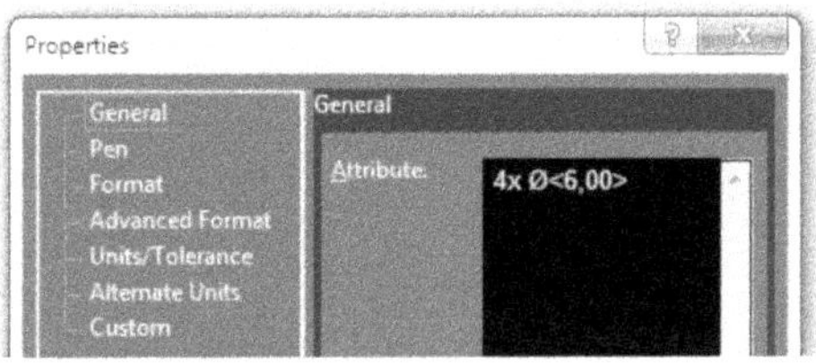

As can be seen in the following figure, the diameter symbol and the quantity of holes have been added. The measure remains associative and adapts to changes. If the number of holes changes, this must be adjusted manually in the holes dimension properties menu shown before.

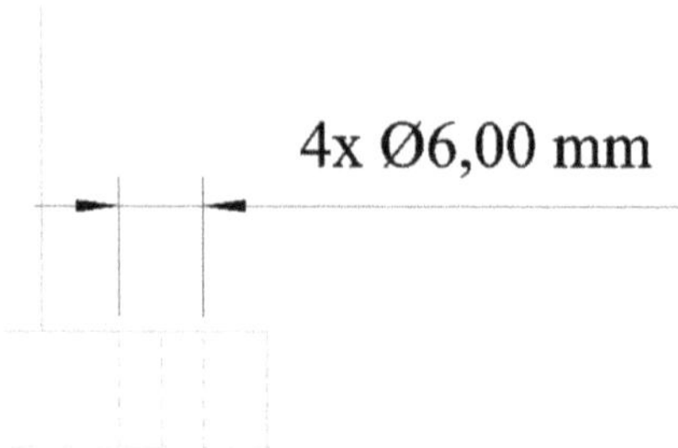

13. In this step, a text window is created in the lower left area of the drawing sheet.

    ➔ Activate the command "Text"  in the left toolbar.
    ➔ Click where the text should be placed.
    ➔ Enter "Crane hook 100x40x68" and jump to the next line with the "ENTER" key.
    ➔ There you should write "Scale 1:1".
    ➔ Select the font size 5 mm in the "Properties Toolbar".

    ➔ Use the "Finish" command  in the "Inspector Bar" to finish typing and the text box is created.

14. Now add all other dimensions and text windows in the drawing sheet according to the template shown below. You can find out more about the subsequent moving of dimensions with the help of the "Edit Tool" in chapter 4.6.

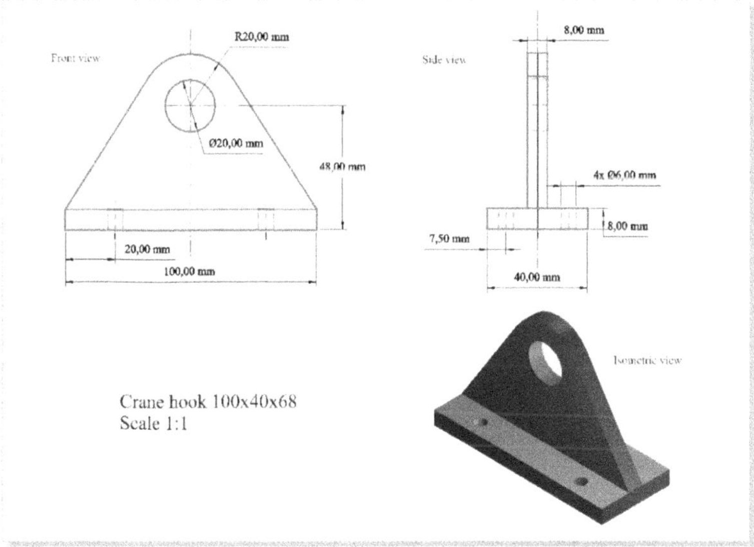

15. You will now print the present drawing. If you do not have a correct printer or a PDF printer installed, you can skip this step.

→ Click on the "Print" command .

→ You may be asked if the page margins should be adjusted automatically. Confirm this with "YES".

→ Start the printing process with "OK".

The "Print" menu closes.

16. A drawing derivation of the crane hook has now been created with the aid of viewports and dimensioning commands. In the further course of this chapter you will intervene in the editing history of the component and make small changes. Finally, you will see that because of these changes to the model, the viewports and the dimensions in the drawing derivation are automatically updated.

→ Jump back into the model space.

➔ Change to the view “Isometric_SE” .

➔ Activate the “Hidden Line”  render mode.

➔ Click on the circle sketch of the crane eyelet (shown in the following figure in magenta).

➔ Select the option "Circle" in the “Selection Info” palette that may be displayed.

It is the circle of the 2D drawing used to create the extrusion.

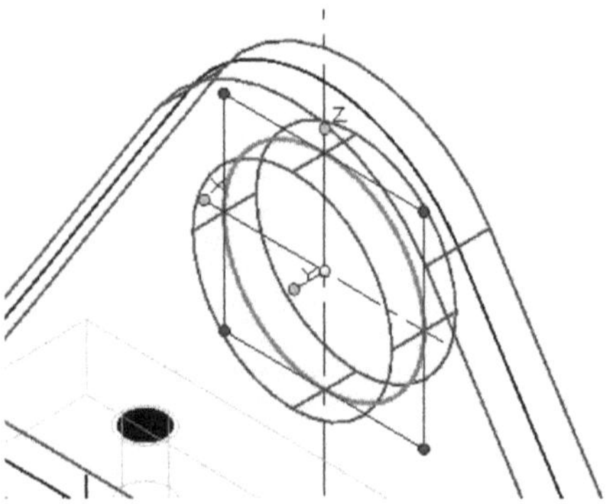

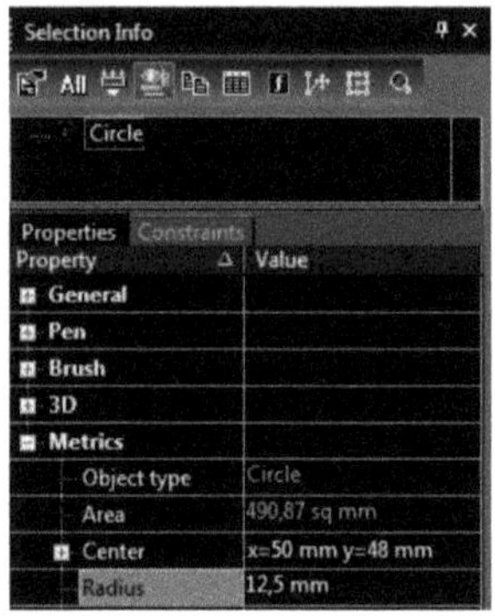

When you have selected the circle, look in the “Selection Info” palette.

➔ Open the section "Metrics".

Geometric object properties are listed here.

➔ Overwrite the radius with the value "12.5".

➔ Press the "ENTER" key.

The circle and the hole created by it have now increased accordingly.

17. You will now access the editing history of the component in order to increase the bore diameter.

➔ Select the 3D body of the crane hook.

Click on an edge of the 3D model with the "Select" tool. Since it is a part structure, it is displayed in green. Stored 2D sketches are displayed in blue.

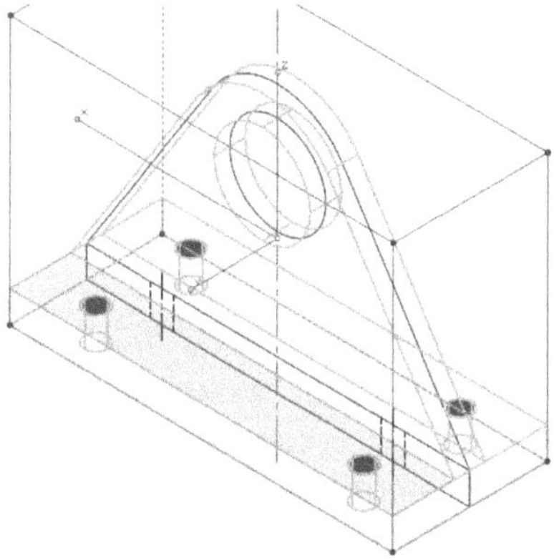

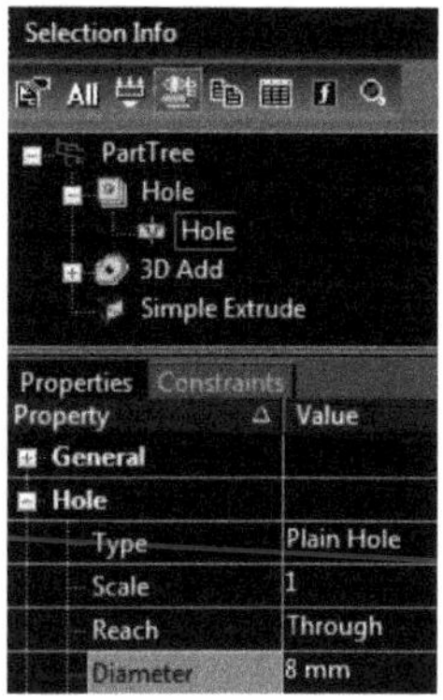

If you click too close to a 2D object, the selection menu may open. There you should select the option “Part”. This is the 3D body. If you accidentally select a 2D object, end the selection with the “ESC” key. Take another look at the “Selection Info” palette. The holes have been added to the “PartTree”.

➔ Unfold the above listed folder structure.
➔ Select the blue symbol labeled “Hole".
➔ Then expand the object properties "Hole" as showed above.
➔ Change the hole’s diameter to 8 mm.
➔ Confirm with "ENTER".

All four holes have increased accordingly in the model.

18. Changes in model space are automatically inherited by the viewports in the paper space.

    ➔ Switch back to the paper space.

    There you can see that the dimensions of the crane eyelet and the holes have been adjusted.

This completes the final task of the "Getting Started" chapter.

2 General overview / Program structure

2.1 User interface

2.1.1 Default user interface

After installing the software and opening it for the first time, the default interface of the program is loaded. This will be shown on the next page. The central element is the model space, which is surrounded by menus, toolbars and palettes. The program interface information such as the number, sorting or position of the toolbars is stored locally in a workspace template file on the PC, which is located in the following path: "Documents/ TurboCAD® 2017 Professional x64 DE/ Config". The path may vary slightly depending on the operating system and the TurboCAD® version you are using. The files which save all the User Interface's settings the endings ".xcfg" and ".xml".

By default, the following files are saved inside the "Config" folder:

LTE_1024_TCPRF.xcfg
LTE_1024_TCPRF.xml
LTE_1280_TCPRF.xcfg
LTE_1280_TCPRF.xml
TC_1024x768pro.xcfg
TC_1024x768pro.xml
TC_1024x768pro_pre.xcfg
TC_1024x768pro_pre.xml
TC_1280x1024pro.xcfg
TC_1280x1024pro.xml

These template files are optimized for different screen resolutions. The user interface of TurboCAD® is similar to common CAD applications such as the widely used AutoCAD®. Toolbars, palettes and menus are arranged around a drawing area and allow quick access to the necessary drawing commands. The following figure shows the most important components of the program's User Interface after installation. How to customize the User Interface to you own needs is described later in this chapter.

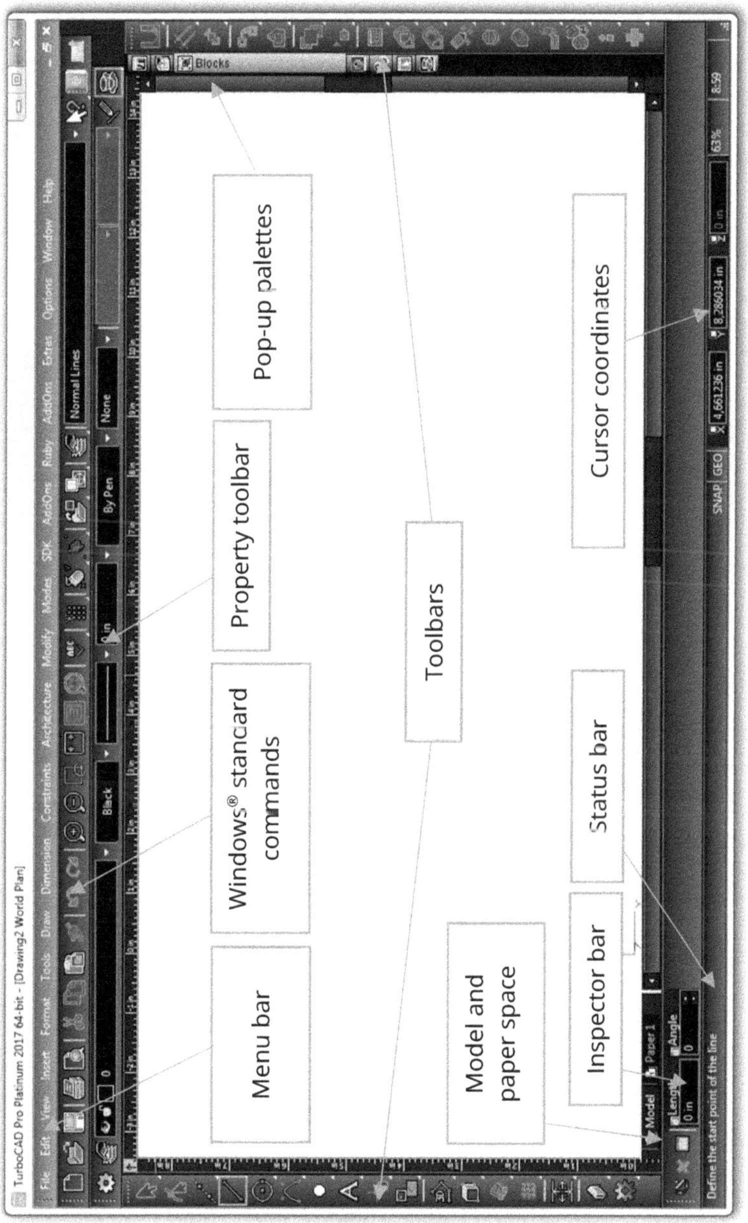

Figure 2-1 User interface after software installation

2.1.2 Loading, changing, and saving the User Interface

The User Interface can be customized by the user. Commands can be individually added to toolbars and thus adapted to their own needs. This makes it easier to find frequently used commands and thus optimize the workflow. Right-clicking on an empty area next to a toolbar will open the "Customize" menu window. This is also found in the "Tools/ Customize" menu. Here you will find information about the User Interface of TurboCAD® in the menu "Options". The drop-down menus under "Load From:" and "Save In:" contain the template files listed in the previous chapter. All template files, which are located in the folder path shown on page 68, are displayed here and can be loaded and saved as and when needed. The preparation and use of your own template will be explained later in the chapter.

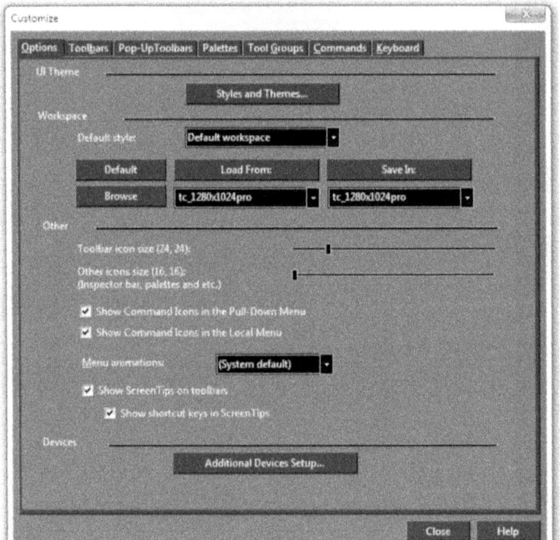

Figure 2-2 "Customize" menu

All toolbars in the user interface have a dotted line on the left or top side. If you move the mouse over this line, the mouse pointer changes into a four-arrow symbol.

Figure 2-3 Exemplary toolbar

By clicking and holding down, the toolbar can now be detached from the anchor at the edge of the screen and either placed in a free floating position or anchored again somewhere else. Under "Tools/ Customize/ Toolbars", pre-sorted toolbars can be added or removed. The following choices should be marked, as these bars contain useful tools and information:

- **Property**
  Allows direct access to layer, line, and brush properties.
- **Inspector Bar**
  The "Inspector Bar" is used to enter values for modifying tools. It also provides information about the size and position of selected parts, as well as allowing them to be moved or scaled.
- **Menu bar**
  Contains TurboCAD's® program menus (see Figure 2-1).
- **Standard**
  Includes, in addition to the Windows® "Open", "Save", and "Print" commands, general commands such as "Zoom" and "Undo".

To save your own User Interface, you must first enter the desired name for the template file under "Tools/ Customize/ Options/ Workspace/ Save In". Clicking "Save In" will automatically create the two template files with the extensions ".xcfg" and ".xml". Changes to the User Interface can then be saved in this newly created template file. In companies with several CAD workstations, the design of a uniform User Interface is recommended. It is not possible to access these template files on a network server. They must be stored manually on each workstation using the path already mentioned. When changing the company-internal template, this must subsequently be communicated to all TurboCAD® users so that the template file is immediately updated on all computers or overwritten with the newer template file. Changes, such as adding or moving command buttons is possible after loading the file. It should be noted that if you reload ("Load From") the template you set, it will of course be overwritten again.

2.1.3 Visual layout of the User Interface

How you decide to layout the User Interface is certainly a matter of personal taste, however, the custom theme "Office 2003 theme" has the advantage that an activated command is highlighted in orange and thus its status is clearly visible. This can be very helpful, especially for tools that are switched on and off more frequently during the work process. The visual theme of the User Interface can be changed in the "Customize" menu window under "Options/ Styles and Themes...". In the "Customize" menu, the icon size can also be adjusted.

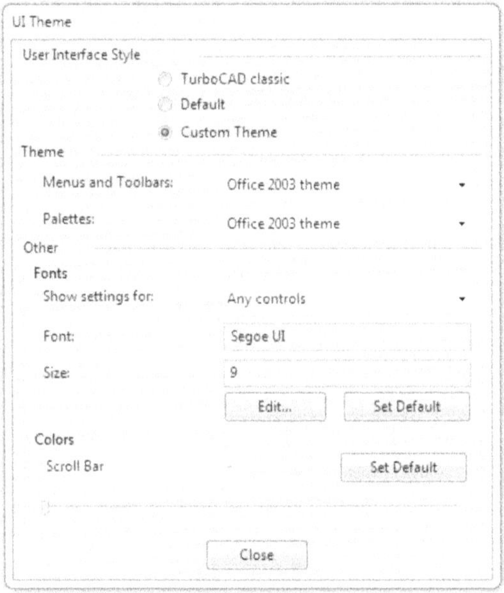

Figure 2-4 "UI Theme" menu

2.2 TOOLBARS

The default arrangement of the toolbars after reinstalling the software is not very intuitive and sometimes slows down the workflow due to constantly having to search for commands. Sensibly dividing the commands into tool groups would be beneficial here. The solution to this problem is to remedy the existing bars by changing or creating your own custom bars. You can edit existing toolbars or create them from scratch. Individual commands can only be removed and added as long as the "Customize" menu window is open. Hold down the "CTRL" key to move commands in both directions. The mouse pointer changes to a gray button with a small cross. The "Commands" menu lists all commands contained in TurboCAD® which can be dragged into the User Interface.

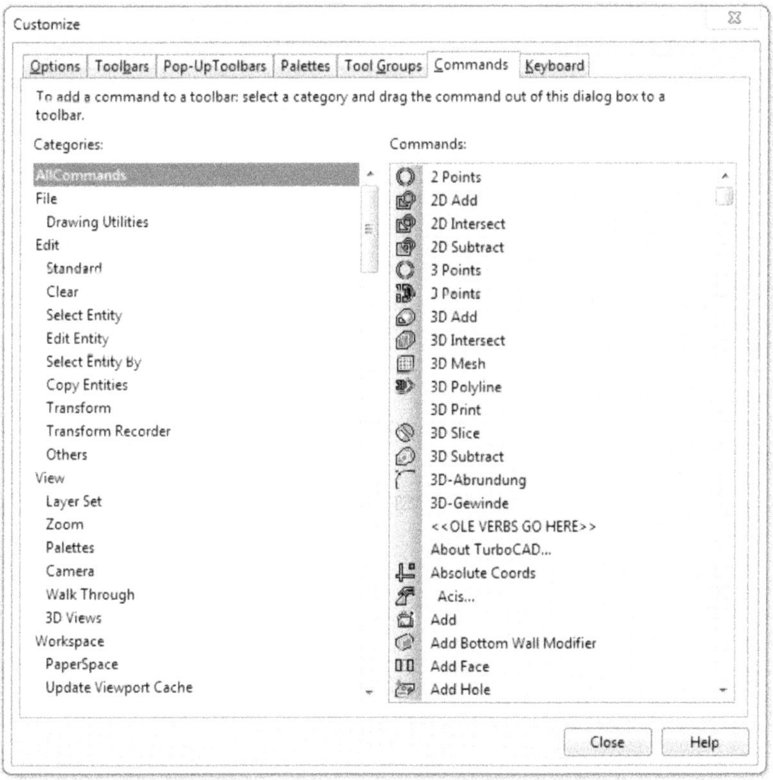

Figure 2-5 Overview of all commands ("Customize" menu)

Below are some of the default toolbars (Figure 2-6), which can be activated under "Customize/ Toolbars". Although commands for toolbars are already summarized here, the use of these bars inevitably leads to an overload of the "User Interface". For example, there are commands that are rarely used in the normal workflow.

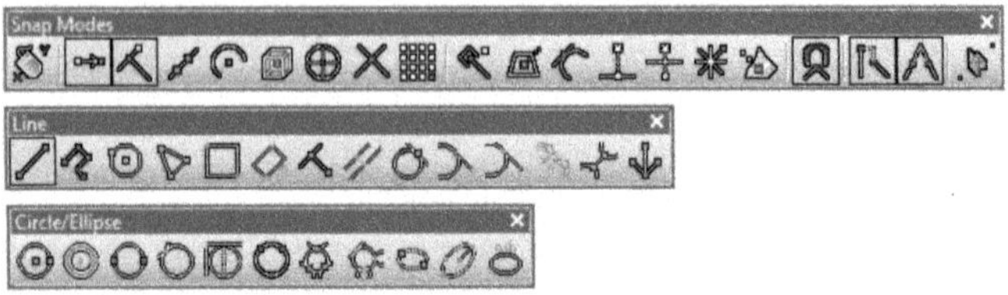

Figure 2-6 By default, available toolbars

To create a new toolbar, you can do the following. Firstly, you need to open the "Customize". Under the heading "Toolbars", a custom bar can be added via the right-hand button "New ..." which you can name however you want. This can then be attached to the screen edge at the desired position.

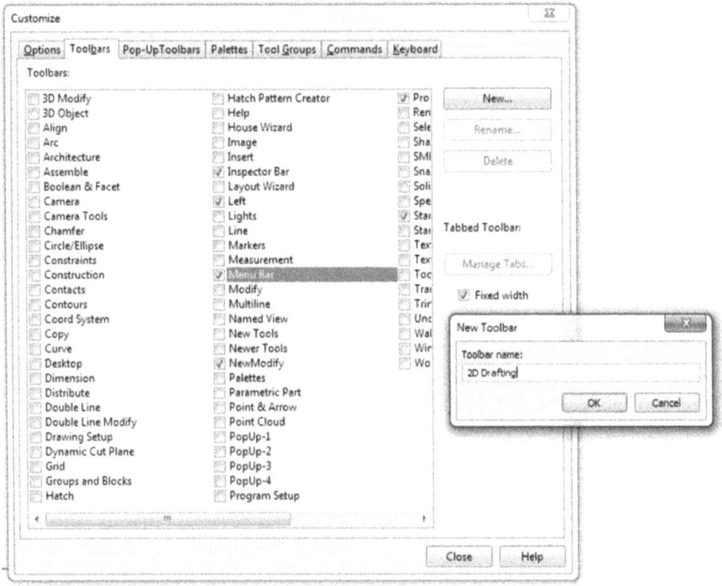

Figure 2-7 Show, hide and create a new toolbar

Command icons can not only be arranged next to each other but also grouped in drop-down menus.

These drop-down menus are indicated by a small black triangle in the lower right corner of the icon. By clicking on the symbol and holding down the mouse button the pop-up menu opens, and all the commands in it can be selected. It is a good idea to put the commands in order based on how frequently you use them. If frequently used commands are located at the top of this menu, time is saved by not having to search for the ones needed each time.

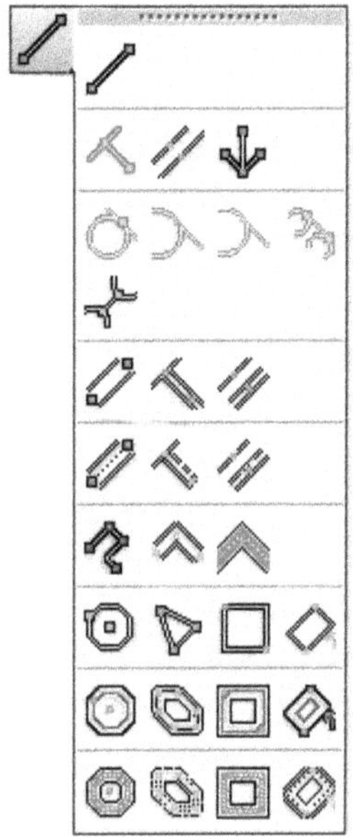

Figure 2-8 Example of a drop-down menu

2.3 Pop up toolbars

Popup toolbars are displayed by right-clicking over the unfolded mouse menu. They allow, quick access to frequently used drawing commands, views or render modes, amongst other things.

The commands that are listed in the pop-up selection can be set under "Tools/ Customize". In the menu item "Pop-Up Toolbars" it is first determined which toolbars are displayed in the pop-up menu.

By default, several toolbars named “PopUp” exist and are selected. These can be edited and provided with the desired commands at your discretion.

2.4 INSPECTOR AND STATUS BAR

By default, the "Inspector Bar", which is located at the bottom of the screen, provides information about the position of selected objects by specifying the coordinates and also allows you to enter values for changing the size, position or scale of an object.

The "Inspector Bar" also contains command buttons. Some commands are permanently available, whilst others are displayed when using a command and are used to set the activated command.

The values displayed in the panel depend on whether TurboCAD® is in 2D or 3D mode. In 2D mode, the Z coordinates are not listed. Therefore, it is easy to recognize which mode you are working in. The values listed can be set in the "Selector 2D Properties" or "Selector 3D Properties" menu. This is divided into "General", "Selector 2D" and "Selector 3D", so that they can be configured differently (more in chapter 3.4).

Below the "Inspector Bar" is the "Status Bar". This informs the user about the current status of a command or prompts for the next action. Specifically getting to know the commands, prompts and descriptions of the next steps inside the "Status Bar" is very helpful.

Furthermore, the "Status Bar" shows the coordinates of the mouse pointer, the zoom factor and the time of day. The "SNAP" button can toggle snap options on and off, allowing access to snap settings (chapter 4.2).

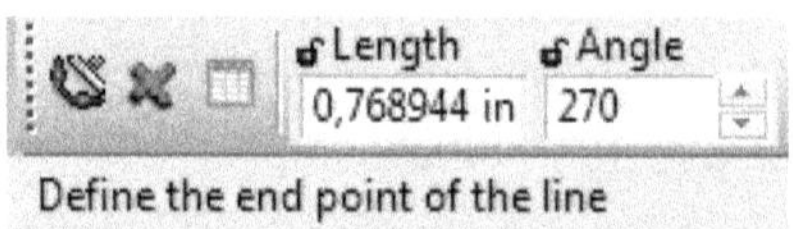

Figure 2-9 "Inspector Bar" and "Status Bar" when using the "Line" command

2.5 MODEL AND PAPER SPACE

In TurboCAD®, a distinction is made between a model and a paper space. The model space is usually intended for creating parts and sketches. The paper space, on the other hand, is used to create the drawing sheet with the full-scale views and drawing information.

If a scaled drawing is to be derived from the drawn model later on, the drawing in the model range on a scale of 1:1 (1 cm of the real part is equal to 1 cm in the CAD model) is appropriate. The desired scale is then set later in the paper space, so that even large drawings can find their place on a standard paper format. The paper space corresponds to the later printout. Here, views of the part drawn in the model space, can be positioned on the sheet, and so on. They can also be provided with dimensions and labels.

You can switch between model and paper space by clicking on the tabs in the bottom left of the screen. You can add different paper spaces and rename them. This can be used, for example, to create drawing derivations from a part on different sheets. Here each paper space can be edited individually (sheet formats, viewports, scales, etc.).

Dimensions and text entries are often made in the paper space. This ensures a consistent font size for later printing.

In companies with several CAD workplaces, the font size and type or layer properties, the properties that determine the visual appearance of the drawing sheet, should be prescribed and enshrined in the standard templates. The creation and use of a standardized drawing template is explained in Chapter 3.3.

2.6 PALETTES

Palettes are menus, which can be anchored to the edge of the screen and provide the user with important information, tools or other work aids. They can be opened as hover menus which only expand and remain open when the mouse cursor is moved over them or if adjustments are made in them. When they are not in use they automatically close after a view seconds. These space-saving menus allow for the model space to have more room. Like toolbars, palettes can be distributed to other screens to maximize the model space even more. In the "Customize" menu, palette properties can be changed, such as defining the time that they remain open. The main 2D drawing and 3D construction palettes are shown below.

The palettes are located under "Tools/ Palettes" or in the standard "Palettes" toolbar.

Figure 2-10 Standard toolbar "Palettes"

Design Director 

The "Design Director" manages layers, layer groups, work planes, views, paper areas, and lighting. More in 2.7, 5.8 and 5.13.

Blocks 

The "Blocks" palette contains all the drawing-internal blocks as well as the external block references. Blocks can be created and edited with the "Blocks" palette open. More in 7.2.

Library 

The "Library" palette is used to manage the various symbol libraries and allows the extraction and storage of frequently used drawing parts which are stored externally. More in 7.3.

Drafting 

With the aid of the "Drafting" palette, true-to-scale views, sections and detailed views of 3D objects can be saved and transferred to the paper area. More in 5.12.

Selection Info 

The "Selection Info" palette displays information such as the object type, dimensions, or position in the drawing of the selected drawing objects.

Object properties can be accessed and changed. Processing steps such as grouping or Boolean 3D operations are chronologically displayed here and thus allow an intervention in the previous work steps (see chapter 5.7).

By default, the "Selection Info" palette displays only 300 objects and operations. This value can be increased under "Options"  in the upper left area of the palette. When creating large assemblies and parts with a large number of processing steps, the preset value is often exceeded.

Figure 2-11 "Selection Info" palette options

2.7 LAYER / DESIGN DIRECTOR

Layers contain information such as line width, type, color, and display order. These can be managed in the “Design Director” ("Tools/ Palettes/ Design Director"). All drawing objects can be assigned to individual layers. By default, there is a layer toolbar above the drawing area, which is displayed under "Property" in the "Toolbars" menu for showing and hiding toolbars.

Figure 2-12 Property Toolbar

If an object is selected in the model or paper space, the layer that this object is on is indicated in the property toolbar. It also shows whether the individual values (pattern, width, color, etc.) are removed from the layer ("By Layer") or whether this information is manually overwritten. If a value is entered manually or a selection is made in the property toolbar, it overwrites the values stored in the layer.

If these values are managed in the active layer, they can also be changed simultaneously in the “Design Director”.

For example, should a color be changed, not every single line or every single object has to be selected. The change can be made once in the “Design Director” which will automatically transfer said change to all of the objects on the layer.

The following explains the layer scope of the “Design Director”. By clicking on the individual panel headers, the values can be sorted.

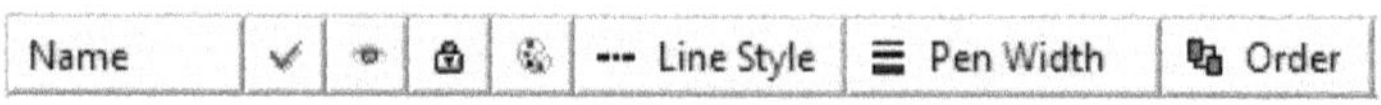

Figure 2-13 Layer information in the Design Director

Name

The layer name can be chosen freely. The layer "0" is always present by default and cannot be renamed or deleted. Drawing tools are initially set so that created objects are automatically placed on the "0" layer. This also applies to groups, blocks, or viewports. As more layers are added, individual drawing tools can be linked to specific layers. More in chapter 3.3.

Active

The active layer is marked by a green tick. Only one layer can be active at a time.

Visible

Layers can be individually faded in and out. Only the layers that have eye icons are visible in the drawing. By pressing the "Alt" or "CTRL" key, multiple layers can be selected and faded in and out simultaneously.

Lock

A layer can be locked. This means that the objects lying on this layer cannot be selected or changed. A locked layer has a "lock icon" in the "Design Director".

Color

Different colors can be selected to visually distinguish between lines and objects. It should be noted that lighter colors are often difficult to recognize when printed later on or displayed on screen. These should either be avoided, or the line strength should be increased. The color white, as well as very light gray tones are converted by default from TurboCAD® into black, because otherwise they would not be seen on the white background. This setting can be deactivated under "Options/ Drawing Setup/ Background Color" if necessary.

Line Style

In "Line Style", predefined styles like "CONTINUOUS", "DASHED", "DASHDOT" and many more are to be chosen. Different layers can be easily distinguished in black and white print or a copy. You can also create your own line styles and add them to the selection (see chapter 3.2). The list of existing line styles can be found under "Options/ Drawing Setup/ Line Styles".

Pen Width

The higher the value that is set, the thicker the line that is displayed. If a pen width of 0 mm is specified in the Design Director, the width specified under "Options/ Drawing Setup/ Display/ Defaults" will be used. The value of 0.25 mm allows accurate reading of printed drawings and enables the common printers to print the lines clearly.

Order

The order indicates the drawing order of the layers. The higher the value, the further towards the foreground the layer is, covering layers with a smaller value. This is especially useful when working with different layer colors and therefore the order is important.

When a drawing is finished, always check that the drawn lines and objects are on the right layers. For this, the "Select By" function can be used (as described in chapter 7.6).

In general, it is desirable to design drawings so that other users who work on them at a later date are automatically provided with sufficient information. Naming the layers helps enormously here.

> If different people are working on a file, a separate layer can be created as a comment layer so that other can identify your own processing. Notes in the model or paper area can then be inserted in the corresponding positions, placed on the appropriate comment layer and thus displayed and hidden as desired. TurboCAD® provides the ability to hide individual layers in the viewports for rendering paper-drawn objects in the model space. Thus, comments in the model space, which are intended only for the editors of the file, are automatically excluded from printing. Creating and editing viewports is described in more detail in chapter 6.1.

2.8 OBJECT PROPERTIES

The object properties include general settings such as color, layer, hatch, or object-specific settings. Basically, any object that can be selected by the "Select" tool has its own object properties. These vary depending on the object type. Object types are line objects, 3D primitives, part structures, blocks or viewports, amongst others.

The object properties can be accessed, viewed and edited in several ways. By default, the object properties menu shown below can be opened by double-clicking with the left mouse button on an object. Since it is possible to set which action follows a double-click (chapter 3.4), this does not always work. The menu can also be opened by right-clicking on the object and then selecting the "Properties ..." command. If an object is selected, this command is also shown on the far left in the "Inspector Bar".

Some of these object properties are also in the "Selection Info" palette (chapter 2.6) and can be edited there. Depending on the property of the object and the changes the user wants to make, it is sometimes helpful to look at the object properties menu. A quick intervention via the "Selection Info" palette is also possible.

In the following step, the use of object properties is explained by using a cylinder as an example (3D command "Cylinder").

Figure 2-14 Object properties of a cylinder (3D primitive "Cylinder")

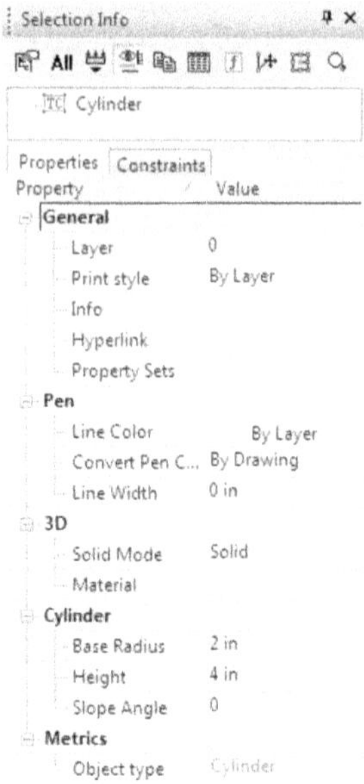

Figure 2-15 Object properties of a cylinder (3D primitive "Cylinder") in the "Selection Info" palette

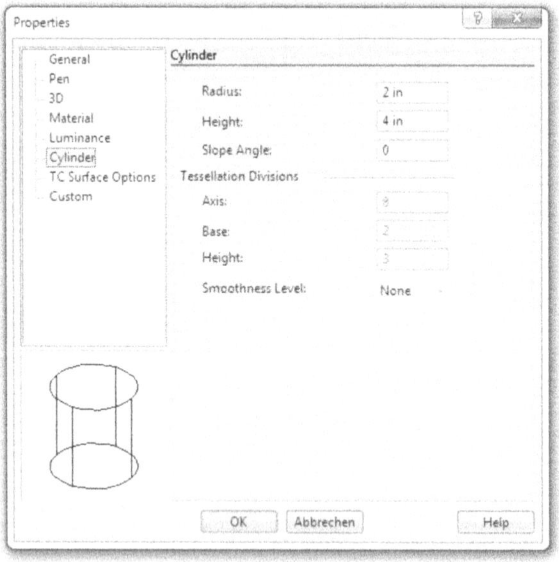

Figure 2-16 Properties menu "Cylinder"

General

The input field "Attributes" on the first menu page of the object properties is empty for most object types. Some objects, such as dimensions, groups, or text boxes, provide information here. For example, a dimension shows the measurement value, a text box the text you type manually, and a group the group name.

A dimension value, which is controlled by the length, diameter or angle of the dimensioned object, is surrounded by less than (<) and greater than (>) symbols (example: <17,3>). If this value is overwritten manually without these symbols, the dimension number loses its connection to the object and length or size changes are subsequently no longer recorded. If the manually entered number is deleted and <> is once again set in the “Attribute” field, the dimensioning value is automatically determined and the connection to the object is restored.

> The “Attribute” window can also be used to enter keywords that can be used in a report query (chapter 7.5) or to search for objects (chapter 7.6).

In the “Selection Info” palette (Figure 2-15), this value can be found under "General/ Info" and can, if necessary, be changed faster here than opening the object properties menu. This is especially true for text fields within groups. In the "Selection Info" palette, the group in the upper display area can be opened and the text (listed in the "Info" field) can be changed.

> The hyperlink may point to network paths or a website. For example, suitable product data sheets, instructions or other documents can be called up quickly.

Each drawing object lies on a specific layer. This is listed in the object properties under "General". If the layer is to be changed, a drop-down menu can be used to select the currently available layers of the drawing.

Depending on the selected object, additional object-specific settings are available.

Pen

With few exceptions, the "Pen" menu offers the same setting options as the standard "Properties" toolbar (chapter 2.7), which is located at the top of the screen. Line style, width, and color can be set here as well. The object properties menu provides the ability to align the line pattern. If this command is activated, the line pattern will be started from the middle of a line. For symmetrical drawings, such as the center mark shown below, the orientation of the pattern provides a much better image.

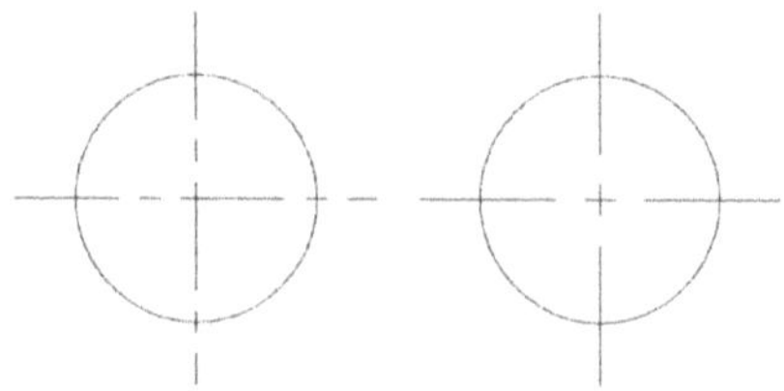

Figure 2-17 Line pattern orientation (Left: disabled, right: enabled)

Pattern, color and width can also be controlled by the layer previously set under "General". To do this, the value "By Layer" must be selected in the corresponding drop-down menus. For 3D objects, some values such as "Pattern" or "Alignment" cannot be changed. For 2D objects, the "Brush" menu is also available. Here too, some settings can be controlled via the standard "Properties" toolbar. In addition, scale, angle and origin can also be set here. For 3D objects, the menu is omitted.

3D

In this menu you can choose between “Solid”, “TC Surface” and “SMesh”. A more detailed description of the three types and their differences can be found in the program help.

Often crucial to the user is that important change tools such as e.g. “Fillet Edges”, “Chamfer Edges”, or “Shell solid” can only be applied to objects that are solid. Thus, the surface and mesh models are not immediately available for 3D construction within TurboCAD®.

The "Thickness" option (another menu sub-item) works similarly to the "Simple Extrude" command (see also Figure 5-12). Thereby a solid or a closed surface body is created from a closed profile, and surfaces are created from open profiles. For 3D objects this sub-item is not available. Finally, below are further settings for the graphical representation of 3D objects.

Material

Here materials can be selected and thus the visual appearance of the object beyond the use of standard colors can be changed. The material selection refers exclusively to the appearance. There is no material-specific data, such as the density for weight determination over the volume deposited. More in chapter 5.13.

Luminance

Luminance creates additional light sources. This feature makes it possible to provide 3D objects with a luminosity. More in chapter 5.13.

Cylinder

This menu is an object-specific menu. Depending on the type of object and the command used to create it, the menu name and the setting options contained therein vary. With a cylinder, which was created by the command "Cylinder", the radius, height, or slope angle can be subsequently entered here. These are values that had to be specified in the "Inspector Bar" when the cylinder was created. Accordingly, changes can be made in the object properties menu shown below or also in the "Selection Info" palette (Figure 2-15).

TC Surface Options

Here, the number of surface segments can be controlled of round shaped objects such as the cylinder, a cone, or a sphere. The smaller the number, the coarser the rounding is simulated. This option is only available for "TC Surface" objects. This setting does not only refer to the representation, but also to the mathematical model. Figure 2-18 shows a cylinder made as a "TC Surface" and provided with only 14 approximation lines. Edges and surfaces can be snapped and processed here.

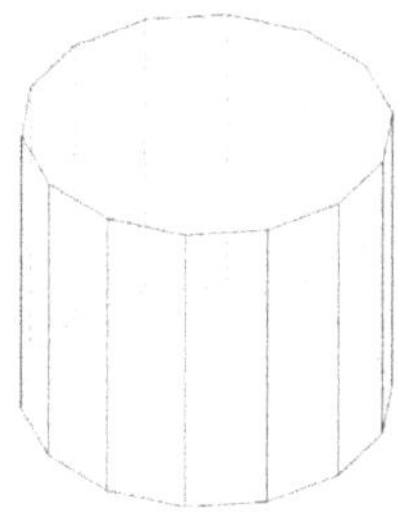

Figure 2-18 Cylinder as TC Surface with 14 approximation lines

Custom

Here, partially predefined information can be added to the objects so that they can be output in automatic reports. This is described in more detail in chapter 7.4.

3 PROGRAM SETUP

This chapter deals with the program setup after the reinstallation. The installation is largely automatic. Installation paths can be chosen freely. The default pre-set folder paths are recommended. If you refer to file storage paths later in this book, these are usually the default paths suggested during the installation.

The system requirements of the manufacturer must be observed. If you are planning to use TurboCAD® in 3D mode, you should specifically check your graphics card recommendations and compatibility.

TurboCAD® can be controlled by a 3D mouse and thus enables easy navigation in 3D space.

The system settings, which are mainly found in the "Options" menu, are divided into two sections:

The “Program Setup...” panel controls program settings such as the layout of the User Interface, toolbars, file paths, graphics settings, and mouse options. These settings are automatically saved after closing the software. Central administration of these settings is not possible. They must be set individually after reinstallation at each workstation.

In the menu area "Drawing Setup..." you can manage grids, drawing units, standard angles, layer and line styles. All these settings are stored within the drawing and therefore can be saved in a drawing template (chapter 3.3). This template can be stored locally on the computer or centrally on a network server. User settings, the use of drawing templates and the benefits of the key user concept are discussed later on in this chapter.

3.1 PROGRAM SETUP / USER SETTINGS

The user settings cannot be managed centrally but must be set on each computer. The following gives you an insight into the existing menus and their functions. The following explains the existing menus and their functions. The settings shown are for guidance only. The individual setting options of the submenus shown below are only briefly described. If more information is required here, you will find a complete explanation of all settings in the online or offline help section of TurboCAD®.

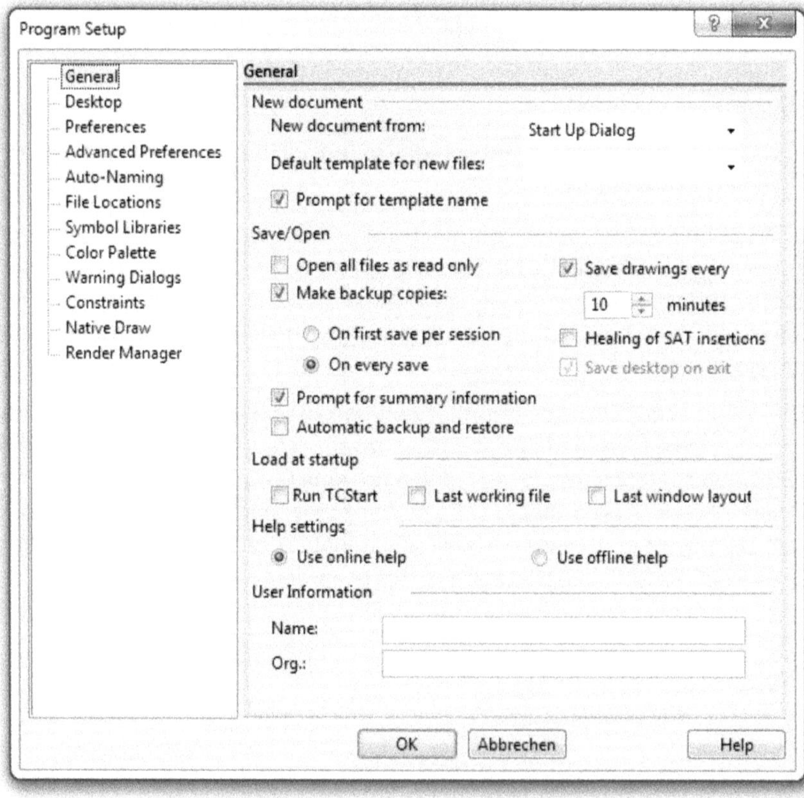

Figure 3-1 User Settings – Program Setup - General

In the area "New document" you can set which templates are selected as soon as a new document is created. The integration of a custom standard drawing template is covered in chapter 3.3. If the item "Prompt for template name" is selected, a selection window appears when opening a new document in which different templates are available.

If the name and company are filled out under "User Information", they are automatically transferred to the file info when saving.

Automatically saving the drawing every 10 minutes should adequately secure the editing of a document and reduce the loss of steps in the event of a system failure.

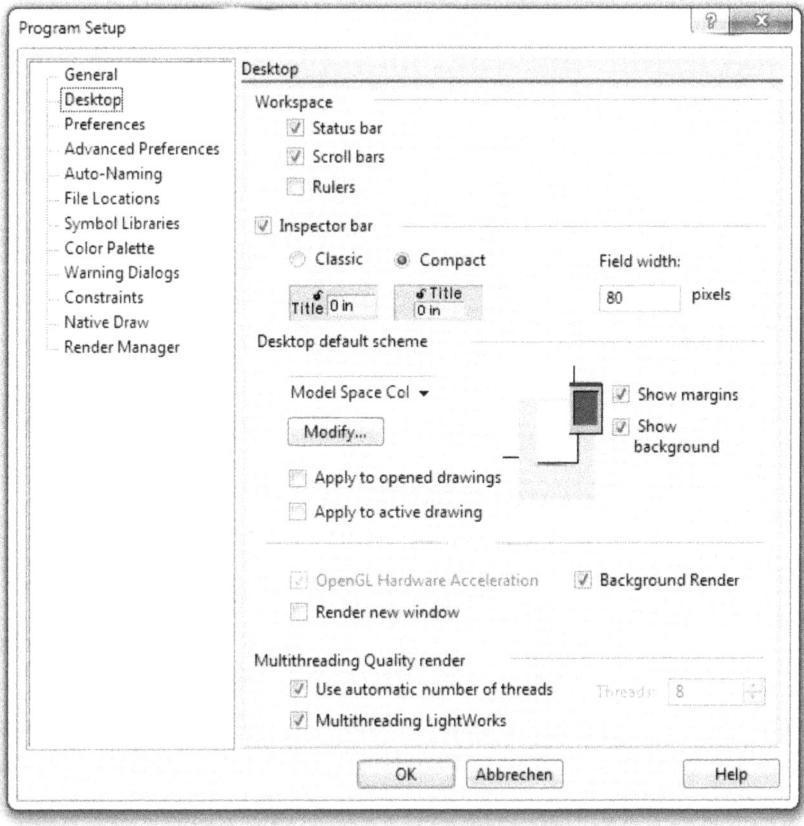

Figure 3-2 User Settings – Program Setup - Desktop

In the menu "Desktop" settings can be made on the User Interface. A panel box width of 80 pixels is a good compromise between good readability and the use of available space. So, in 3D mode, there is room for all of the necessary fields (for X, Y, and Z coordinates).

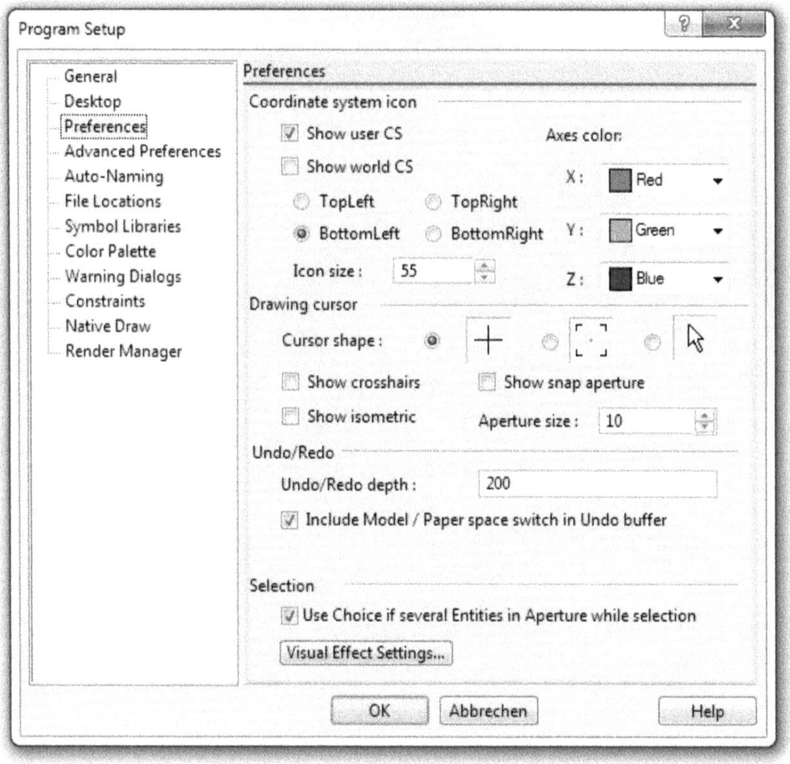

Figure 3-3 User Settings – Program Setup - Preferences

In the "Preferences" menu under "Coordinate system icon" the “User coordinate system” and “World coordinate system” menus (Chapter 5.4) can be shown or hidden. The axis colors are set by default in the colors blue, green and red, which facilitate orientation especially in 3D space.

The item "Use Choice of several Entities in Aperture while selection" under the "Selection" option can be turned on or off as needed. This is helpful when there are many different objects in a small space. A selection menu then helps to select the right object.

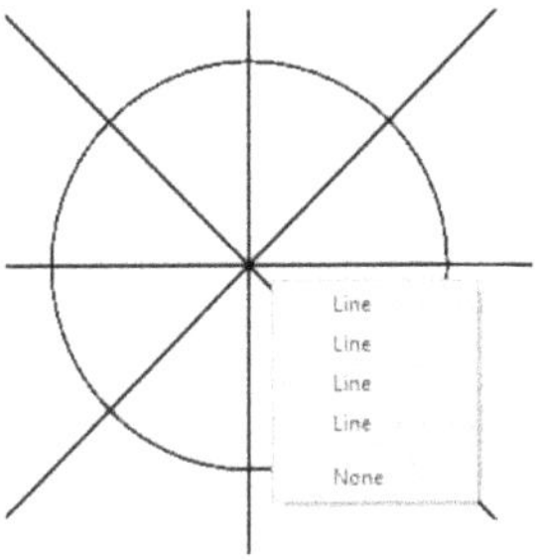

In the example shown, with the "Select" command activated, the left mouse button was clicked in the center of the circle. If the selection list is activated, a menu appears after clicking in which all lines are listed that are close to the cursor. This applies to all tools that require objects to be selected before execution. These include, for example, the commands "Select", "Object Trim", "Fillet2D" and also the dimensioning tools. When selecting the lines in the list, the corresponding line is highlighted. If the selection list is deactivated, TurboCAD® itself selects a line.

The selection aperture of the mouse, which can be set under "Drawing cursor", is decisive for the selection of drawing objects or using snap options. The value in "Aperture size" determines the size of the selection aperture. Only objects or snap options that are within that imaginary selection circle when clicking will be selected.

A value of "10" is a good choice here, as objects can easily be selected without too many other non-required possible objects hindering the process. If the "Show snap aperture" option is activated, a circle on the mouse pointer shows the exact size of the imaginary selection aperture. There are another cursor shapes offered in the menu shown above which also visually display a selection frame and helps to show how "sensitive" the mouse selection is set.

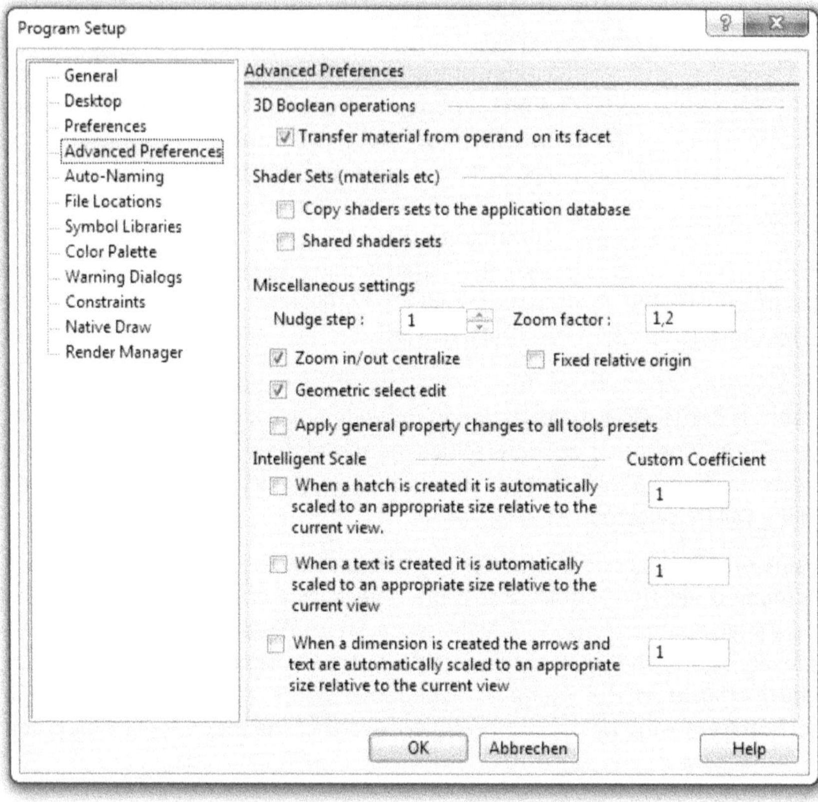

Figure 3-4 User Settings - Program Setup - Advanced Preferences

The "Advanced Preferences" menu is a new addition from the 2017 version and contains miscellaneous settings like material appearance, zoom or scale settings. If activated, material from one object is transferred onto another during a 3D Boolean operation (chapter 5.5).

The default zoom factor of 2 usually results in large jumps. A value of 1.2 is recommended. The "Zoom in / out centralize" option automatically centers the screen in the middle of the mouse pointer during zooming with the mouse wheel.

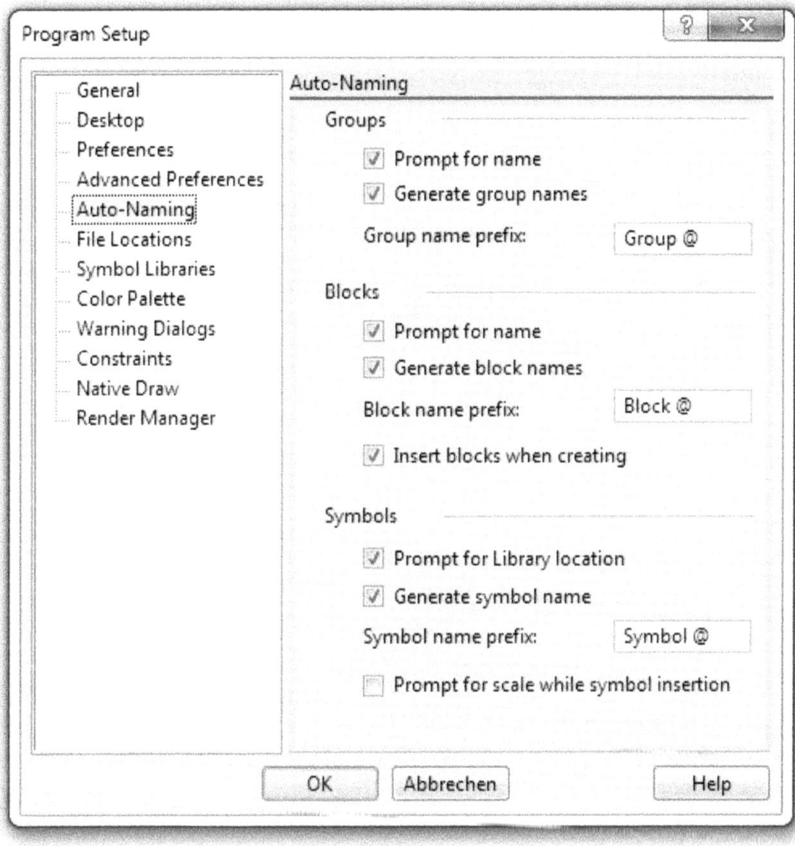

Figure 3-5 User Settings – Program Setup - Auto-Naming

For groups, blocks and symbols (explained in chapters 7.2 and 7.3), in the "Auto-Naming" area you can specify whether a name must be entered during creation. If, for example, you create a group with the settings shown above, the name "Group @" (@ symbol as a wildcard for a consecutive numbering) is automatically entered in the group's "Info" field. The name can be changed any time afterwards in the "Selection Info" palette in the "General" area.

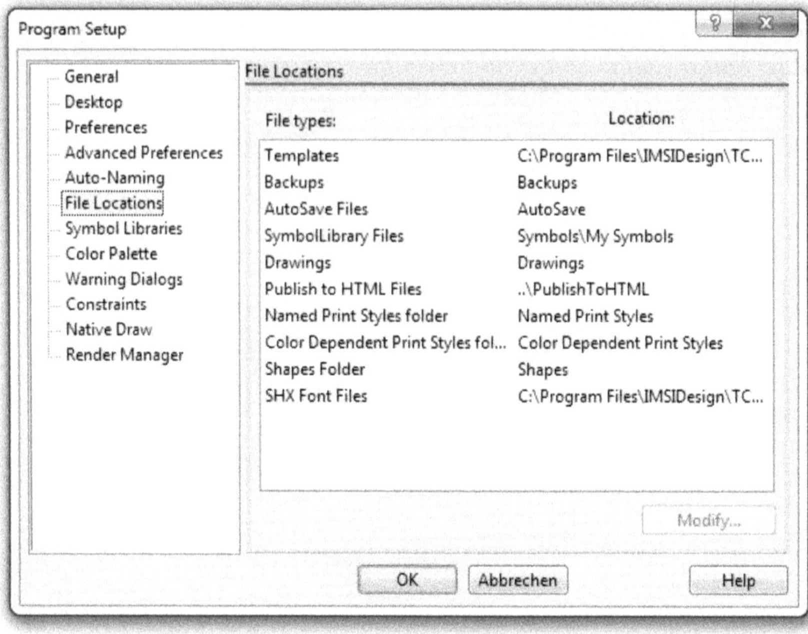

Figure 3-6 User Settings – Program Setup – File Locations

File paths can be set in the menu item "File Locations". For example, you can specify network paths as drawing template storage locations to allow multiple users to access the same template from the network. File paths of backup copies, print styles or fonts can be managed here.

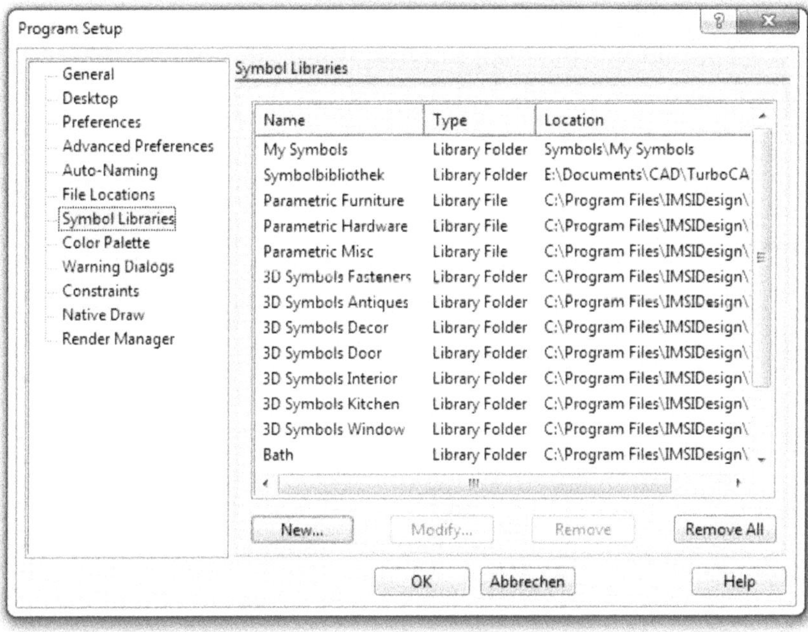

Figure 3-7 User Settings – Program Setup – Symbol Libraries

The menu item "Symbol Libraries" provides an overview of the existing symbol libraries. Libraries can be managed in this menu or in the “Library” palette. The use of symbol libraries is covered in chapter 7.3.

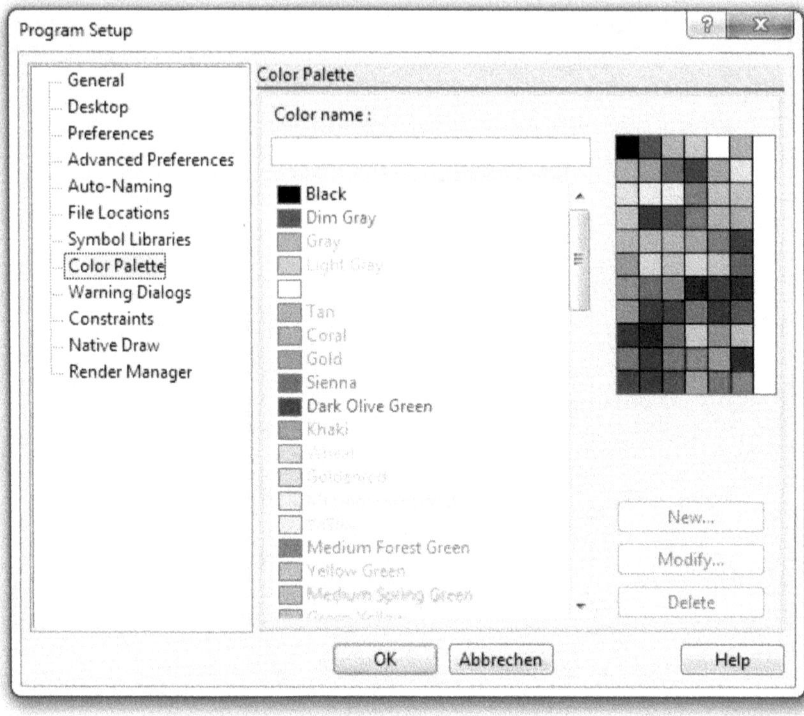

Figure 3-8 User Settings – Program Setup – Color Palette

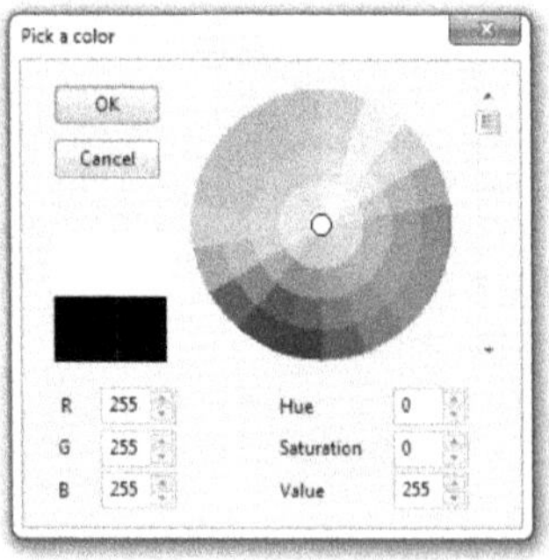

In the “Color Palette” new colors can be created and existing ones can be changed or deleted. If a new color is to be added, the color name must first be specified. You can then create a color stating the hue, saturation, and brightness under “New ...”. This can then be used for example for layers.

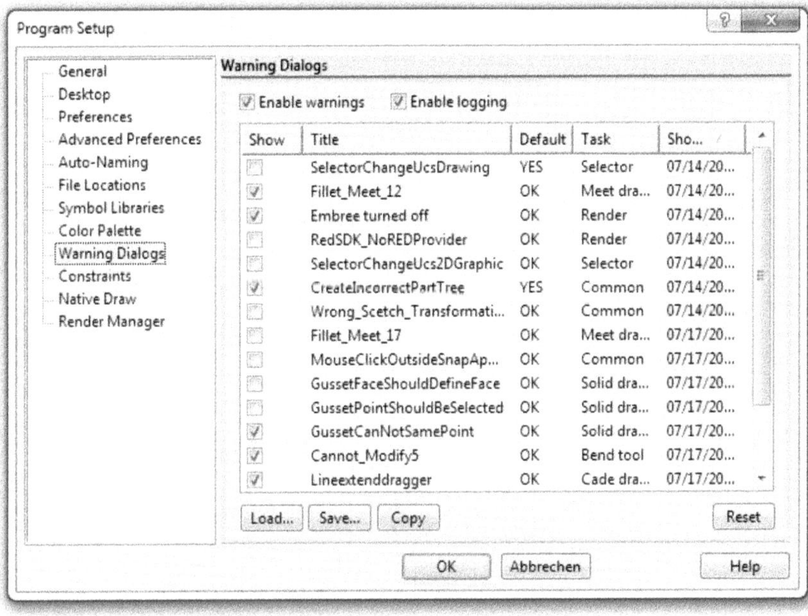

Figure 3-9 User Settings – Program Setup – Warning Dialogs

It is possible to suppress system messages if they appear too frequently and disrupt the workflow. Suppressed messages are listed in the menu item "Warning Dialogs" and can also be reactivated there.

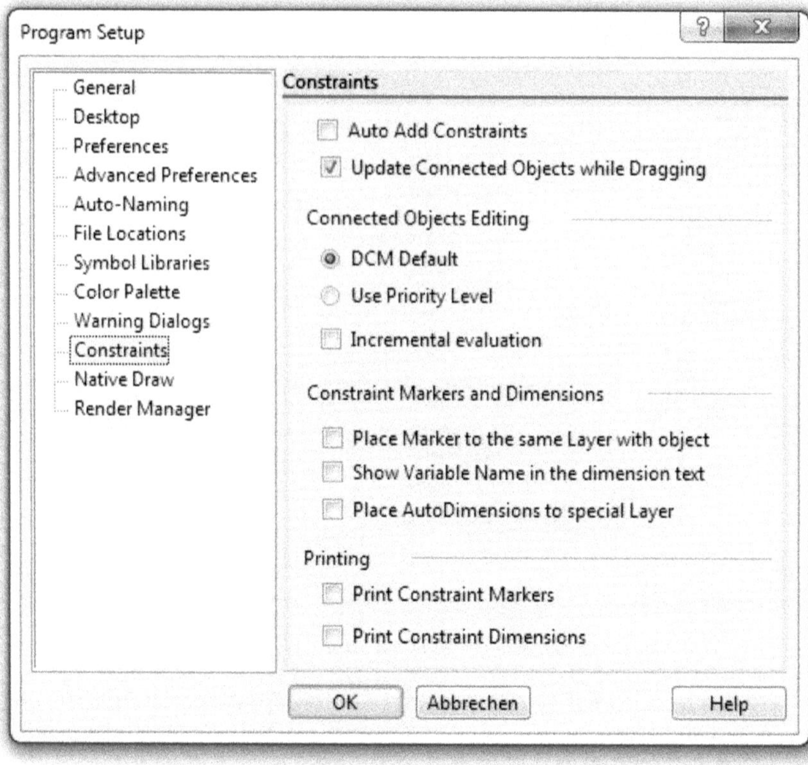

Figure 3-10 User Settings – Program Setup - Constraints

If constraints are used, their settings can be managed under "Constraints". These can be added automatically or manually. On which layers the constraints markers and dimensions are set and whether they are displayed and printed, can also be set in the menu shown above. Constraints are described in Chapter 4.9.

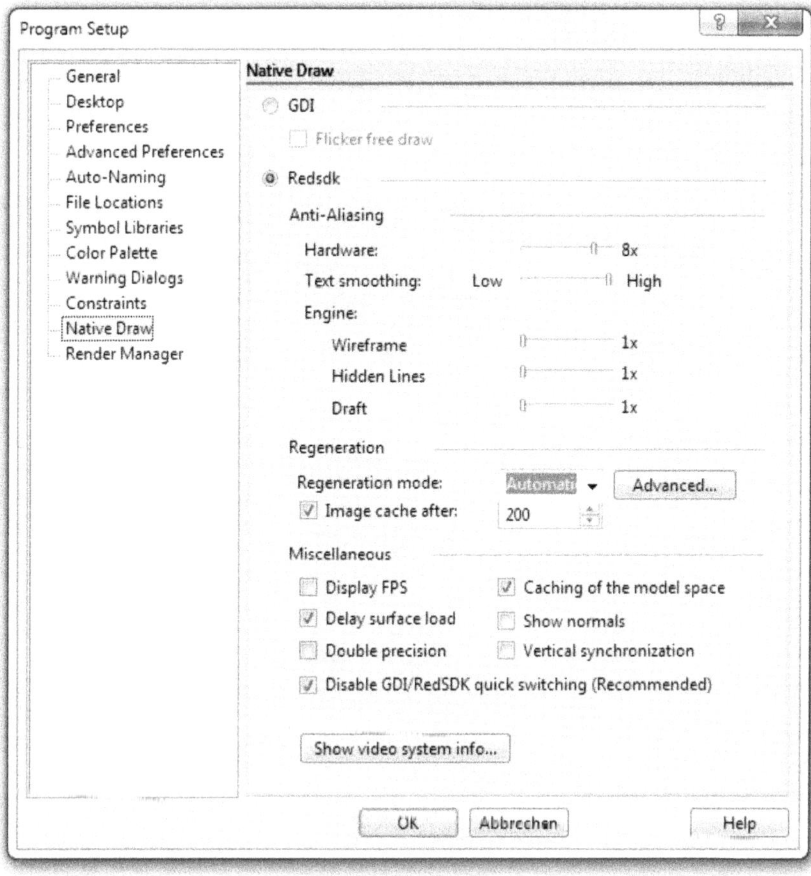

Figure 3-11 User Settings - Program Setup - Native Draw

In the menu item "Native Draw" one of display modules "GDI" (CPU-based) or "Redsdk" (OpenGL acceleration) can be chosen. Depending on the existing CPU and graphics card, the drawing speed in the 2D area can be improved.

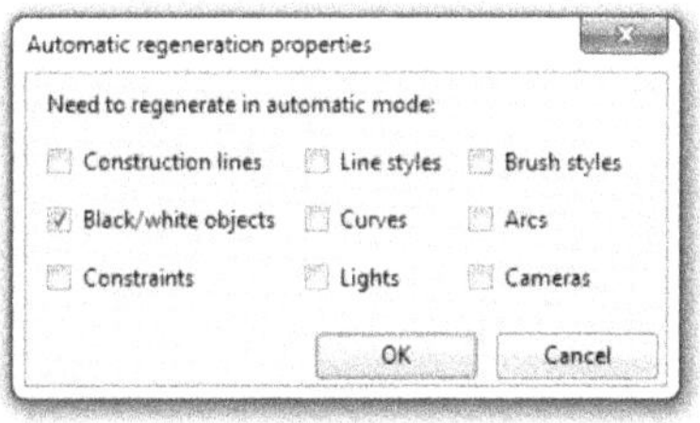

In addition, "Advanced ..." can be used to specify which objects are automatically regenerated during the zooming process. The more points you select, the more detailed the objects will be displayed. Depending on the computing power and the drawing size, however, this can lead to higher loading times. The whole drawing can be updated manually by pressing the "F5" key.

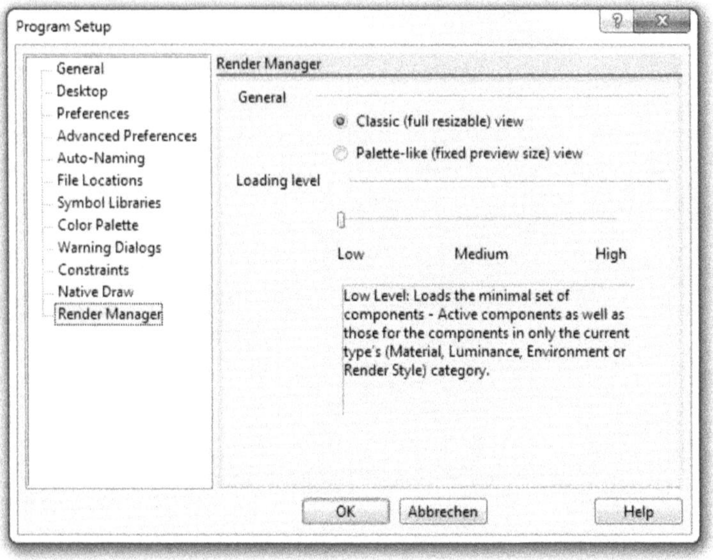

Figure 3-12 User Settings – Program Setup – Render Manager

3.2 DRAWING SETUP

The drawing settings only apply to the drawing that is currently open, unlike the program settings. The drawing settings can be stored in a standard drawing template and thus it can be ensured that the desired drawing settings are always used when creating a new drawing.

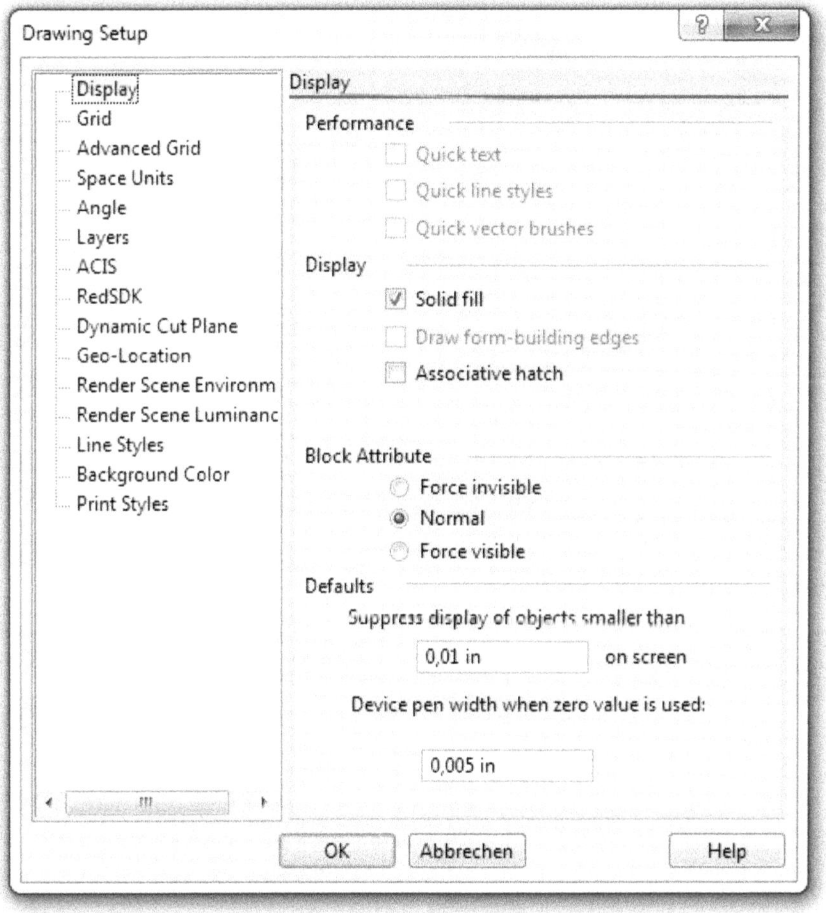

Figure 3-13 Drawing Setup – Display

Of particular note in the "Display" menu, is the value "Device pen width when zero value is used". This specifies the line width for lines that have been given a line value of 0 mm, either in their object properties or in their corresponding layer. 0.25 mm is printed by most printers without problems and is still easily recognizable as a thin line on the printout.

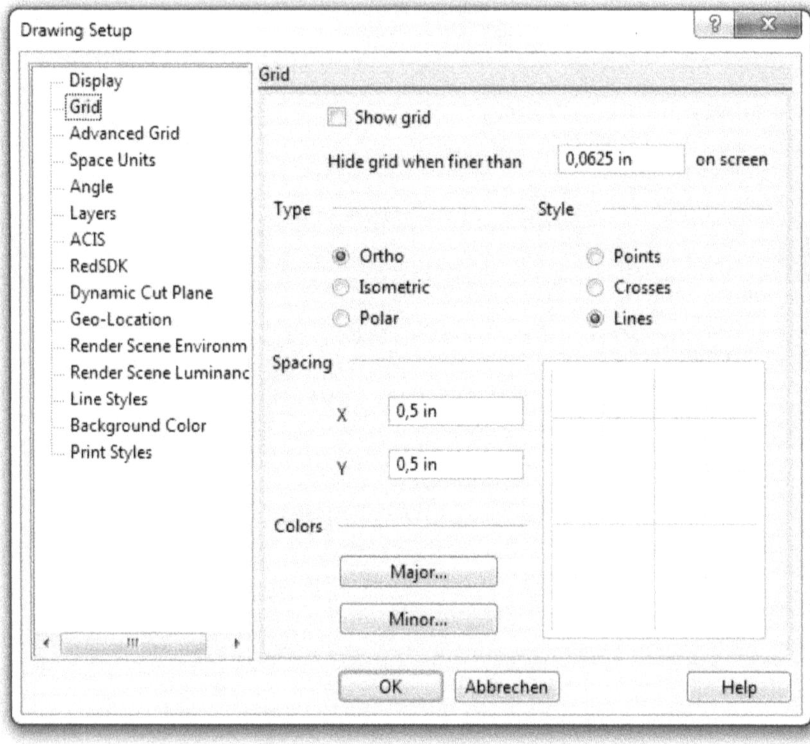

Figure 3-14 Drawing Setup – Grid

The "Grid" and "Advanced Grid" menus control the type, spacing, and display of the grid (chapter 4.8). It can be selected between "Ortho", "Isometric" or "Polar", the line spacing can be defined and its visual appearance adjusted. The use of the grid will be highlighted later in the book.

Settings for the grid density, the division between fine and coarse grid and the alignment are controlled under "Advanced Grid". Offset in X and Y coordinates as well as an offset angle can be entered.

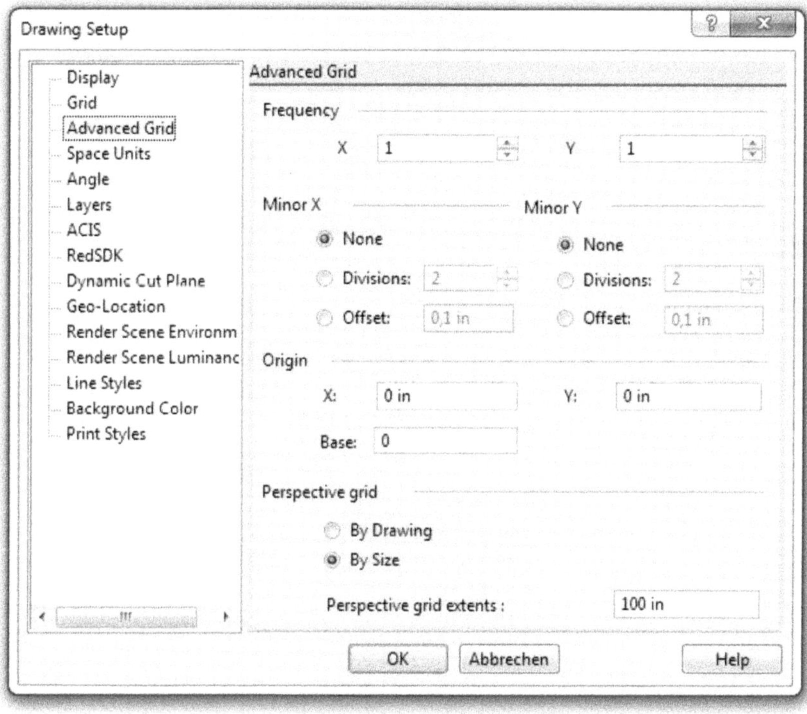

Figure 3-15 Drawing Setup – Advanced Grid

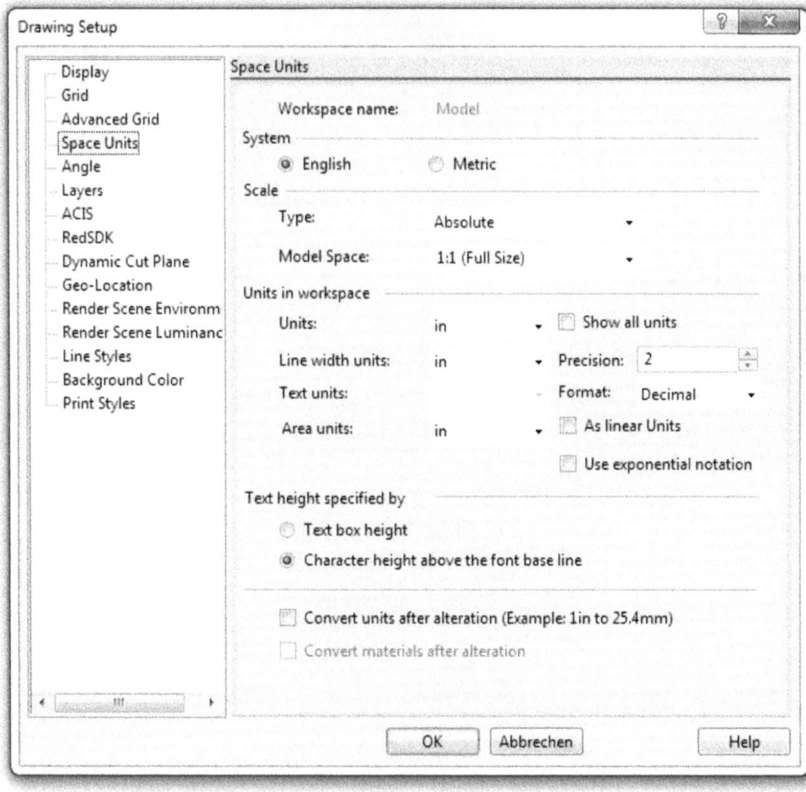

Figure 3-16 Drawing Setup – Space Units

The "Space Units" menu manages the drawing scale and the unit system. The "Precision" option controls the decimal places for dimension inputs, e.g. in the "Inspector Bar". Whether the value entered for the text size refers to the height of the letters / numbers or the text field height can also be defined.

If a drawing is imported which uses a different unit system, the option "Convert units after alteration" can be used. If this option is not selected, 1 inch will be converted to 1 mm. If the check box is marked with a tick, 1 inch will be converted to 25.4 mm. After importing, you should then use dimensions or query tools to check whether the conversion has worked how you wanted.

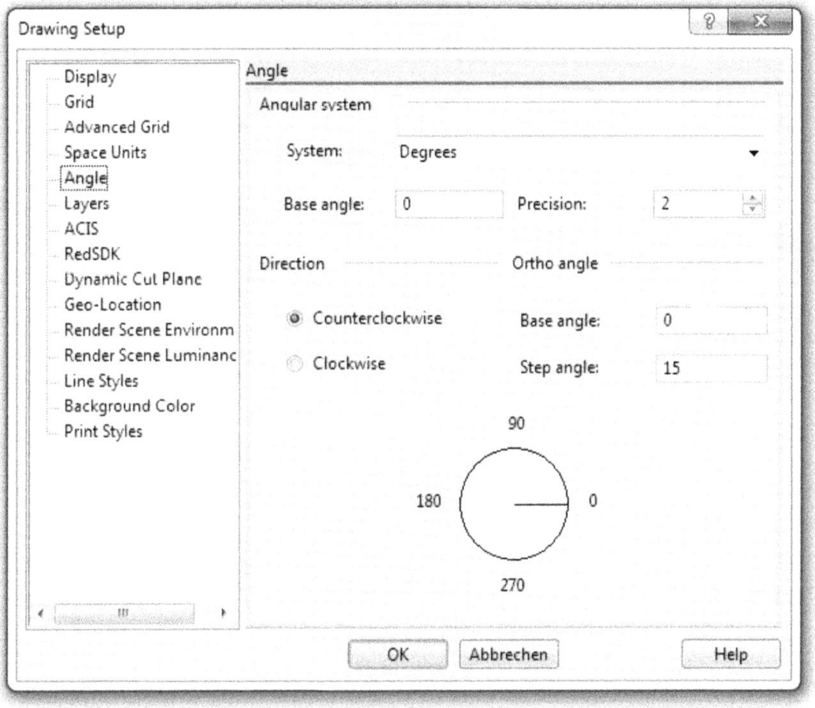

Figure 3-17 Drawing Setup – Angle

The angle system, which controls the rotation of objects via the "Inspector Bar" or the use of the "Ortho" mode (chapter 4.2), can be adjusted in the "Angle" menu. The settings here allow the angle system to be adapted to imported and maybe rotated drawings. The base angle defines the starting point of the angle system. The "Precision" value defines how many decimal places are taken into account analogous to the previously explained unit system (Figure 3-16). Entered values with more decimal places than set under "Precision" are automatically rounded up or down. For the angle system which controls the "Ortho" mode, the base and step angle can be set separately.

Figure 3-18 Drawing Setup – Layers

The "Layer" menu provides an overview of the layers and layer groups in the drawing in the same way as the "Design Director". All settings made here are taken over one by one in the "Design Director". Layer and layer sets can be added, deleted and edited. The handling of these settings is much easier in the "Design Director" (Chapter 2.7). The redundant "Layer" menu described here only serves as an overview.

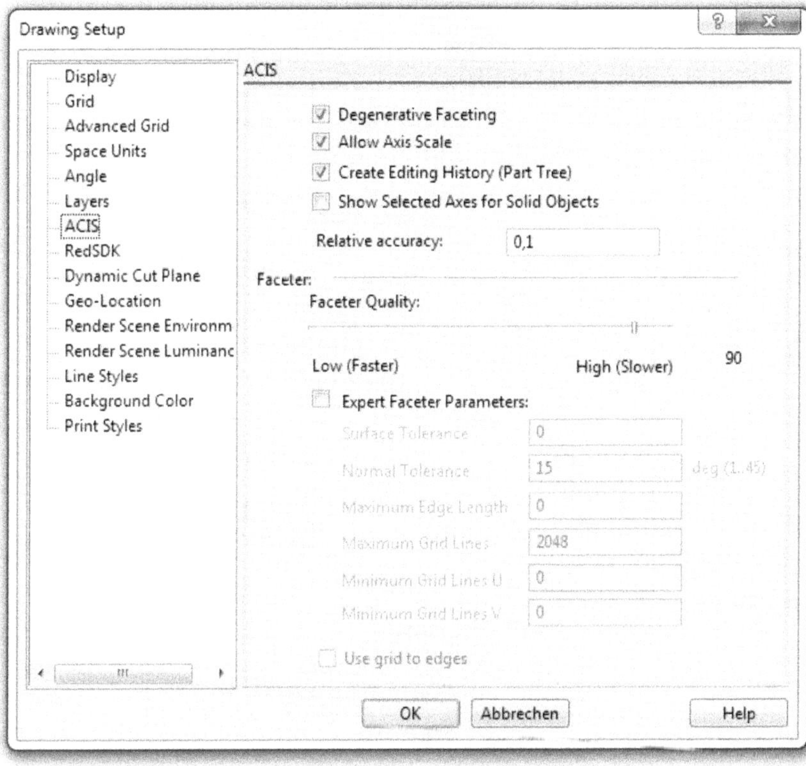

Figure 3-19 Drawing Setup – ACIS

When using TurboCAD® to create 3D objects, the "ACIS" and "RedSDK" menus are important. Here the display quality and the rendering mode "Hidden Line" are controlled (Chapter 5.13). An important point is "Create Editing History (Part Tree)". The "Part Tree" lists all processing steps of a component in chronological order and can be viewed in the "Selection Info" palette. For history-based modeling (chapter 5.7), which is the ability to intervene in previous drawing commands and to be able to change them, activating the part structure is essential.

If this is not desired, this option can be deactivated for performance reasons. Thus, the part history would not be recorded and, consequently, the processing steps of the part will not be reloaded again and again.

The facet quality controls the visual "softness" of the curves. If it is set low, curved lines are visually subdivided into straight single lines and the impression of a polygon is created.

The higher the value is set, the smaller these individual pieces become, until at some point they visually merge into one curved line.

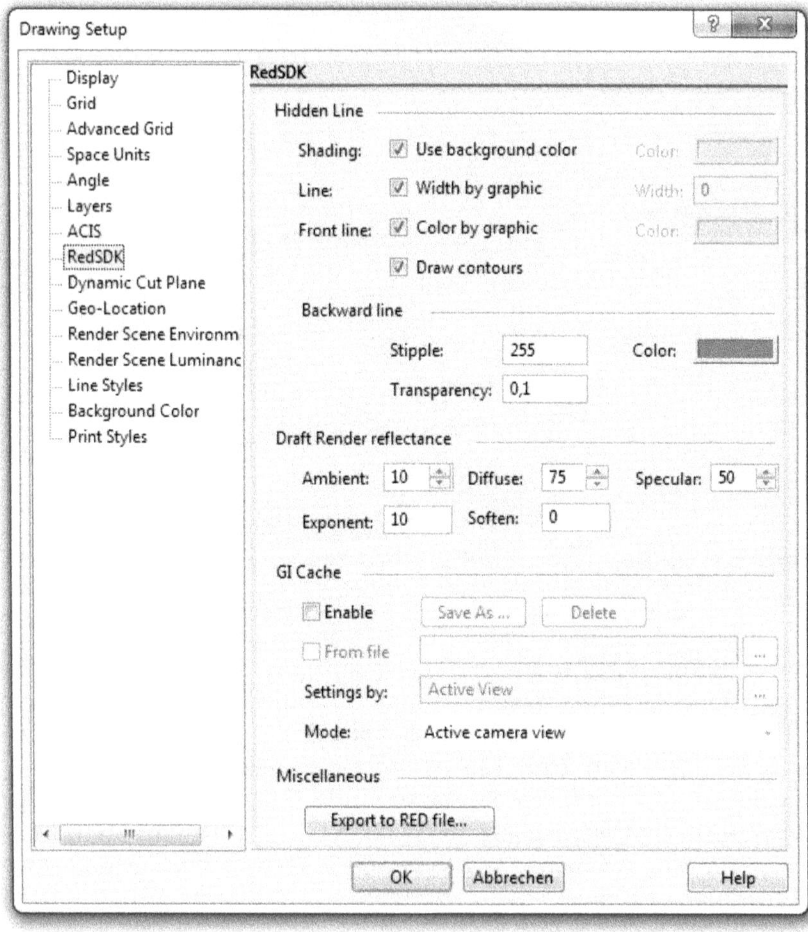

Figure 3-20 Drawing Setup – RedSDK

Properties of rendering modes "Hidden Line" and "Draft" are controlled in the "RedSDK" menu. The various render options for displaying 3D objects are explained in more detail in chapter 5.13.

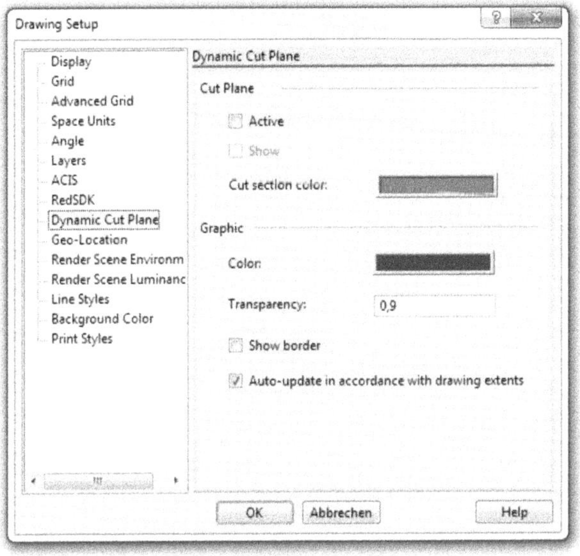

Figure 3-21 Drawing Setup – Dynamic Cut Plane

The "Dynamic Cut Plane" can be used to create temporary and interactive section views of a drawn 3D solid or assembly. The cutting plane can be moved freely and rotated and cuts the component according to its position. This allows glances into the interior of the model without having to delete or split parts or areas. Contours or surfaces cut in this way are only visual as this process gives a projection of what the object would look like if the part was actually cut away. They cannot therefore be snapped or otherwise used. The optical properties of the cutting plane are controlled in the "Dynamic Cut Plane" menu.

The "Dynamic Cut Plane" can be moved or aligned with the standard toolbar shown below.

Figure 3-22 Standard toolbar "Dynamic Cut Plane"

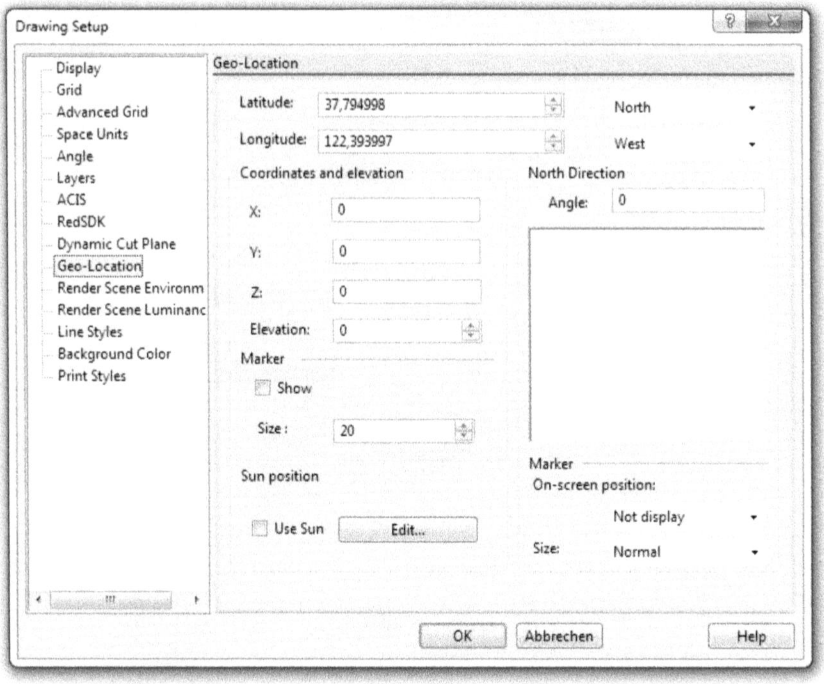

Figure 3-23 Drawing Setup – Geo-Location

The menu item "Geo-Location" offers the possibility to store geographic coordinates in a drawing. This should be interesting for architecture or landscaping users.

For photorealistic rendering, you can also enter the position of the sun in this menu and thus create a natural and realistic illumination of the model.

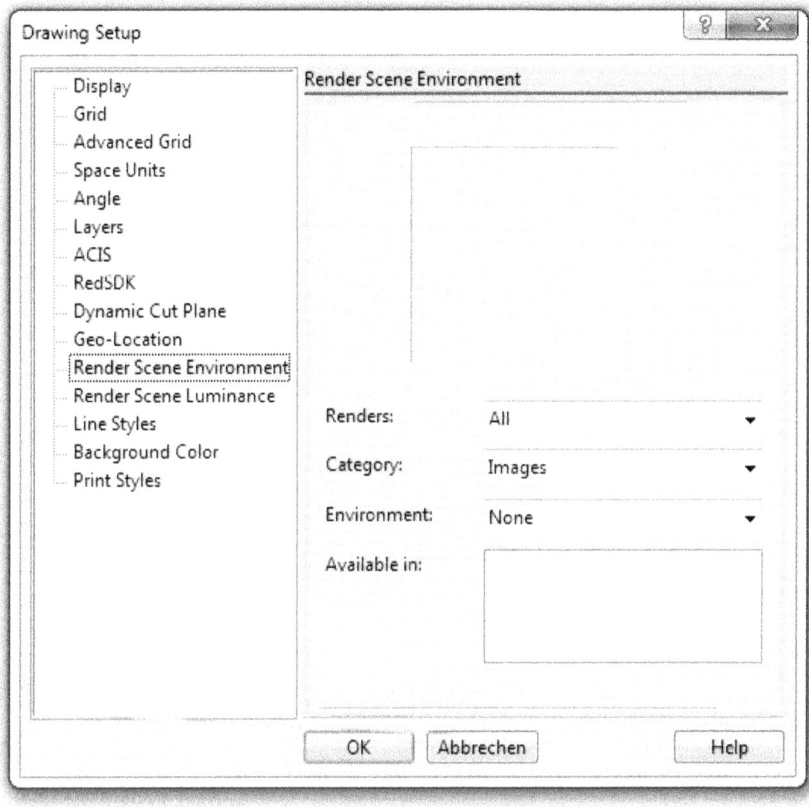

Figure 3-24 Drawing Setup – Render Scene Environment

In the "Render Scene Environment" and "Render Scene Luminance" menus, background graphics can be added both behind and in front of the model for a deep-realistic rendering. You can also set luminance for the entire drawing or individual objects.

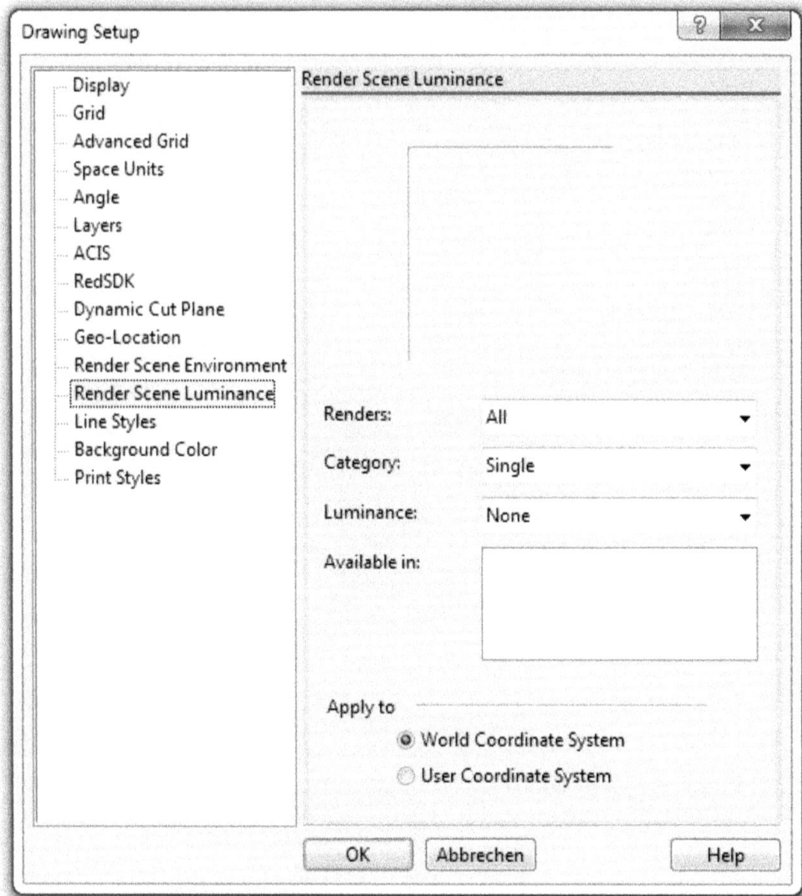

Figure 3-25 Drawing Setup – Render Scene Luminance

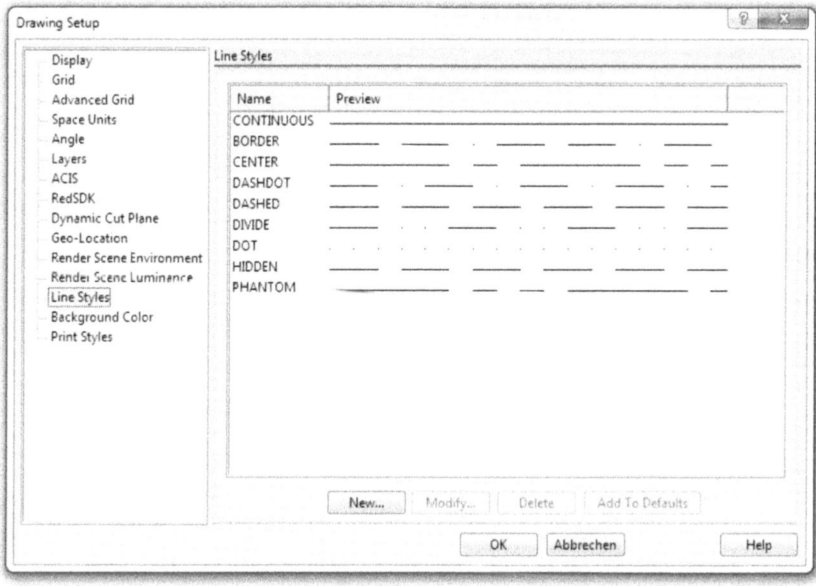

Figure 3-26 Drawing Setup – Line Styles

In the menu "Line Styles" all defined line styles are listed. Only the line styles listed here can be assigned to objects and layers. Line styles can be created, deleted, and changed here. To create your own line styles, a variety of icons are available. They can be selected from the elements: “Dash”, “Dot”, “Space”, “Shape” and “Text”.

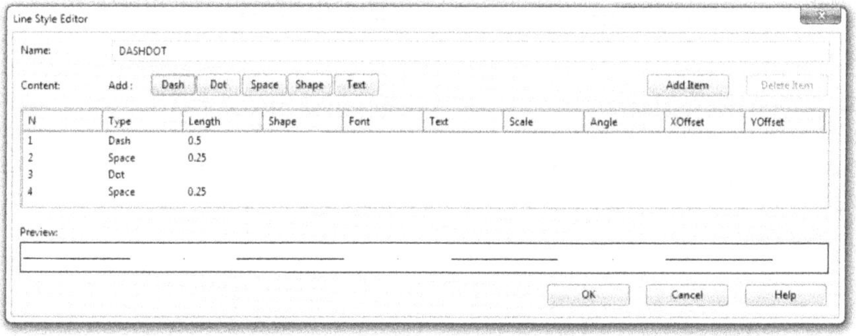

Figure 3-27 Line Style Editor

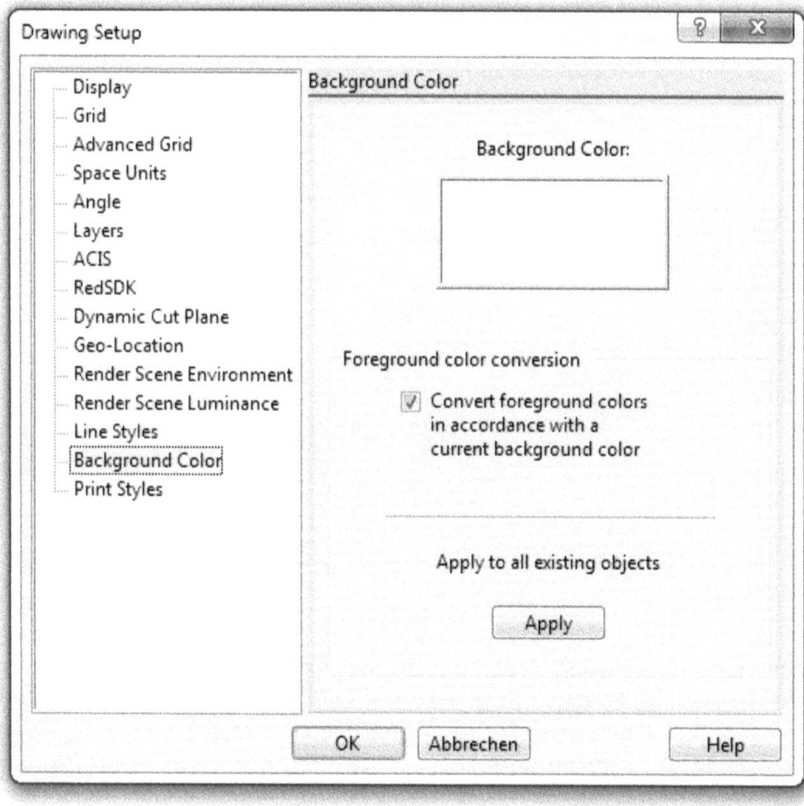

Figure 3-28 Drawing Setup – Background Color

The "Background Color" menu is limited to selecting the background color and the option to invert objects of the same color as the selected background color so that they remain visible and don't disappear from view. For example, white lines on a white background are displayed in black. Since this can be set for individual drawing objects in their settings, the "Apply" button enables overwriting.

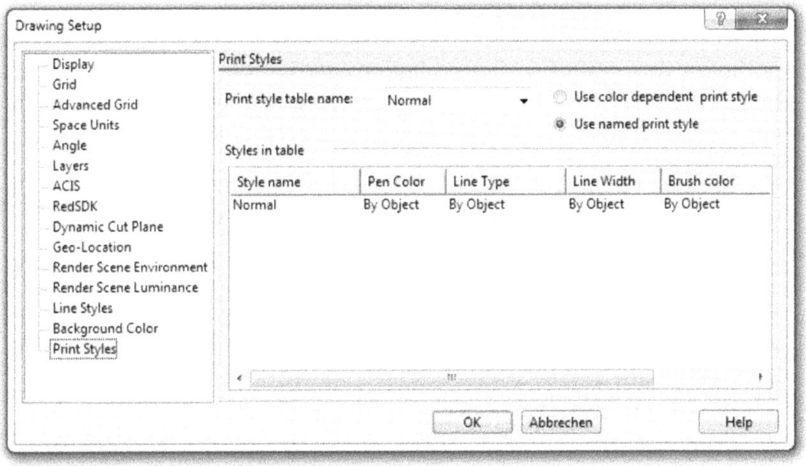

Figure 3-29 Drawing Setup – Print Styles

The different print styles determine the colors, line styles, or brushes of objects as soon as the drawing is printed. The representation on the screen, which is primarily controlled by the layer and object settings (chapter 2.7), remains unaffected.

The desired print style can then be selected during printing in the printer menu.

3.3 Drawing template

In a company with several CAD workstations, it makes sense to use a standard drawing template. It is desirable that a cross-user standard is set in which font, font size, drawing formats, drawing header, etc. are set and preset.

TurboCAD® provides the ability to create a drawing template, place it centrally on a network server and load it automatically when a new drawing is opened.

This drawing template can contain the following information:

- Paper spaces with drawing borders, title block, and company logo
- Predefined standard layers
- Text styles
- Lighting to visualize 3D objects
- Tool settings
- Space unit system

A drawing template that has the file extension ".tct" is created and loaded as follows.

First, a new document is created with the selection "New from Scratch". The opened document will now be edited according to your own ideas. If the selection window shown in Figure 3-30 does not appear when opening a new document, you must first select "Prompt for template name" under "Options/ Program Setup/ General" in the "New document" menu item.

Care must be taken when creating and maintaining the drawing template, as it is used by all users. Errors quickly multiply among a large number of users. Changes to a drawing template have no effect on previously created drawings. The template is used only when creating a new drawing, and then does not retain any association.

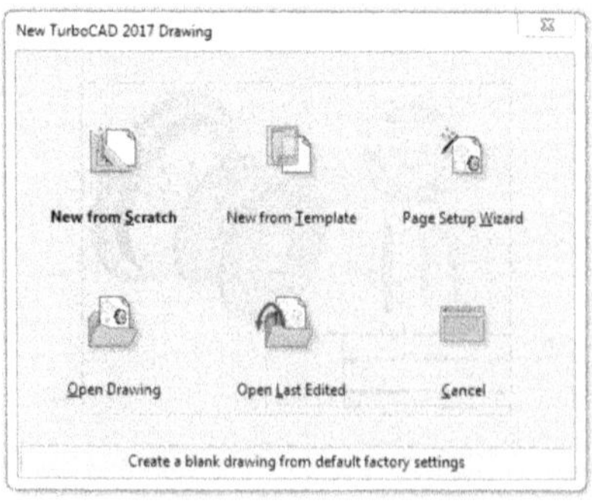

Figure 3-30 New TurboCAD 2017 Drawing

Paper space with a title block and frame

The standard template can store common sheet formats, so you do not have to add them when creating drawing derivations. For the different sheet formats (for example, DIN A4 to A0 in landscape and portrait format), the title block and frame can be implemented, which contain the company logo and, if necessary, some pre-filled information.

Standard layers

When creating a drawing template, layers should be preset that are used by all users. In addition to the classic layers such as contour, dimension, hidden or centerline, there are also industry-specific layers, such as different media in piping and instrumentation diagrams.

Unit system

The desired units (mm, inches, etc.) can be set in the drawing template and define how many decimal places are displayed.

Lighting

If TurboCAD® is used exclusively in the 2D area, the lighting in the drawing template does not have to be adjusted. Any document opened without a template initially has no lighting. If also drawn three-dimensionally, it is advisable to add lights which, when switching to a rendering mode, illuminate the modeled objects sufficiently to allow a realistic view. The lighting settings are under "View/ Lights ...". TurboCAD® suggests activating the default lighting when switching to a render mode. This is sufficient in most cases but can be edited yourself.

The arrangement and intensity of illumination within the standard drawing template can be chosen according to taste. The distance of the points of light in the standard template to the origin (x=0, y=0, z=0) can be adjusted according to the average expected object size. If smaller objects are usually modeled, the points of light can be moved closer to the origin. This creates a very natural illumination. In chapter 5.13 the visualization of 3D models will be discussed further.

Figure 3-31 Arrangement of lights

Tool settings

Individual commands can be provided with appropriate layers. If, for example, you want to assign different layers for contour, dimensioning or 3D objects, you can link these with the corresponding commands. This is done by right-clicking on the corresponding command symbol. In the menu which opens, the layer under "General" can be selected and confirmed with OK. If you then use the corresponding command, TurboCAD® automatically activates the previously set layer. Example: If the "Text" command is linked to a separately created text layer from the start, created texts are automatically placed on it and can then be faded in or out if necessary, or formatting properties can be changed in the "Design Director".

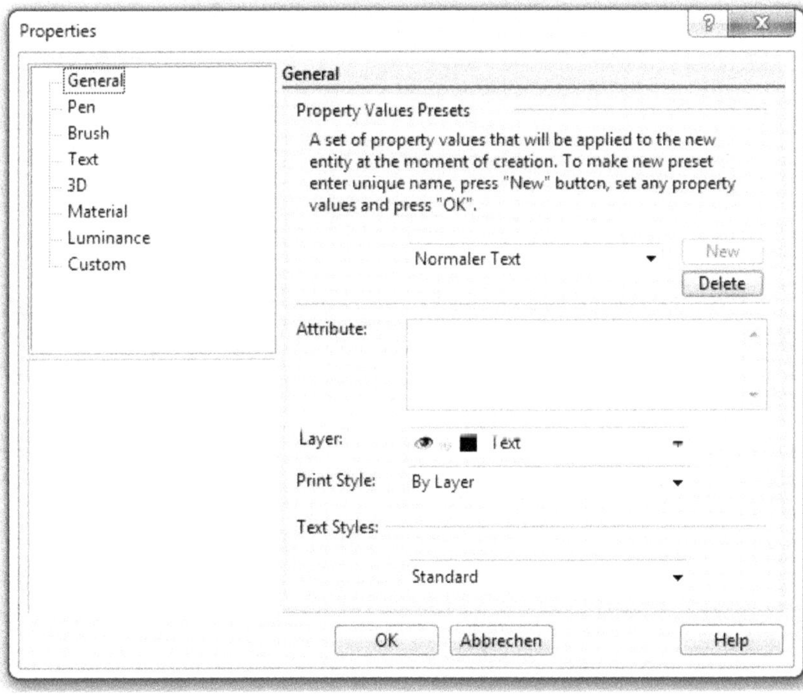

Figure 3-32 Linking command properties to a Layer.

3.4 SELECTOR PROPERTIES

The "Selection Properties" menu allows the configuration of the selection tools and how they interact with the coordinate systems and the "Inspector Bar". In this menu you can define what you want double-clicking to do. For example, you can define whether double-clicking on an object opens the object properties (Chapter 2.8) or activates the "Edit tool" (Chapter 4.6). It is also possible to set to which coordinate system the input values (for example when moving an object) in the "Inspector Bar" relate.

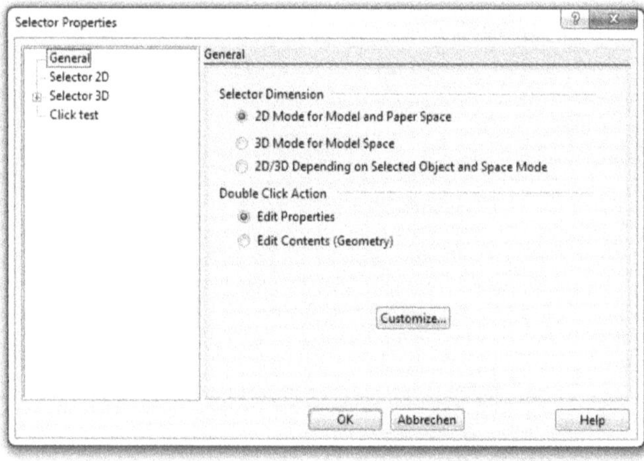

Figure 3-33 Selector Properties - General

The different coordinate systems and their use are explained in chapter 5.4. Under "Customize" the actions by double-clicking for different objects, features, etc. can be defined. A drop-down menu offers various actions to choose from.

Figure 3-34 Customize Double Click Action

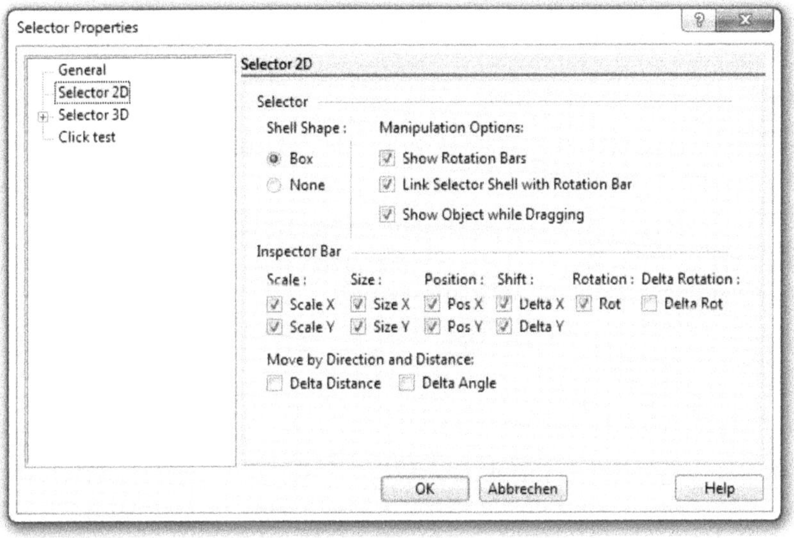

Figure 3-35 Selector Properties – Selector 2D

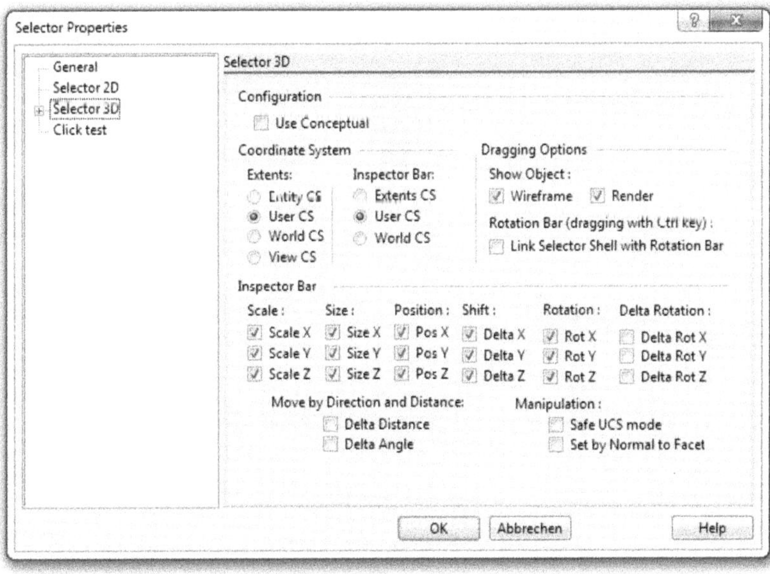

Figure 3-36 Selector Properties – Selector 3D

3.5 KEY USER CONCEPT

If a company has several CAD workstations, and if TurboCAD® is to be installed and managed across all of them, the naming of a key user is recommended.

The following explains the activities and benefits of having a key user for the company and its colleagues:

- Maintenance of software installation and setup
- Contact person for all users who have questions and problems
- Designated user of the software's hotline
- Collection point for improvement suggestions and new features of a program update
- Training of colleagues as and when the company needs it
- Management of standard templates and symbol libraries

In order to enable the key user to carry out these tasks, they should regularly undergo further training and, if necessary, go to training courses. Thus, they can also decide for the company, when the change to a new program version should take place.

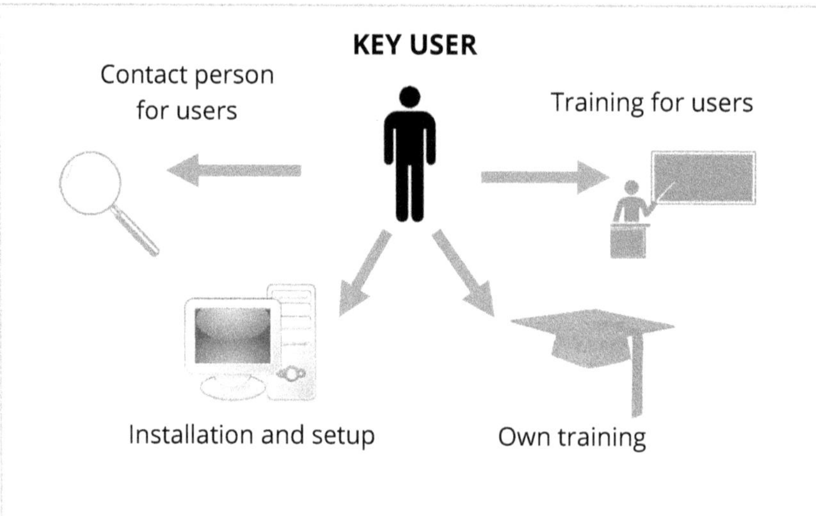

Figure 3-37 Key-User concept

4 Two-dimensional drafting

4.1 Basic 2D drafting tools

The simplest but most commonly used basic two-dimensional drawing tools include the simple line, the rectangle, and the circle. The main this that these commands have in common is that they are defined with two mouse clicks. After clicking on the corresponding command symbol, the first mouse click in the model space sets the starting coordinates. This starting coordinate is a line end point for the simple line, one of the four corners for the rectangle or the center of the circle for the circle command "Circle Center and Point". With the second click you define the angle and the length of the line, the edge lengths of the rectangle or the radius of the circle.

Table 2 Exemplary comparison of the most important 2D basic tools

"Line" 	**"Rectangle"** 	**"Circle Center and Point"** 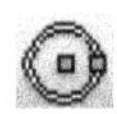
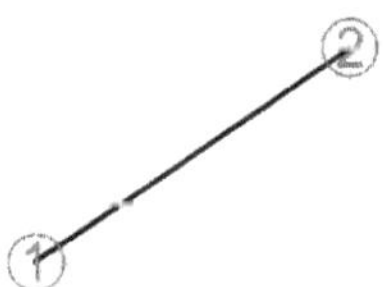	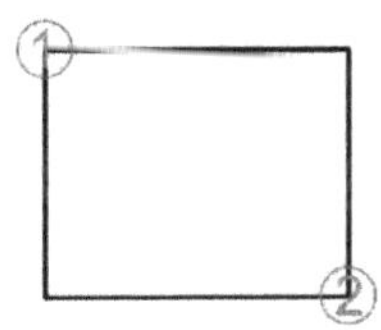	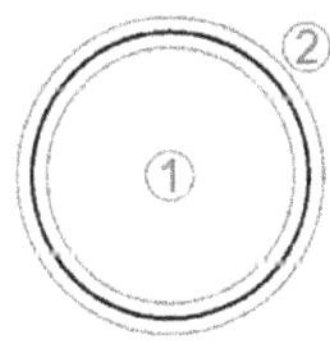

The drawing commands usually remain active after an object has been created, so that the command is executed again by clicking again in the model space. These simple geometries can be placed freely in the model space.

The question quickly arises as to how lines can be aligned horizontally, vertically or at a certain angle. To do this, there are several possibilities.

"Ortho" mode 

The "Ortho" mode allows you to draw at predefined angles. These can be defined under "Options/ Drawing Setup/ Angle". If the "Ortho" mode is activated, a line tool can be used to draw the lines only in these angular steps. Likewise, objects can only be moved in this type of grid.

Because this command is frequently turned on and off, it is useful to use a keyboard shortcut or appropriate positioning on the desktop. Keyboard shortcuts can be assigned in the "Customize" menu (Figure 2-2) in the menu item "Keyboard".

The "Extended Ortho"  mode is another snapping tool. When enabled, horizontal and vertical guides will appear on which points can be snapped. For this, the mouse must first be held stationary at the starting point for a short time. The guides will be displayed shortly afterwards. These guides are always located on the work plane (Chapter 5.8). This must be taken into account when using this command in the 3D mode.

Input of coordinates

If the line command is activated, the "Inspector Bar" at the bottom of the screen contains a "Length" and Angle" box. If the starting point is set, the line can be defined by specifying the length [mm] [1] and angle [°]. The unit system can be changed under "Options/ Drawing Setup/ Space Units".

The starting point of all 2D and 3D objects can also be determined by entering the mouse pointer coordinates. If a command is activated, the values are first entered into the X, Y and, if applicable, the Z coordinate fields by pressing the "TAB" key and the command is executed by pressing "ENTER" to confirm.

The starting point is thus at the desired position.

[1] Depending on the selected unit system

"Polyline" 

The polyline is a series of connected single endpoints. If the command is activated, an end point is defined with each mouse click in the model space. If you have set a point incorrectly, the command "One Step Back" undoes the wrong positioning of the point. With the command "Close" the last set end point is connected to the starting point of the polyline and thus a closed profile is created. If you select the "Finish" command or press the "ESC" key, the polyline is created, and the command is ended. You can choose between straight line or curved segments. The "Edit Tool" (Chapter 4.6) can be used to move, add or remove nodes later to change the polyline. If the polyline is exploded with the "Explode" command, intended to break up groups, the segments lose their connection to each other and single lines are created.

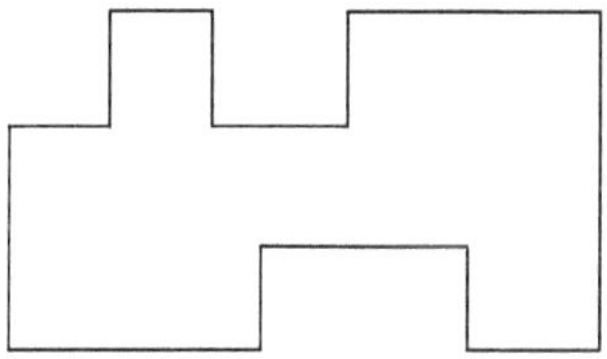

Figure 4-1 Application example - Polyline

"Revision Cloud" 

To create revision clouds to highlight changes, use the "Revision Cloud" command under "Draw/ Curve/ Revision Cloud". The use of this command is similar to the "Polyline" command described above. If you have set a point incorrectly, the command "One Step Back" undoes the wrong positioning. With the command "Close" the last set end point is connected to the starting point of the revision cloud and thus a closed profile is created.

Figure 4-2 Example: Revision cloud

Spline and Bezier curves

Using the various spline tools, smooth and homogeneous curves can be created. For this purpose, different reference points are usually set between which the spline line runs according to the selected command. Then with the "Edit Tool" all control points and tangent directions can be adjusted, and the curve changed. In addition, in the object properties, among other things, the fineness of the curve is influenced by the number of segments and it can be chosen between "Spline" and "Bezier" curve types.

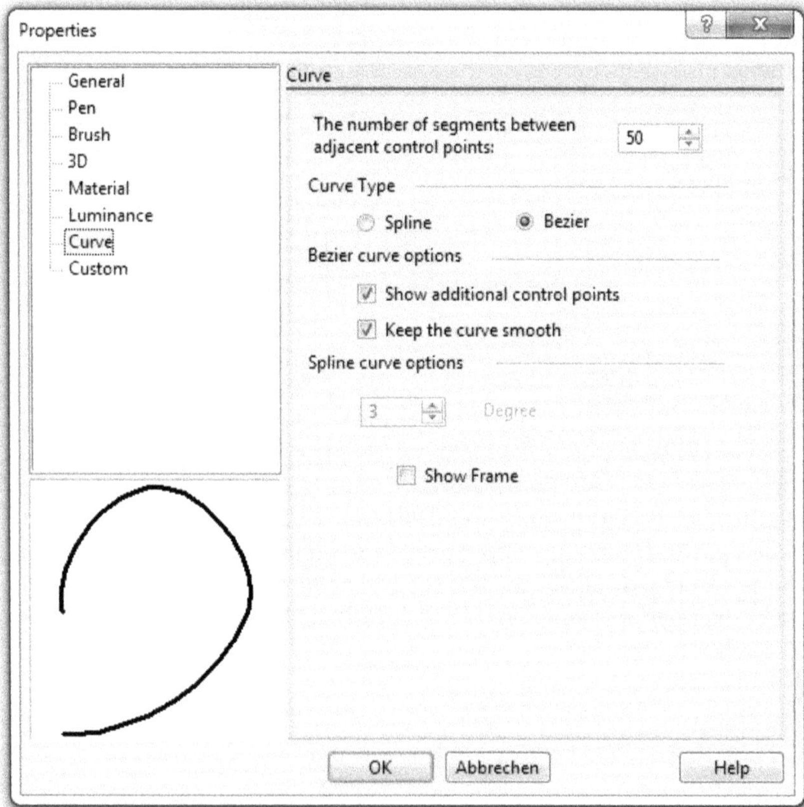

Figure 4-3 Properties of a spline curve

"Spline By Control Points" 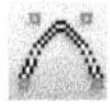

Each click determines the position of a control point (blue). The spline curve then runs accordingly within the set points.

Figure 4-4 Example: "Spline By Control Points"

"Spline By Fit Points" 

The spline curve runs through all points that are defined by the user. The control points are automatically placed in the required position. If these control points are subsequently moved, the spline line no longer passes through the insertion points (black). There is no connection.

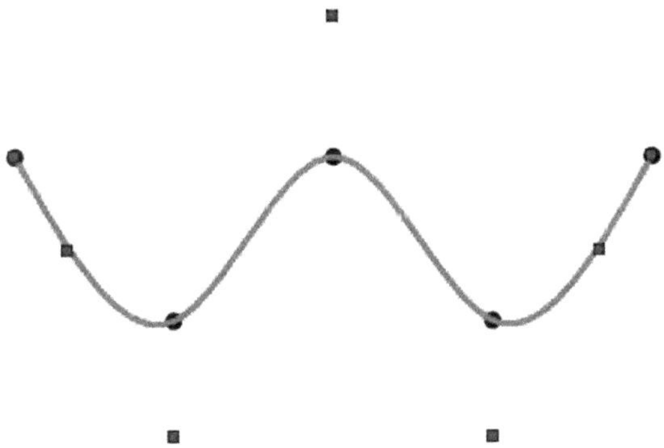

Figure 4-5 Example: "Spline By Fit Points"

"Bezier" 

In contrast to the other two spline tools, the Bezier curve offers the possibility of influencing the tangent directions. As a result, this curve can be adapted more flexibly and lends itself to free-form surface modeling.

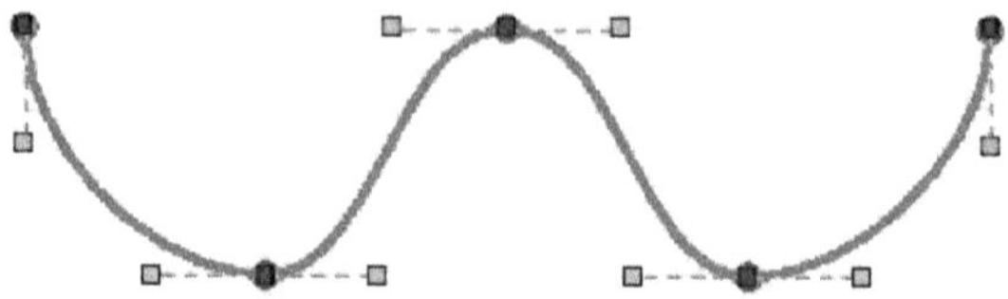

Figure 4-6 Example "Bezier"

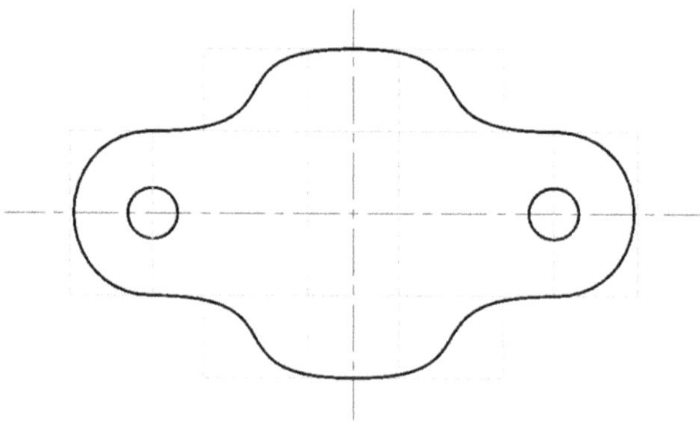

Figure 4-7 Application example - Spline

4.2 MANAGE SNAP MODES

Snap modes allow precise snapping of points such as endpoints or midpoints of lines. For example, if you want to add another line to a drawn line, the exact connection of the end points is not possible freehand without the snapping tools. It may seem this way at first glance, but if zoomed in on the corresponding spot, we can see that the two lines are not connected properly. Two examples are shown in the following table:

Table 3 Example: Drafting without snap tools

NORMAL VIEW	DETAIL ENLARGED
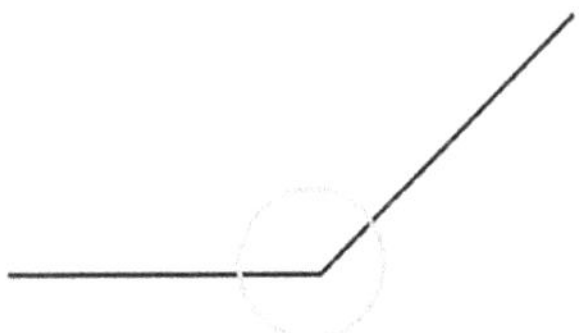	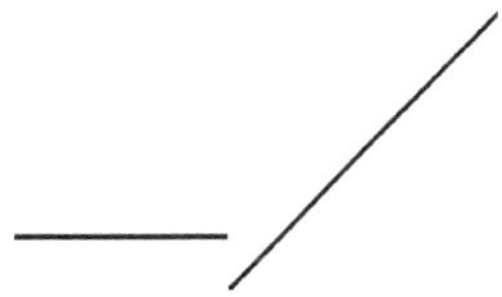
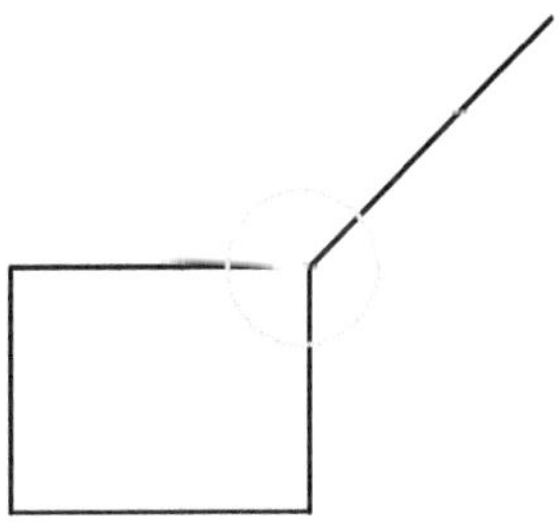	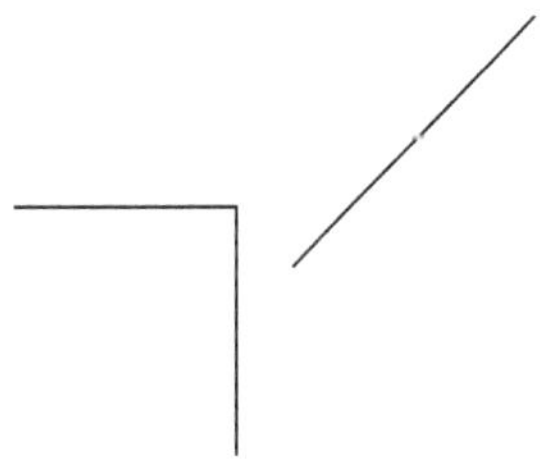

In order to enable accurate drawing and to be able to optimally use other editing tools, the use of the object snap, both in 2D and in 3D drawing, is essential.

The most important snap modes are shown in the table below:

Table 4 Important snap modes

"Vertex"	
"Middle Point"	
"Center"	
"Intersection"	
"Quadrant Point"	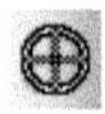

There are several ways to manage the snap modes. One way is to do this is by right-clicking on "SNAP" in the bottom right-hand corner of the screen which opens the "Drawing Aids" menu (Figure 4-8). This contains a list of snap options for selecting and deselecting. It should be noted that the first three selection items of the capture options are only to be activated if they are needed, as they could otherwise suppress or influence the other snap tools. If you encounter problems with the usual snap modes while drawing, it is worth taking a look at this menu.

> It should always be ensured that not too many snap modes are activated at the same time. This can limit the functionality due to the fact that the possible snap points interfere with each other.

Snaps can also be equipped with different priorities.

The use of the snap modes and the setting of priorities must be set by each user for themselves in order to find the optimum for their own working method.

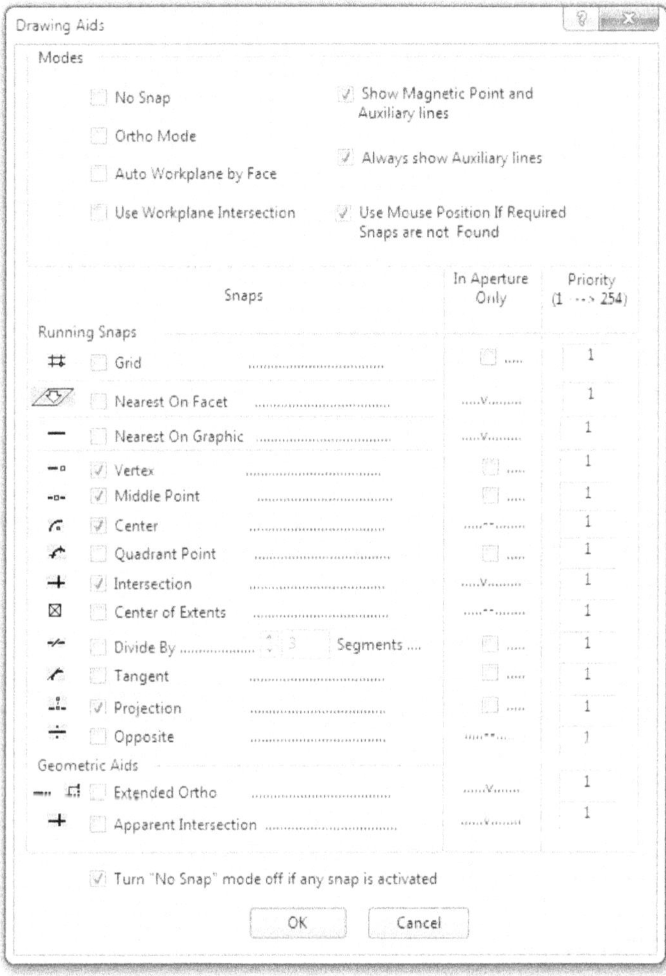

Figure 4-8 Snaps in the "Drawing Aids" menu

For faster access to the snap tools, it is possible to create a corresponding toolbar on the edge of the screen. Here, as already explained in chapter 2.1.2, you can apply your own selection of snap tools or use the standard "Snap Modes" toolbar.

The “No Snap”  command automatically disables all snap tools. If this is activated, there are no snap modes available. If the lowest selection point "Turn "No Snap" mode off if any snap is activated" is selected in the "Drawing Aids" menu (Figure 4-8), the command "No Snap" will automatically switch off as soon as a snap mode is manually activated.

Also, via the "SNAP" button, which is located in the “Status Bar”, all snap modes can be switched on or off at once. Please note that the command "No Snap" and the button "SNAP" are not linked; they can be turned off individually. However, if one of them is turned off, there will be no snap modes available. There is no added value in this unusual division of one function into two different buttons. This just creates confusion. If no snap modes are available, both the "No Snap" command and the "SNAP" button must be checked to see if either of them has been deactivated.

A third way to apply snap options is explained below.

While a drawing command is already active, individual snaps can still be changed if too many others automatically appear in the area in which an object is to be snapped. If, for example, you have set the starting point of a line and want to use only a special snap mode for the end point, you can select it by right-clicking, and choosing the desired snap mode in the "Local Snap" menu. Only this selected snap will be then offered. If this snap mode is then executed, the selection is resolved, and all other snap modes become available again. Keyboard shortcuts can be used to speed up the selection of snap modes and thus the workflow.

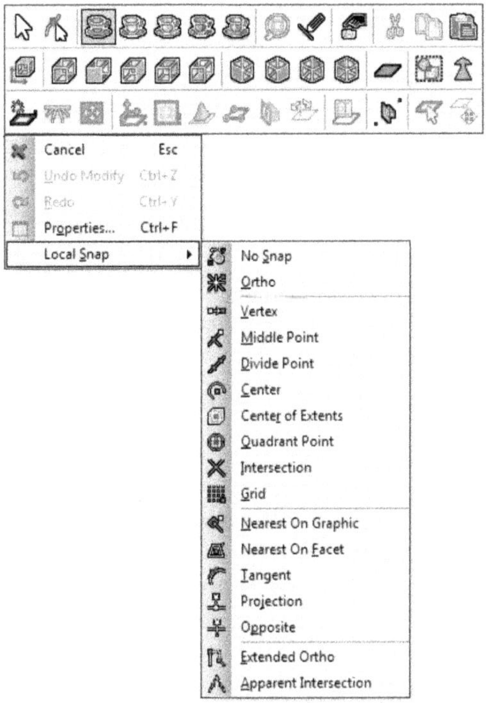

Figure 4-9 Selection of a snap option during an active drawing command

4.3 MOVE, COPY & RELOCATE THE REFERENCE POINT

When an object is selected, a reference point is displayed in the center of the selection frame. The selection frame includes the extent of the object or all selected objects. The reference point is shown as a yellow dot. At this, the object can be moved and positioned on other objects.

The valve symbol shown below illustrates a problem that sooner or later any user of TurboCAD® will be confronted with. For example, if you want to move the valve symbol to the end of a pipe line, the default position of the reference point in the middle of the selection frame is not helpful. However, the reference point can be moved.

If you move the mouse over the reference point while holding down the "CTRL" key, the mouse symbol changes from an arrow to a hand symbol . If you now click on the dot while holding down the "CTRL" key, the reference point now sticks to the mouse pointer. The "CTRL" key can then be released. The reference point can be arbitrarily set down anywhere, not only on the valve symbol itself. When setting the reference point down, snap modes can and should be used. Otherwise no exact positioning of the reference point or the part is possible.

The reference point of the valve symbol can now be placed in order to be connect it to the pipe line. Also, the reference point can be attached directly to the mouse pointer by pressing the "D" key. For larger objects, searching or zooming in to the reference point may be omitted. This keyboard command is useful in everyday life to speed up the workflow.

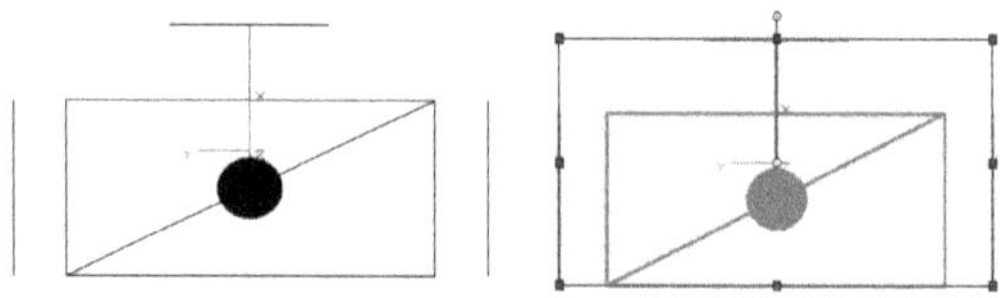

Figure 4-10 Object selection by reference point

It should be noted that for a group of objects or a block, the position of the shifted reference point is retained even if the group is deselected and re-selected. For individual objects such as lines, the reference point automatically returns to its default position when re-selecting.

If the reference point of a group or a block is offset but needs to be reset to its standard position, which is in the middle of the object selection frame, the command "Default Reference Point" can be used. This is located in the "Inspector Bar". This command is greyed out, if the point is already on the standard position.

There are three ways to copy objects:

"Rubber Stamp"

If an object is selected and the "Rubber Stamp" is activated in the right-click pop up menu or the "Inspector Bar", a copy of the previously marked object is saved with each further click in the model or paper space. The object is placed at the reference point.

If objects are not to be distributed freely, but to be deposited at defined points, the appropriate positioning of the reference point is required. The copying stamp can be deactivated by pressing the "ESC" key or selecting another command.

If a 3D object contains an editing history (Chapter 5.7), the "Copy Stamp" is not available for duplication. In this case the command "Make Copy" can be used.

"Make Copy"

The "Make Copy" command behaves similarly to the "Copy Stamp". It can be activated, however, without having to select an object. After the command has been activated, a copy is generated when moving an object. Even when moving the reference point or the rotation points, a copy of the selected object is created, which then lies exactly on the old object.

The "Make Copy" command remains active after one use. It must be deactivated manually after copying.

> To prevent duplicated copies, due to forgetting to deactivate the "Make Copy" command after using it, the "STRG" key can be pressed while moving a part at its reference point. This temporarily activates the "Make Copy" command.

False copies, which are exactly on the original part, are not immediately recognizable. So sometimes many lines or objects lie on top of each other, especially in drawings in which reference points are often moved. For larger objects with a large part structure in the 3D area, this can lead to significant performance losses since all these objects are calculated in the background.

The following chapter shows ways to detect duplicated and superimposed objects.

CTRL+C und CTRL+V

Copying and pasting via the "CTRL" key in combination with the keys "C" (for copying) and "V" (for pasting) also works in TurboCAD®. All objects can be copied in this way. As a rule, the objects are inserted in the center of the screen and are selected after insertion.

4.4 Detection of superimposed objects

Activation of the selection list

By activating the selection list in the program settings ("Options/ Program Setup/ Preferences/ Selection"), underlying objects are automatically made visible when the selection list appears because the program is unsure which line to select.

An example can be seen in the following figure. Here are two identical lines on top of each other. If you select the visible line, the selection list opens so the program can clarify which line is intended to be chosen.

Figure 4-11 Recognition of duplicate objects through the selection list

Color change in 3D render mode

If copies of a 3D object are accidentally made, this is indicated by a change in the color of the object. The more copies you make, the brighter the color will be.

This recognition is only possible in the render mode "Draft" and if there is another existing object with the same color as a reference.

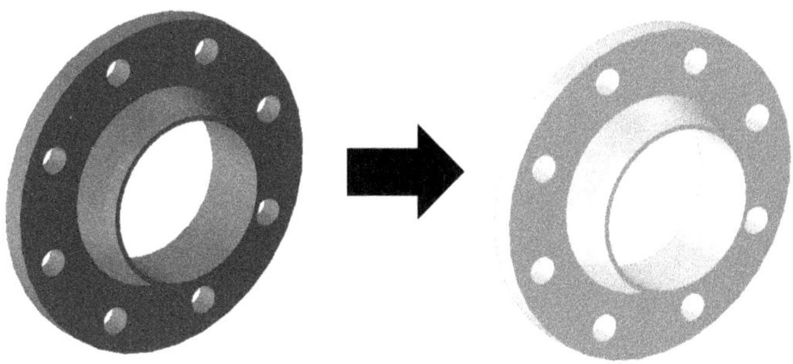

Figure 4-12 Optical identification of superimposed parts

Check through the "Selection Info" palette

Checking through the "Selection Info" palette is theoretically possible, although not always suitable. If you mark certain areas of the drawing, the "Selection Info" palette displays an overview of the selected drawing objects. If this listing of the number of certain objects does not match the drawn one, discrepancies can be identified.

Detection by chance

If you use editing commands around lines (e.g. to trim) but you see no change, this can also be an indication that there are double lines on top of each other.

4.5 Editing and Modifying 2D Objects

In order to make changes to existing 2D objects, TurboCAD® offers a wide selection of tools for trimming, lengthening, rounding off, mirroring, plus many more.

Some of these commands are put together in the standard toolbar "Modify".

Figure 4-13 Standard toolbar "Modify"

A small selection of these change tools is shown below.

"Object Trim" 

The "Object Trim" tool uses selected 2D objects as cutting edges and removes protruding or intervening objects. What a cutting edge is and what should be removed is defined by the order of selection.

"Split Entity" 

The "Split Entity" command divides objects such as lines or circles into individual segments.

"Stretch" 

This command moves all nodes marked in the selection window, such as endpoints or vertices, according to the input. If an object is selected entirely it will be moved. If only a few nodes are selected, the object is stretched and the shape changes accordingly.

"Fillet2D" and "Chamfer"  

With these commands, corners can be rounded or provided with a chamfer.

The "Polyline" command option  automatically captures and rounds off all corners of a polyline.

4.6 EDIT TOOL

The "Edit Tool" provides the ability to move line nodes to selectively modify drawing objects. It can be activated in three ways; via an icon in the "Inspector Bar", in the pop-up menu by right-clicking or in the "Edit" menu.

If the "Edit Tool" is activated, the mouse pointer contains a black dot. If you click on a 2D object, the nodes are displayed as blue squares. These can now be moved freely or by entering coordinates in the "Inspector Bar".

By holding down the "CTRL" key, nodes can be added to lines (symbol of a black square with an arrow) or removed (garbage bin symbol).

Figure 4-14 Edit a rectangle by adding and moving nodes ("Edit Tool")

Also, on 3D objects useful modifications can be made with the "Edit Tool". With the blue arrow symbols, flat surfaces of 3D bodies can be moved freehand or with dimensions in the "Inspector Bar".

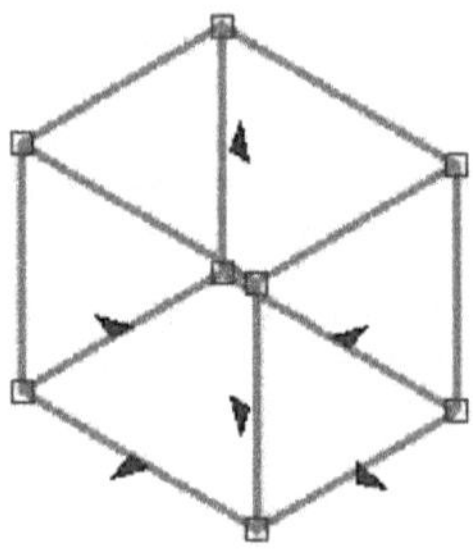

Figure 4-15 Modifying a 3D body through the "Edit Tool"

The "Edit Tool" is also used to move set dimensions. If you select a dimension with the editing tool, blue nodes are displayed, as shown by way of example in Figure 4-16. Based on this, the position of the dimension can be changed.

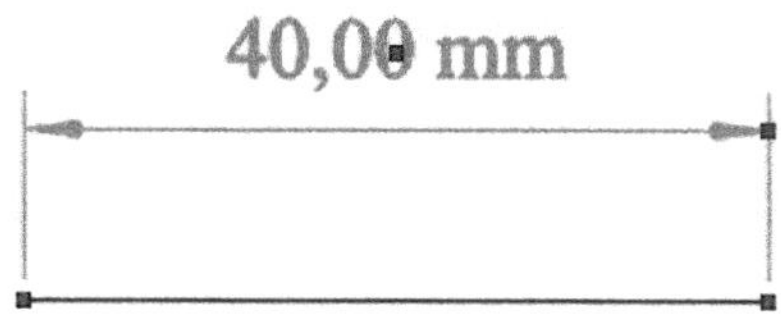

Figure 4-16 Selected dimension ("Edit Tool")

By clicking once on the node, which is on the measurement number, it can be freely moved and placed. The dimension lines automatically adapt to the position of the dimension. The node on one of the dimension arrows allows you to set the height of the dimension line. The dimension number stays at its relative position to the dimension lines.

It also displays node points where the dimension is applied to the drawing object. These points can also be moved which changes what is measured. As can be seen in Figure 4-16, the dimensioned line is displayed in blue. This signals that at least one of the two dimensioning guides points towards the line object.

4.7 DRAWING IN XY COORDINATES

Although drawing in 2D mode means drawing on the XY plane, parts may be shifted in the Z dimension as well. For example, this can occur when external data is included.

The Z dimension is not locked in 2D mode, but instead it is only hidden. For 2D drafting, the standard view "World Plan" is used; a view frontally on the XY plane. Thus, a displacement of parts in the Z dimension can't be easily detected.

Table 5 Unintentional offset in the Z direction

"World Plan" 	**Rotated View**
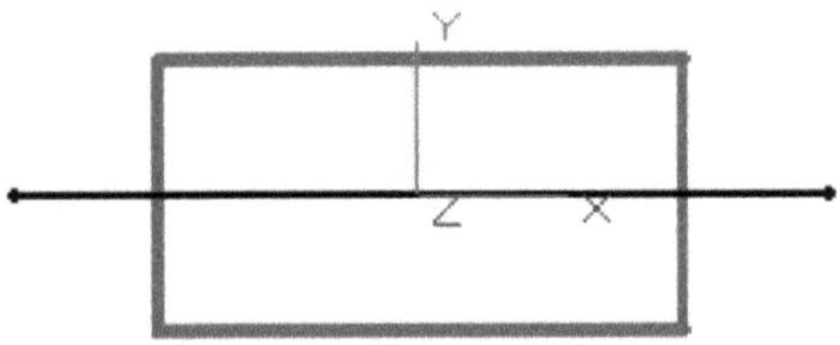	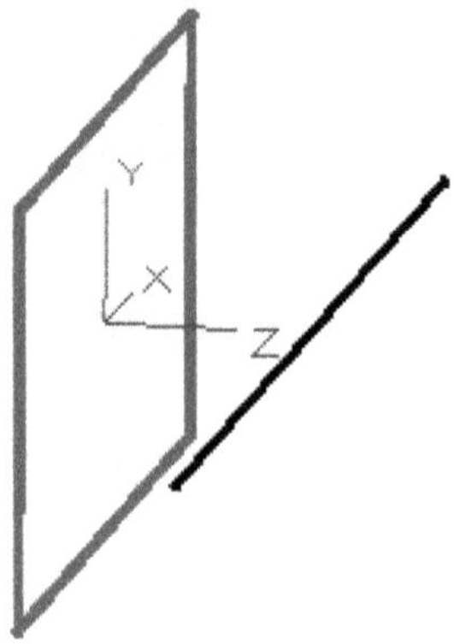

If the entire drawing is marked and the 3D mode is activated, the size in the Z-dimension can be determined. If all lines are on the XY plane, this size must be 0. If the value is not 0, lines or objects are shifted in the Z dimension. This can be seen in the 'Rotated View' section of Table 5 above. A value that is greater than 0 will show a protrusion of the line in the Z dimension.

These can then be determined individually and set back to the XY plane. A simpler and usually faster solution is "flattening" the drawing. To do this, first select everything and enter the value 0 in the field "Size Z" of the "Inspector Bar" and confirm it.

Now, all lines are on a plane parallel to the XY plane although they are not necessarily on it. This is indicated by a value greater than 0 in the "Pos Z" field of the "Inspector Bar". If you set this value to 0, all lines are on the XY axis.

If you want to trim lines that are both wrongly not on the XY plane, and thus have no real intersection, the following error message appears.

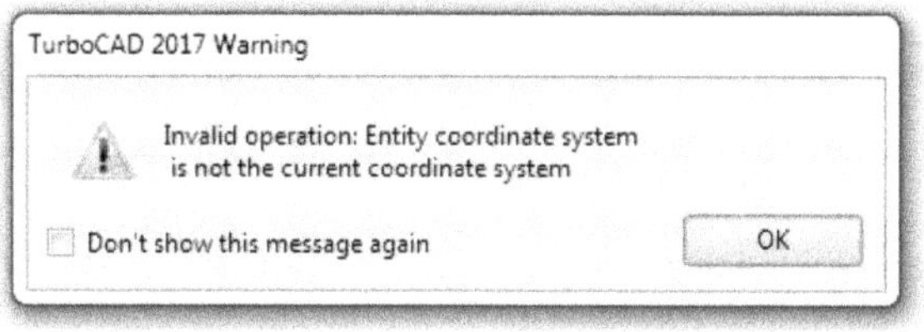

Figure 4-17 Possible error message with a trim command

This is a clear indicator of a shift of the lines in the Z dimension.

4.8 GRID

For simple 2D components, flowcharts, or isometric views, a grid can be used whereby a grid of the desired mesh width is laid in the model space, thus facilitating the drawing of simple geometries.

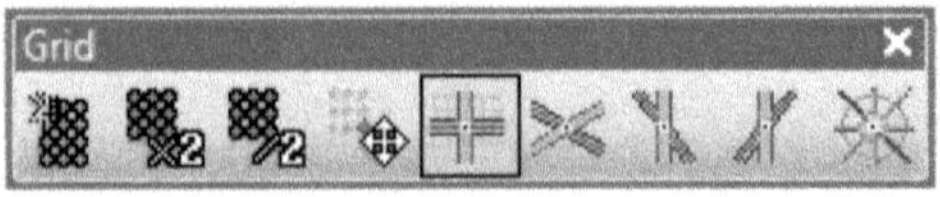

Figure 4-18 "Grid" toolbar

The "Show / Hide grid" command displays the standard preset ortho grid with a line spacing of 5 mm. Changes to the grid can be made in the drawing options under "Options/ Drawing Setup/ Grid" and in the "Grid" toolbar. Grid spacing can be chosen freely, the visual appearance of the grid can be influenced, and different types of grid can be selected. The following figures show different types of grids.

To snap the grid with line commands, the grid snap must be activated. The possibility to do so can be found in the "Drawing Aids" menu, which can be opened by right-clicking on the "SNAP" icon located at the bottom right of the screen next to the mouse pointer coordinates.

It should be noted that when the grid snap is on, gridlines will be snapped, even if the grid is set to hidden. Whether the grid snap is activated or not should always be checked, as it often suppresses other snap modes which may inadvertently snap false points in the model space.

The grid is always flat on the work plane. For example, if this is placed on a surface of a 3D body that does not correspond to the XY plane of the "World coordinate system", the grid is offset accordingly and allows use on the newly set work plane.

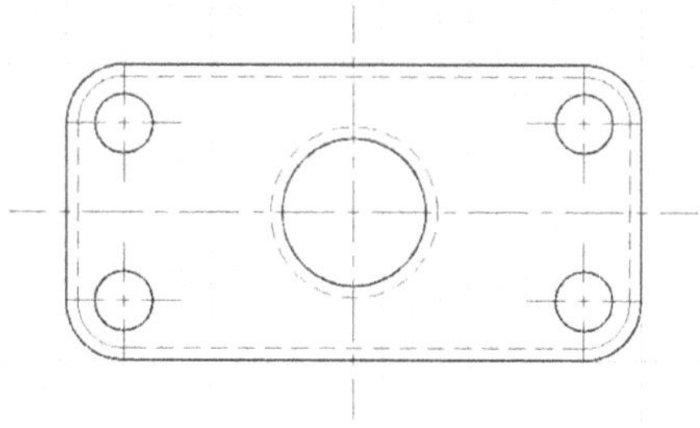

Figure 4-19 Example of an ortho grid

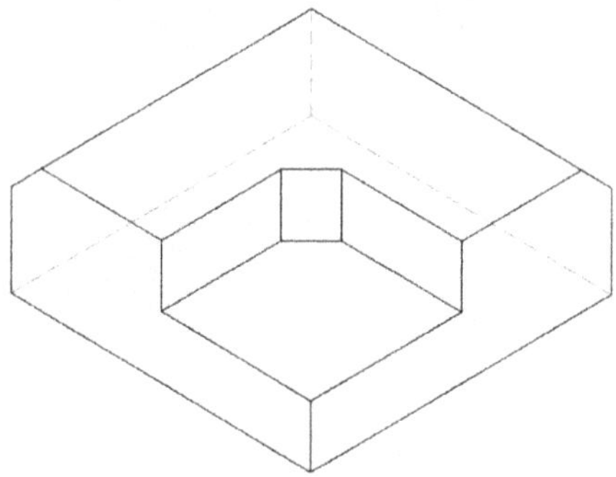

Figure 4-20 Example of an isometric grid

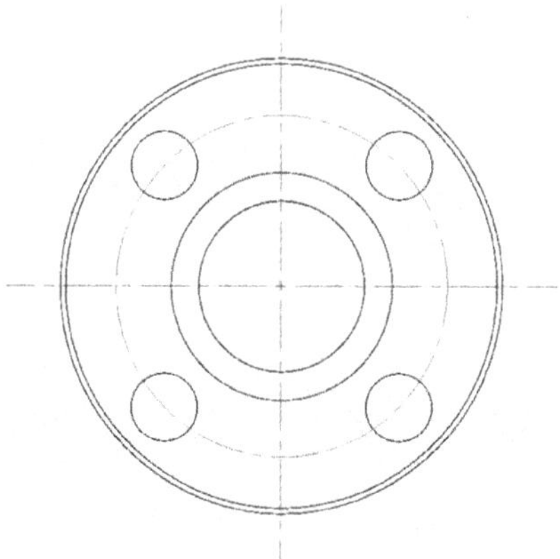

Figure 4-21 Example of a polar grid

4.9 CONSTRAINTS

The constraints can be used to define positional relationships between line objects. Constraints can be activated from the "Constraints" toolbar as well as in the "Constraints" menu.

The following groups can be distinguished:

Position to each other	**Properties**	**Position in space**
Coincident	Equal Radius	Fix Geometry
Parallel	Equal Length	Horizontal
Perpendicular		Vertical
Tangential		
Midpoint		
Concentric		
Symmetric		

Figure 4-22 Standard toolbar "Constraints"

To set a constraint, first the corresponding command has to be activated and then the line or lines one after another are to be selected. Constraints are displayed as small green symbols (attached to the lines). These constraint markers can be selected and deleted individually by pressing the "Remove" key.

By default, a separate layer "$CONSTRAINTS" is created for these markers. With this layer, the markers can then be faded in and out.

Constraints cannot be applied to 3D objects. The menu "Options/ Program Setup/ Constraints" contains more settings (chapter 3.1).

The "Auto Add Constraints"  command automatically adds matching position relationships to existing 2D objects. To do this, first activate the command, then select the appropriate lines and execute the command by pressing the "Finish" command. In the command options inside the "Inspector Bar" certain relationships can be deselected so that they are not added.

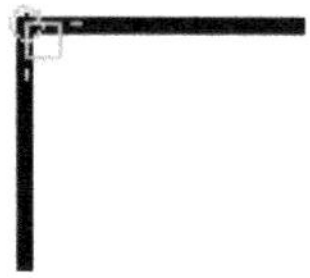

Figure 4-23 Constraints "Coincident" and "Perpendicular"

The “Selection Info” palette provides an overview of the existing constraints. When an object is selected, all existing constraints are automatically listed in the “Constraints” submenu (Figure 4-24). In the example shown above, the corresponding constraints "Coincident" and "Perpendicular" were added to the lines.

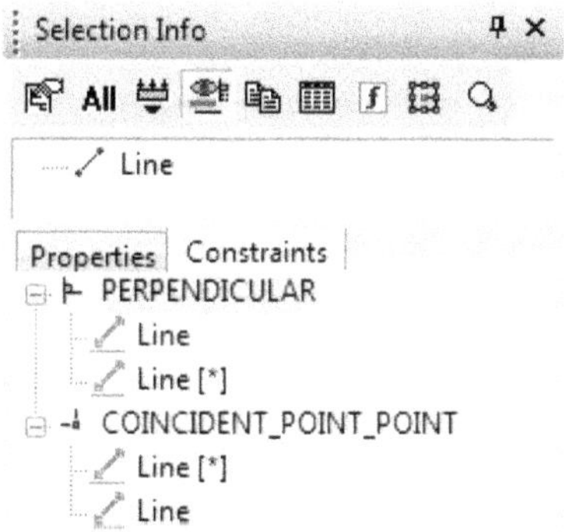

Figure 4-24 Listing of the existing constraints of a selected line in the “Selection Info” palette

4.10 Drawing compare

To compare two drawings and make the changes visible, TurboCAD® offers the "Drawing Compare" tool. This is located under "Tools/ Drawing Compare...".

In the window shown below, the paths of the drawings to be compared must first be specified. If you now press the "Compare" button, a message will first appear as to whether differences have been discovered or not. In the next window you have the possibility to view the differences via a command line arranged above.

The "Diff" command is a good way of showing just the differences between the two drawings.

This tool only applies to 2D drawings.

> It is particularly suitable for drawings in different revision levels to make any differences to old revisions visible if they have not been sufficiently identified.

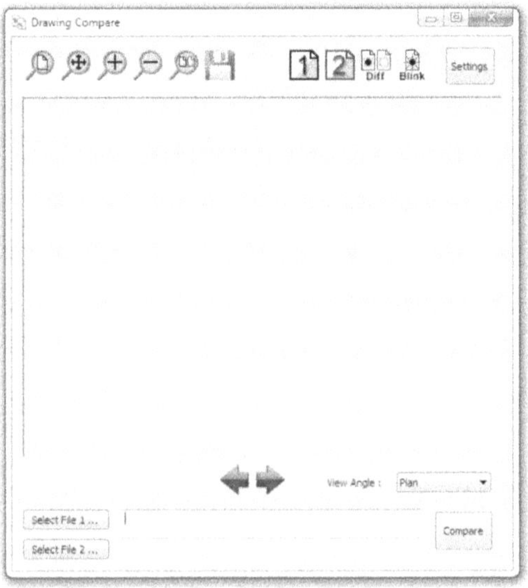

Figure 4-25 "Drawing Compare" tool

4.11 Isometrics

Isometric drawings can be generated in two ways in TurboCAD®. Either they are drawn manually, observing all angles and lengths, or an isometric view (standard view) is created from an existing 3D body. The differences are described below. Generally, in isometric projection, the object is represented in its true dimensions. All lines at a 30-degree angle and the vertical lines are drawn without shortening. The Z axis always represents the real height.

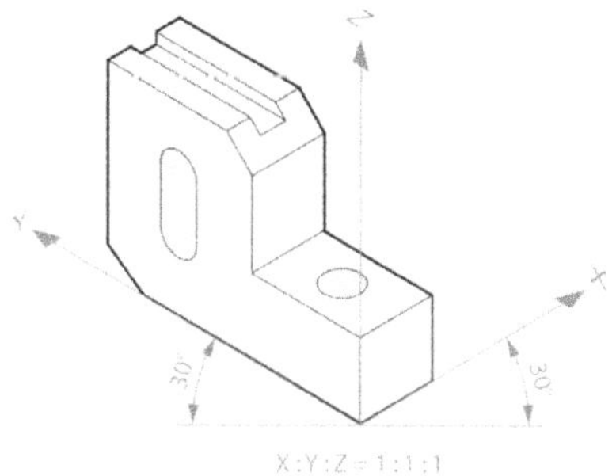

Figure 4-26 Isometric view (© 2014 ARAKANGA)

Drafting

Isometrics can be drawn in 2D while maintaining the required angles. The "Ortho" mode (Chapter 4.1), which works like a kind of raster, helps. If it is activated, lines can only be drawn at preset angles. This is called the "Step angle", which can be defined under "Options/ Drawing Setup/ Angle". With a "Step angle" of 15°, the angles of 30° required for isometric display can be ideally imitated with the "Ortho" mode. In addition, it is possible to display an isometric grid (chapter 4.8) to keep the necessary angles.

Isometric view

3D objects can be displayed in the isometric view (Figure 4-26), placed on a drawing sheet and dimensioned there. It should be noted that this way the lengths in the X, Y and Z directions are not reproduced in the ratio 1:1:1. In this projected view, edge lengths are not displayed in their entirety, as actually required by the isometric representation. This causes problems with the dimensioning in the viewport in the paper space. This is illustrated in Figure 4-28. Here the 3D model of the example cube has an edge length of 30 mm, and a standard isometric view has been selected. The green dimensions were added in the model space, and the red ones at a viewport in the paper space.

Currently, this problem can only be avoided by placing dimensions in the model space. This can be done with the dimension commands "Parallel" and "Smart" (Chapter 6.2).

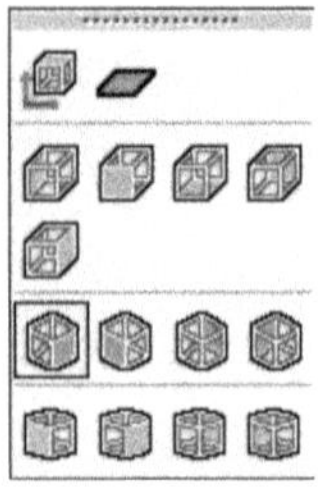

Figure 4-27 Standard views

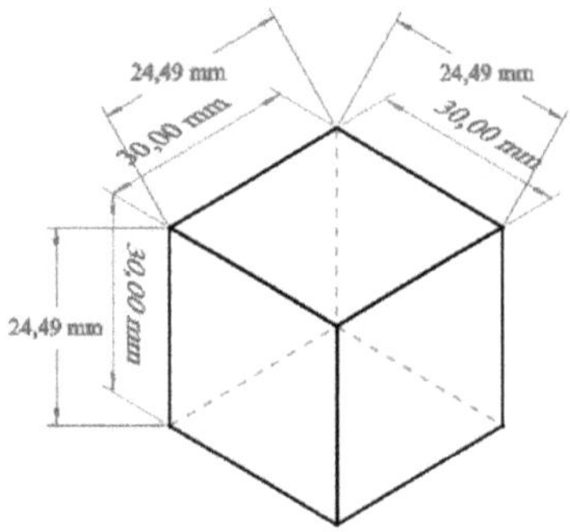

Figure 4-28 Differences in the dimensioning of isometric objects in the model and paper space

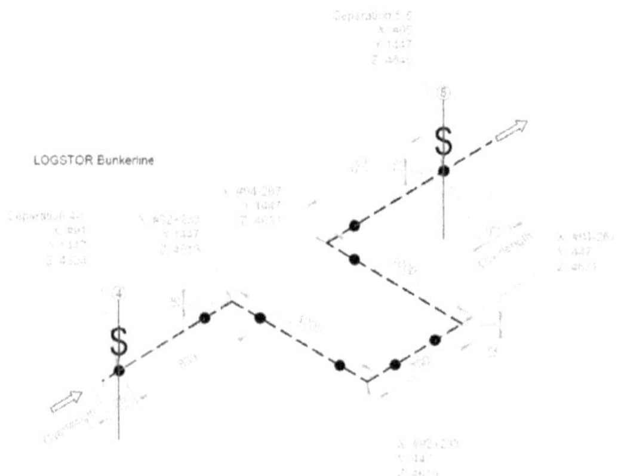

Figure 4-29 Example of a pipe isometry

4.12 AUTOMATIC NUMBERING

In addition to the manual placement of text windows and numbers, the marking tools can also be used for numbering. The corresponding toolbar "Markers" can be activated in the "Customize" menu (see Chapter 2).

Figure 4-30 Toolbar "Markers"

If some tools in this toolbar are missing after activating it (the toolbar may be inserted as seen here ), they can be added later. To do this, the corresponding commands can be dragged and dropped from the "Customize" menu under "Commands" (a list of <u>all</u> commands in TurboCAD®) into the existing toolbars of the user interface.

The formatting of the numbering (font size or frame) can be changed to adapt it to your own standards. One of the marking commands must be chosen. While the command is active, the following options appear in the "Inspector Bar" at the bottom of the screen:

Figure 4-31 Markers properties

Here the option "Mark Properties" (the wrench symbol) has to be selected.

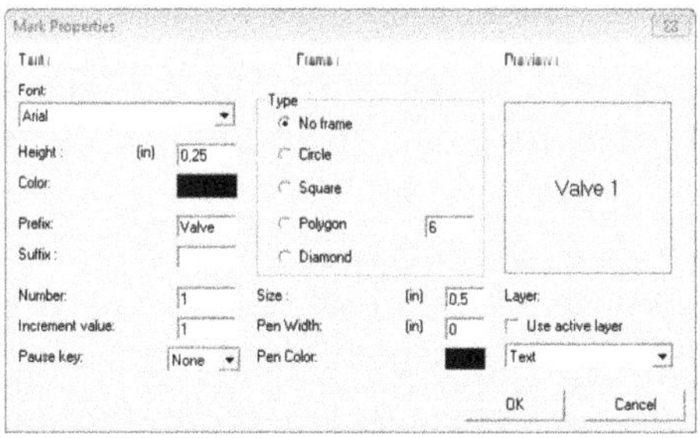

Figure 4-32 "Mark Properties" menu

In the menu "Mark Properties" the numbering can be formatted. In addition to font size and type, layer assignments, frames, prefixes, and suffixes as well as the counting interval can be set.

4.13 Piping and Instrumentation Diagram

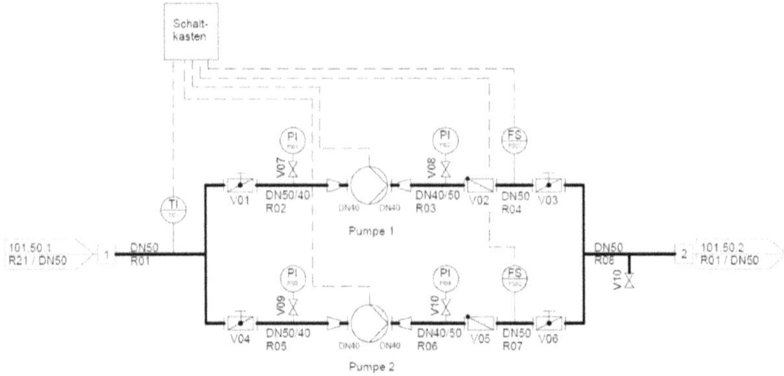

Figure 4-33 Example of a P&ID created in TurboCAD®

In the 2D mode, TurboCAD® has all the necessary tools to create professional piping diagrams. Important features include:

- Layer structure (chapter 2.7)
- Parts library (chapter 7.3)
- Parts with custom properties (chapter 7.4)
- Reports (chapter 7.5)
- Drawing templates (chapter 3.3)
- Numbering (chapter 4.12)

The layer structure, which is controlled in the "Design Director", allows various process media and system parts of the diagram to be displayed with different line types, colors and line widths, specifically filtered or hidden by layers.

By using layer sets, for example, different process sequences can be displayed (chapter 7.7).

To ensure a uniform image in all the diagrams, the drawing template can use standard fonts, the same layer properties, and uniform drawing frames. These can be preset by the default template, so no customization needs to be done before creating a diagram. The use of standard symbols enables the "Library" palette.

Creating viewports then transfers the drawn diagram from the model space to the paper space. If the viewport is selected on a scale of 1:1, and if the sheet and printer properties are set correctly, lines, symbols and text windows in the model space, paper space and on the printout, have the same size, ensuring a homogeneous drawing image.

The drawing legend and other textual information can be placed in the paper space.

For the preparation of piping diagrams, the use of standard symbols is recommended. These include all symbols that are frequently used. In the case of a P&ID[1], these are either valves, fittings, measuring points or even certain annotations.

If a valve symbol is created which is supposed to be used several times in the current drawing, the individual lines that are used to create the valve symbol should be grouped. Handling (moving, copying, etc.) is thus easier. Before grouping, the correct layer assignment must be checked. Text windows can also be grouped with them. This might be suitable for valve or measuring point labels.

The use of the symbol library is explained in chapter 7.3.

---

[1] Piping and Instrumentation Diagram

5 THREE-DIMENSIONAL MODELING

5.1 ORIENTATION IN THE 3D SPACE

Unlike the two-dimensional drafting on the XY plane, three-dimensional modeling moves freely in space. Therefore, before starting to draw, it is helpful to orient yourself within the space. The coordinate systems (chapter 5.4) help here.

So that all standard views fit in advance and the drawn objects do not have to be turned afterwards, the "Isometric_SE" view should be selected first. The coordinate system should then be aligned as shown in Figure 5-1. The Z-axis forms the height in the room. The example of the table below illustrates this.

Starting from this view, the objects are to be placed in the room and drawn accordingly.

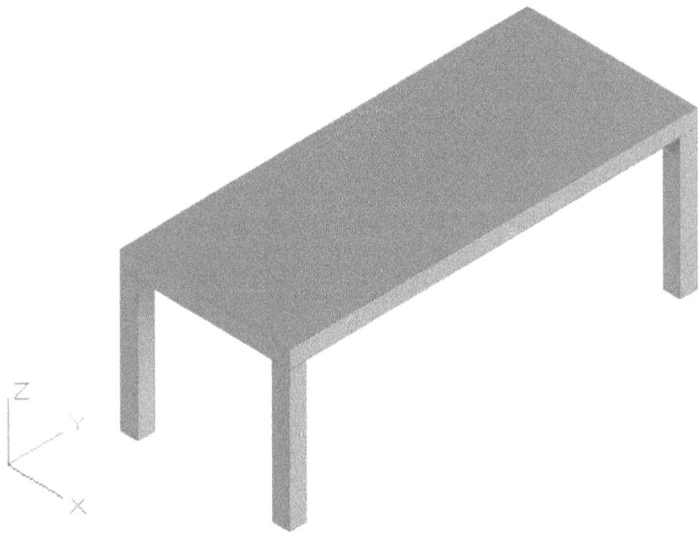

Figure 5-1 Example object for orientation in 3D space

5.2 Render modes

For three-dimensional modeling, the following rendering modes are relevant:

Table 6 Render modes "Wireframe", "Hidden Line" und "Draft"

"Wireframe" 	**"Hidden Line"** 	**"Draft"** 
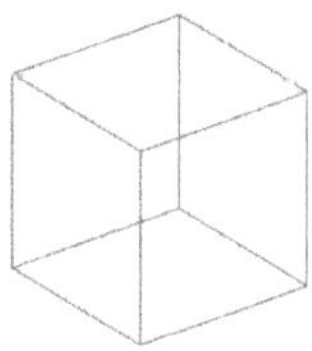	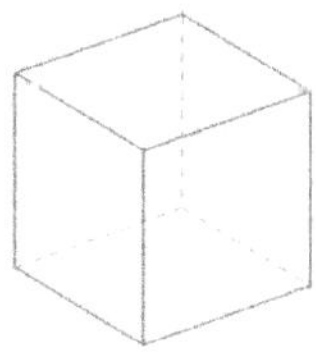	

When working with 3D objects, switching between the above rendering modes as and when required is very common. The "Quality" and "Advanced" rendering modes are more likely to be used for advanced visualization (chapter 5.13) or photorealistic rendering, and less during the actual design process.

The render modes can be changed by clicking on the cup icons shown in Table 6. They are listed in the standard "Render" toolbar.

Figure 5-2 Toolbar "Render"

In addition, they are included as standard in the pop-up menu (chapter 2.3), which opens with a right-click in the model space. This allows quick access to switch to another rendering mode if needed.

When switching between the rendering modes, the following should be noted:

If an object is selected whilst switching between rendering modes, the selected render mode may only be applied to the selected object (Figure 5-3). This can be used in some cases to represent different parts differently.

However, one quickly realizes that this actually quite helpful feature is not mature. If you select some objects and change them from the "Wireframe" mode to the "Draft" mode, only the marked objects are rendered as desired.

All remaining objects stay in "Wireframe" mode. If you want to change another body into the "Draft" mode, or transfer it to the "Hidden Line" mode, the previously set mixed representation will be dissolved.

> If the "Draft" mode is activated, problems can occur when copying 3D objects into another drawing. In most cases, an image file, and not the 3D object, will be inserted. Before copying to another file, you should always first activate the "Wireframe" mode. This does not refer to the copying / duplication of 3D objects within the model space.

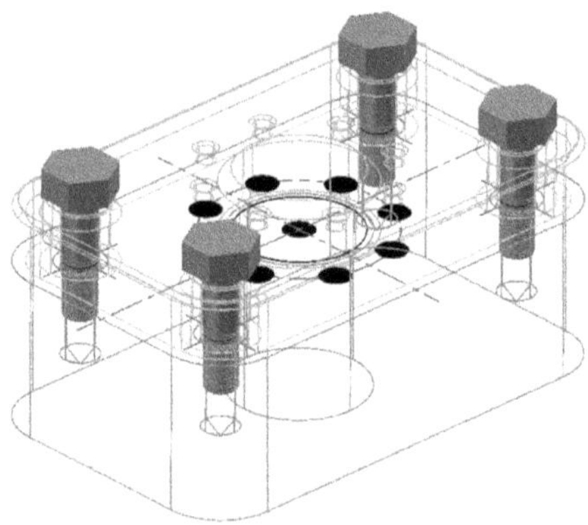

Figure 5-3 Mixed presentation "Wireframe" and "Draft"

The "Wireframe" is ideal for sketch-based 3D objects, making it easier to see 2D sketches. All edges are displayed. The "Hidden Line" mode allows a view into the interior of a model, as hidden edges are shown using dashed lines. For a realistic view of the model, the "Draft" mode is recommended. Surfaces are filled in and shaded depending on the lighting and the chosen color.

For displaying objects, TurboCAD® offers configuration options for both 2D and 3D objects in various menus. Depending on the PC, graphics card and other factors relevant for the graphics, problems can occur in the display of lines or 3D surfaces as well as in performance.

The following are tips on which settings usually lead to a satisfactory representation of all objects.

"Native Draw"

As shown in chapter 3.1, the menu "Options/ Program Setup/ Native Draw" (Figure 3-11) provides ways to change the graphical representation of objects. Depending on which hardware is used, switching between "GDI" and "Redsdk" can lead to a huge improvement if there are any display problems.

If "Redsdk" is activated and supported by your own graphics card (the TurboCAD® help documentation provides a list of supported graphics cards), then there are many useful setting options.

In the menu item "Anti-Aliasing", for example, lines and texts can be smoothed. This can also be set individually for the render modes "Wireframe", "Hidden Line" and "Draft". However, the anti-aliasing is associated with more processing power and therefore lines might be very thin when displayed. Coordinate systems and selection frames are also affected and can be difficult to identify. A healthy compromise must therefore be chosen by the user. Figure 5-5 gives a recommendation of settings that have been proven in various applications.

Figure 5-4 Example: "Redsdk" Anti-Aliasing (Text smoothing)

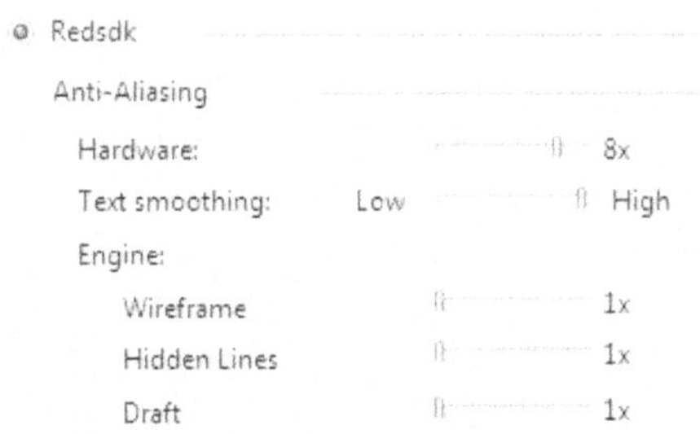

Figure 5-5 "Redsdk" Anti-Aliasing settings recommendations

"Camera Properties"

For each individual rendering mode, you can use the "Camera Properties" menu (Figure 5-6) to specify the rendering type, mode, and other render settings.

For the render modes "Hidden Line" and "Draft", there is the possibility to show 2D objects, such as sketches that serve as a basis for extrusion. If the field "Nonrenderable objects" is checked, 2D objects are also visible, as shown in Figure 5-16.

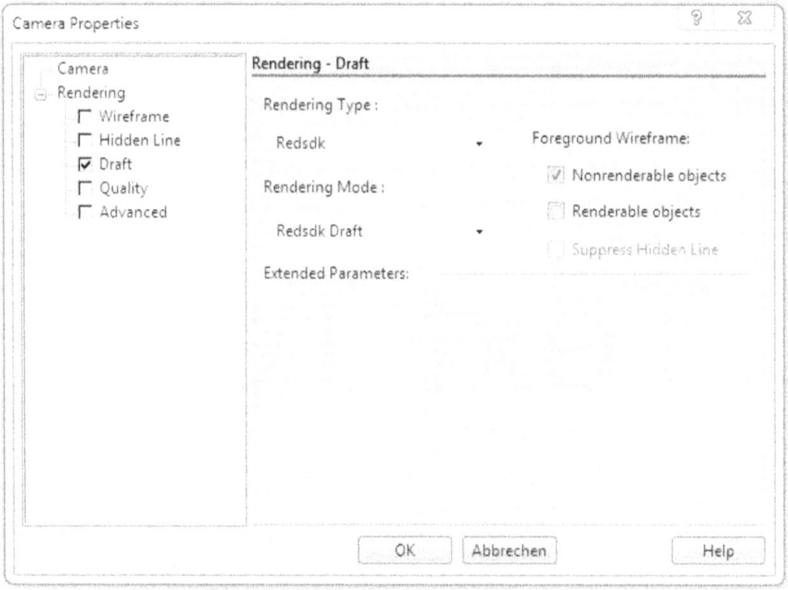

Figure 5-6 "Camera Properties" menu

In the render mode "Hidden Line", the type of render available is "Redsdk" and "Hidden Line".

If the "Hidden Line" rendering type is selected, different settings are available below the selection menus. If "Redsdk" is activated, the display can be adjusted under "Options/ Drawing Setup/ RedSDK".

If the "Redsdk" mode is supported by your own graphics card, the use of the "Redsdk" renderer is recommended for the "Hidden Line" and "Draft" render types, as it enables a detailed and smooth display of 3D models.

"RedSDK"

The "Options/ Drawing Setup/ RedSDK" menu mainly controls the "Hidden Line" render mode in conjunction with the "Redsdk" render type. The settings shown in chapter 3.2 (Figure 3-20) serve as a recommendation.

"ACIS"

In the menu "Options/ Drawing Setup/ ACIS" the facet quality of solids can be set. If this is too low, curved surfaces are displayed angularly. However, this refers only to the visual representation, but not to the mathematical model. The settings shown in chapter 3.2 (Figure 3-19) are recommended here.

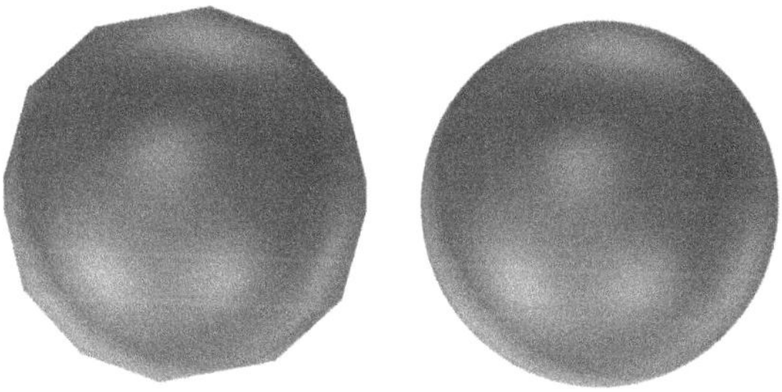

Figure 5-7 Comparison of low to high facet quality (ACIS)

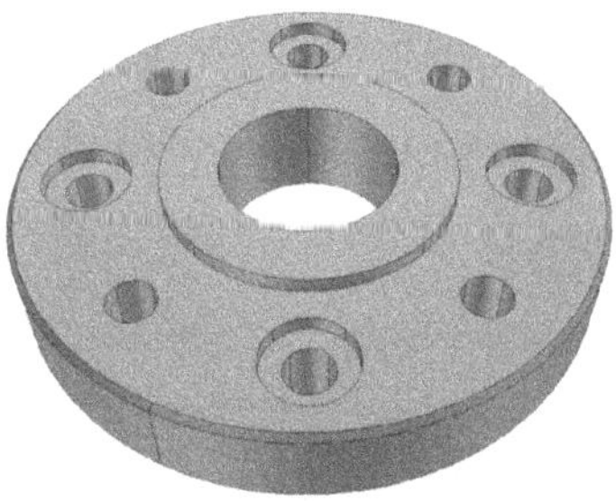

Figure 5-8 Perspective mode

The option „Renderable objects“ (Figure 5-6) displays the contour lines. These are displayed in the object’s color. The thickness of the contour lines can be adjusted in the object properties or the property toolbar. When you combine this with the activated perspective mode („View/ Camera/ Properties...") shown exemplarily in Figure 5-8, you can see a great example of a rendered 3D object. The perspective mode can be disabled by double clicking on the active cup icon shown in Figure 5-2.

5.3 3D MODE

If you start with three-dimensional modelling, the 3D mode should be activated. Assuming that something has already been drawn, this can be done by right-clicking in the model space. The pop-up menu (Figure 5-9) contains the "Toggle 2D/3D" command. In addition, the "Inspector Bar" offers it as well.

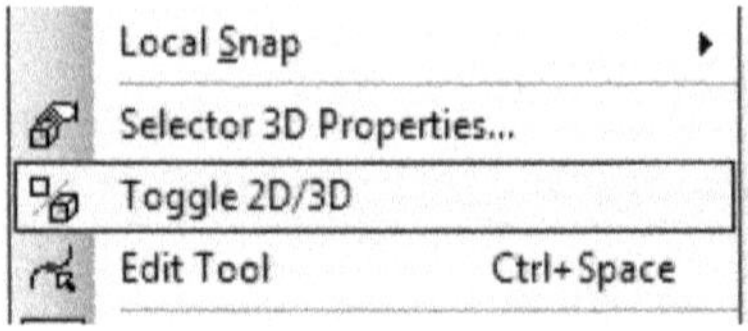

Figure 5-9 Changing between 2D and 3D modes

An easy way to check which mode is active is to look at the "Inspector Bar" or a coordinate system of a selected object. If only X and Y dimension are displayed, the 2D mode is activated. If, on the other hand, all three dimensions are displayed, the 3D mode is active.

The "Extents coordinate system" (chapter 5.4) of a selected object has only one green rotation point in 2D mode and three in 3D mode.

The recognition features are shown in Table 7.

Table 7 Recognition features of the 2D and 3D mode

2D mode	**3D mode**
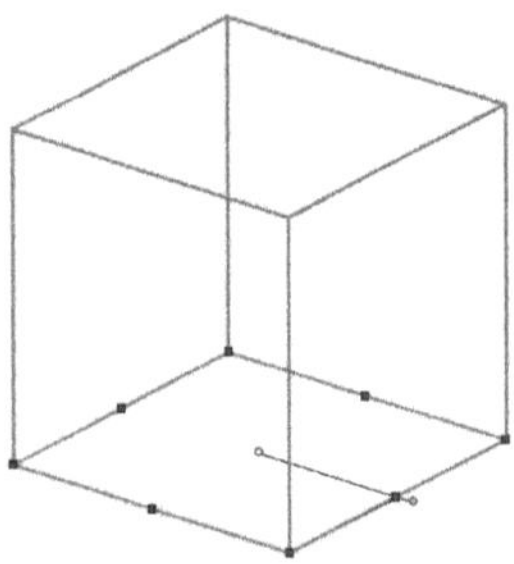	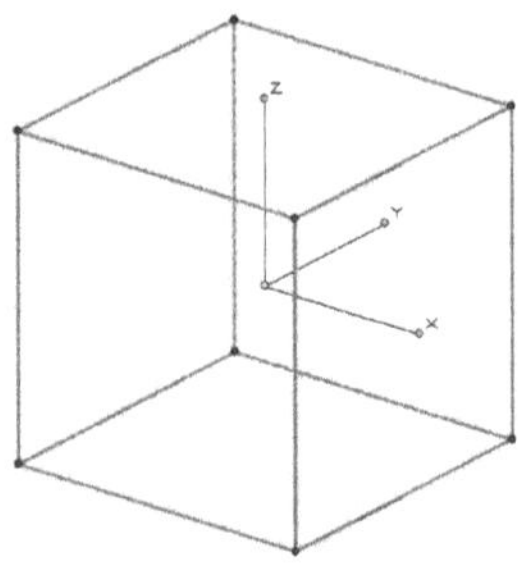
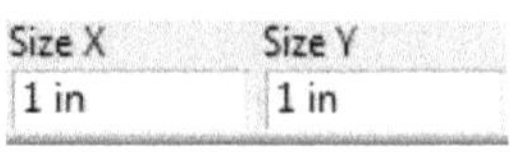	

In general, it is helpful to work with coordinates when modeling in 3D. This greatly simplifies the later editing of complex drawings and the shifting of 3D bodies in space. The snap modes can sometimes cause problems because there may be too many possible snap points in three-dimensional space.

Changing the reference point (chapter 4.3) for moving and positioning 3D objects is indispensable.

In addition, the "Ortho" mode should be disabled, as this also adversely affects the moving and placing of objects. The "Ortho" mode is described in chapter 4.2.

5.4 COORDINATE SYSTEMS

TurboCAD® differentiates between the coordinate systems listed below:

- Entity coordinate system (ECS)
- User coordinate system (UCS)
- World coordinate system (WCS)
- View coordinate system (VCS)
- Extents coordinate system (EXCS)

Of these, however, only three are obviously visible to the user. The following graphic shows these three coordinate systems:

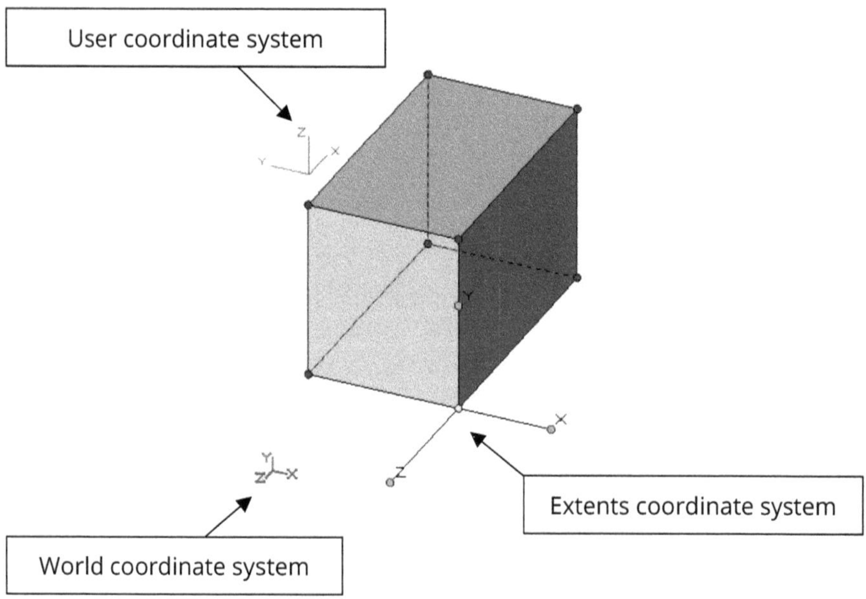

Figure 5-10 Overview of different coordinate systems

World coordinate system (WCS)

The "World coordinate system" is understood to be the overall coordinate system of the model space. Unlike the other systems, it cannot be moved and has no fixed origin. If you choose to show it, it stays in the set corner of the screen and turns accordingly to the view. Initially it is for orientation. The default views of TurboCAD® are also fixed. One could thus speak of a connection between the WCS and standard views.

The following table shows three standard views with the corresponding orientation of the "World coordinate system".

Table 8 Orientation of the "World coordinate system" in different standard views

"World Plan" / "Top"	**"Front"**	**"Isometric_SE"**
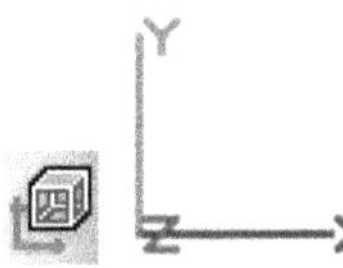	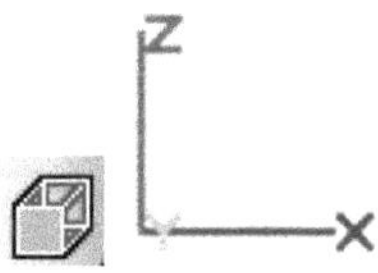	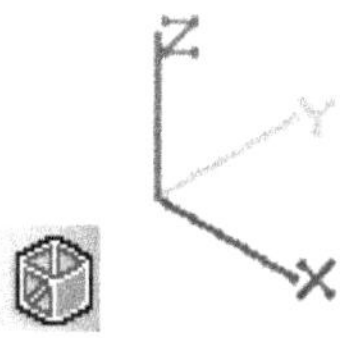

User coordinate system (UCS)

Unlike the "World coordinate system", the "User coordinate system" can be freely moved and aligned. The commands shown in Table 9 on page 180 are suitable for this purpose. The UCS and the work plane (the plane on which 2D sketches can be created) are firmly connected. The work plane always lies on the XY plane of the UCS. The work plane is described separately in chapter 5.8.

Extents coordinate system (EXCS)

The "Extents coordinate system" always sits with its origin on the reference point of an object selection. By moving the reference point or the rotation points (chapter 4.3), the EXCS can be freely changed in its position and orientation.

Working with the coordinate systems

For working with the existing coordinate systems, there are different approaches in TurboCAD®. This depends on whether you are working in 2D or 3D mode and depending on the complexity of the model and the resulting work steps. For two-dimensional drafting there is generally no need to move the work plane or the "User coordinate system", which are both firmly linked. However, when working with complex 3D models, moving the UCS or EXCS is helpful, if not necessary.

It can sometimes be very confusing when you see differently aligned coordinate systems on the screen and when inputs to the "Inspector Bar" do not produce the desired result.

The following recommendations can be made to work efficiently with the coordinate systems:

By meaningfully positioning the UCS, two things can be achieved. On the one hand, the work plane can be placed on body surfaces in such a way as to create any extruded sketches or 3D primitives (chapter 5.5). On the other hand, the UCS can serve as a reference for the value inputs in the "Inspector Bar" and so objects can be moved exactly in any direction.

> In the "Selector Properties" menu, under "Selector 3D/ Inspector bar", you can specify which coordinate system is used to refer to coordinates in the "Inspector Bar". You can choose between the EXCS, UCS and WCS.

In Figure 5-11, the UCS has been placed on the sloping surface of the object. The work plane is therefore coincident with the oblique surface. An object can now be created at this surface. To be able to move this object by specifying distances on the sloping surface, the "Inspector Bar" must be connected to the UCS.

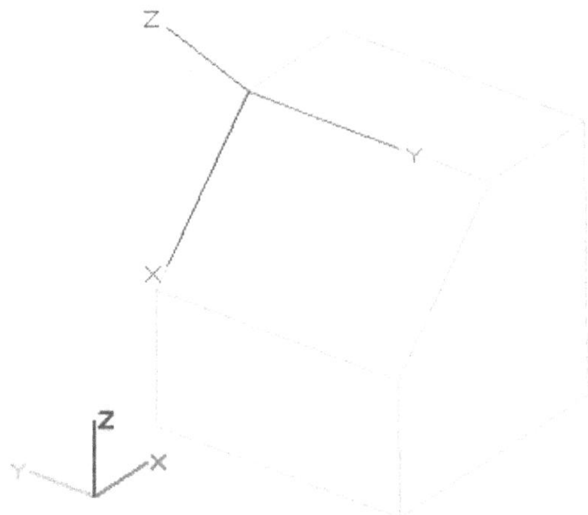

Figure 5-11 Differently oriented world and user coordinate systems

If the user is well-versed in how to move the UCS or the work plane, which is very useful for working in 3D, the UCS is recommended as a reference point for the "Inspector Bar". The settings shown in Figure 3-36 of the 3D selection tool should therefore be applied.

The WCS then serves only as a guide and can be hidden if necessary.

The EXCS is used in this operation only for moving or aligning existing objects based on the reference point or the rotation points.

The following should be noted:

Before saving and exiting a file or before creating a symbol for the library, the UCS should be reset to the normal state, which is identical to the WCS, via the command "Plane by World"  .

This could otherwise be confusing for other users who open and edit the drawing at later on.

When creating symbols for the library, it should be noted that each created part adopts the UCS at the time of creation and stores this as the so-called "Entity coordinate system". This ECS remains in each created part and cannot be changed afterwards.

5.5 EXTRUDING SKETCHES VS. 3D PRIMITIVES

To create 3D objects, TurboCAD® offers geometric primitives (cube, sphere, cylinder, etc.) or the possibility to create these geometries by extruding a 2D sketch. For example, extruding a circle creates a cylinder and extruding a square creates a cube or cuboid.

If used to generate 3D parts by sketches using sketch-based programs such as SOLIDWORKS® or INVENTOR®, TurboCAD® offers this function as well. Sketches can be created on previously placed work planes and extruded into 3D bodies. These can then be processed and merged with existing bodies or subtracted from them.

> When using the extrusion commands described below, such as "Simple Extrude" or "Revolve", it is mandatory to enable the "Use Compound Profile" option if you want to have a connection between the sketch and the resulting 3D solid.

If this option is not active during extrusion, there is no link between the 2D sketch and the 3D body.

If you delete the 2D sketch with which a 3D-body was created, the body will continue to exist. However, you automatically lose the ability to change the 3D body by editing the 2D sketch. Depending on the application, it should therefore be carefully considered which way is chosen with regard to later changes that will be made to the model.

Here the following recommendations can be given:

Working with primitives seems to be more flexible, since a meaningful sequence of commands makes subsequent editing possible through the "Selection Info" palette (chapter 2.6). In the case of simple geometries, such as straight forms, the use of basic bodies is therefore preferred.

If objects are to be generated, such as, for example, natural curve shapes as shown in Figure 5-17, extrusion commands are to be used. These forms are difficult or impossible to replicate with primitives.

A combination of both ways of working is also possible.

TurboCAD® not only offers tools for creating 3D objects, but also many editing tools (chapter 5.6) for merging, separating, or deforming bodies.

Extrude

The normal extrude turns a closed profile into a solid 3D body. If an open profile is extruded, only surfaces are created. This is illustrated in the following Figure 5-12.

The direction of extrude can be controlled by entering a positive or negative extrude height value.

The extrusion can also be carried out evenly on both sides. Once the extrusion has been created, a draft can be added to the "Properties" menu of the created object.

Under "Offset" the wall thickness can be defined. The extruded object is then hollowed out and is opened at the top and bottom.

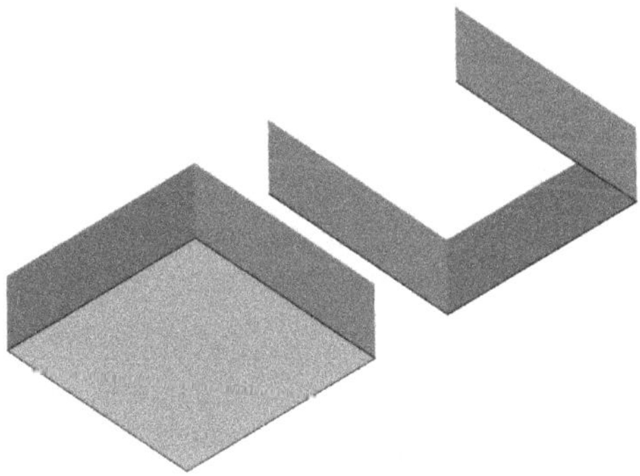

Figure 5-12 Extrude of a closed and open profile

Figure 5-13 Extruded circle with a draft and a offset

Also, from interlacing 2D profiles 3D bodies can be created. The internal profiles are automatically cut out. These remain linked to the 3D body, thus allowing any subsequent changes. This extrude technique is used in the exercise task "Crane hook 3D".

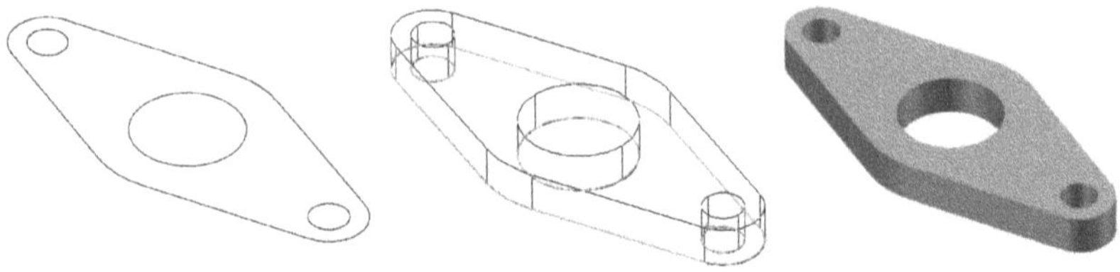

Figure 5-14 Extrude with a compound profile

Another form of extrusion is called the “Sweep”. In this case, an open or closed profile is extruded along a guide line, thus creating a volume or surface body. Line objects such as polylines or splines can be used as guide lines to determine the path of the sweep and therefore the form of the resulting 3D object. Also, 3D polylines or 3D splines can be used.

Position and orientation of the profile to the guide line dictate the resulting shape of the 3D body. Profile and guideline don’t have to touch each other.

In the object properties of the extrusion, further adjustment options such as “Twist Angle” or “Draft Angle” are available.

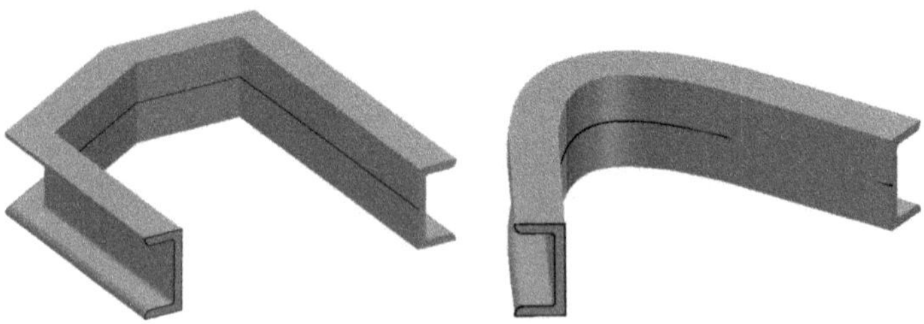

Figure 5-15 Sweep

During revolving, also a form of extrusion, a profile is revolved around an axis to create a 3D body. Here, the revolve angle and the direction of revolving can be specified.

To create a revolution, an open or closed line profile has to be selected first. Then an axis of revolution over two points has to be defined. Alternatively, an existing line element or a body edge can be selected as the revolution axis via the command option "Select Revolve Axis".

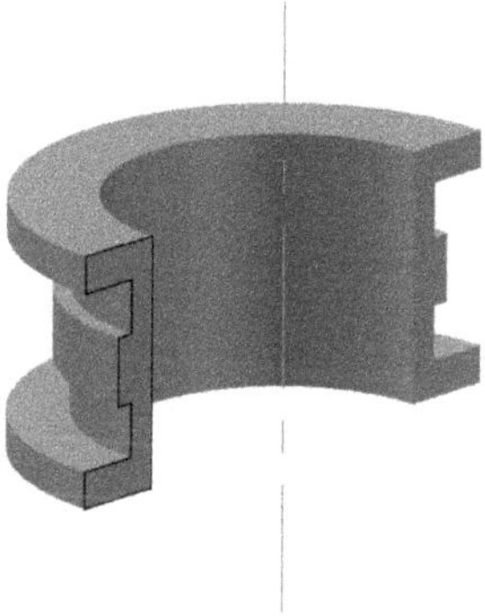

Figure 5-16 Revolved body

With the command "Lofting" several profiles can be connected. By adding guide curves, the shape of the survey can be adjusted between two profiles. All nodes can be moved with the "Edit tool" (chapter 4.6), and the shapes and surfaces can be adapted flexibly.

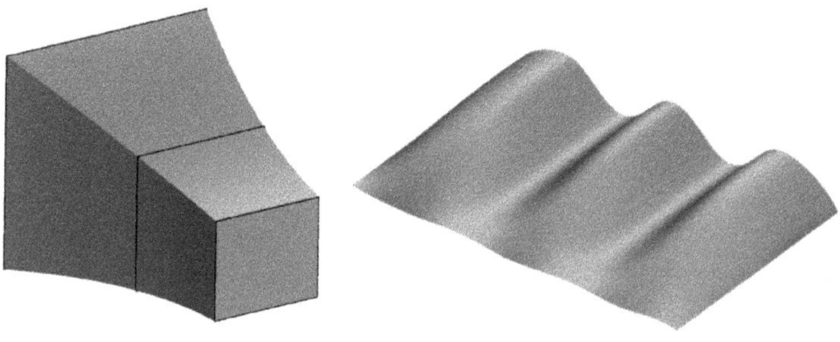

Figure 5-17 Lofting

Primitives

All primitives such as "Box", "Sphere", "Cylinder" or "Torus" can be created with a few mouse clicks, edited in the “Selection Info” palette or their “Object Properties”, and aligned and placed freely in 3D space. 2D sketches which are necessary to define 3D objects are already included in these commands. In comparison to the extrusion commands, they are merged with the 3D object, which makes the handling easier.

Figure 5-18 3D primitives

Standard objects

Commands such as “Spiral”, “3D Polyline”, or “3D Spline By Control Points” can be used to create complex sweeps. 3D polyline and 3D spline curve work analogously to the 2D variant. They are suitable for creating springs, pipe or hose runs.

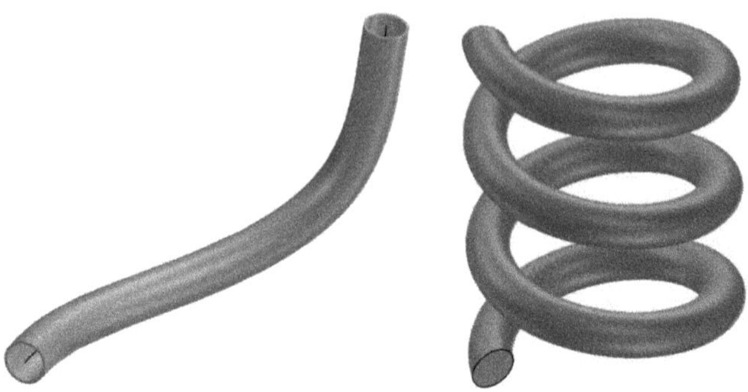

Figure 5-19 3D spline and spiral as guiding lines for a sweep

Boolean operations

Boolean operations include commands for union, difference, or intersection. For example, two volumes can be merged or subtracted from each other. The "3D Subtract" command is well suited for creating molds.

Figure 5-20 Toolbar "Boolean & Facet"

Figure 5-21 Mold created with the "3D Subtract" command

5.6 3D MODIFICATION

If a 3D object has been created by extrusion or the use of primitives, it can be edited with the help of modification tools.

Most commonly used commands are "Fillet Edges", "Chamfer Edges", "Shell solid", "Fillet3D" and "Add Holes".

These are described below.

"Fillet Edges" & "Chamfer Edges" 

These commands round off or chamfer object edges by specifying radius, angle, or offset. While the command is active, different radii can be applied to individual edges or edge courses.

Adding a fillet or chamfer removes material from the outside edges and adds it to the inside edges.

Figure 5-22 Fillet and chamfer

"Shell solid"

The command "Shell solid" thickens the outer surface of an object when entering a positive value and hollows it out when entering a negative value. The entered values correspond to the shell or wall thickness. Individual areas may be excluded from the thickening / hollowing, e.g. to generate openings.

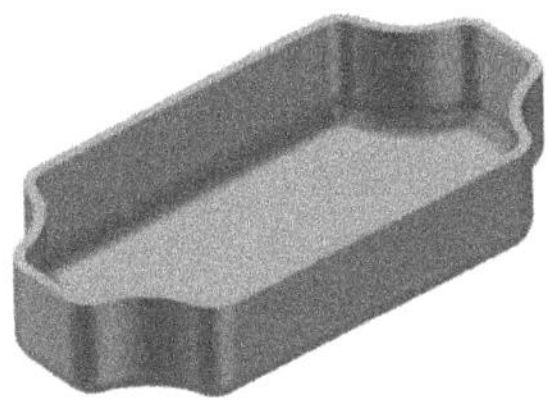

Figure 5-23 Hollowed object with the "Shell solid" command

"Fillet3D"

This tool can be used to round off the edges of 3D polylines. If, for example, a 3D polyline is to be used as the path for a sweep for modeling a pipe, then the bending radii can be introduced. The "Fillet All" command option automatically selects and rounds all edges of a polyline. This can speed up the process of rounding off all of the polyline's edges.

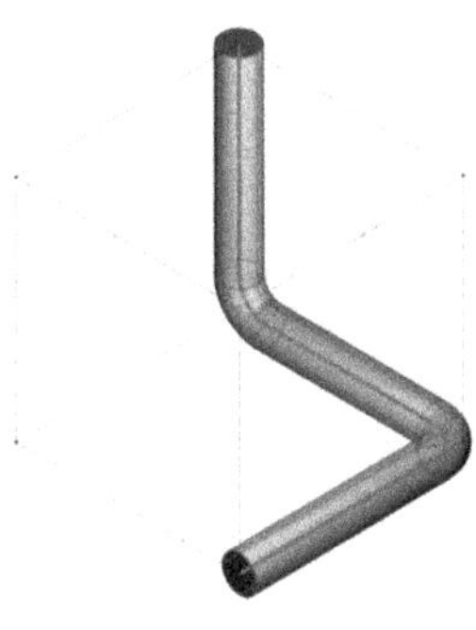

Figure 5-24 "Fillet3D" command to fillet edges of a 3D polyline

"Add Holes" 

The "Add Holes" tool[1] can be used to add different types of holes or pins to a component.

The following types of hole are available: "Plane Hole", "Counter Sink", "Counter Bore", "Counter Drill", "Tapped Hole" and "Boss".

To use the hole tool, one or more 2D points must first be placed on the component. These indicate the position of the hole. If the "Add Holes" command is activated, the "Properties" menu shown below can be opened in the "Inspector Bar". All the necessary inputs to define the holes are listed there. Once all settings have been made, one or more points must be selected after confirming the menu. The holes are then added using the "Finish" command.

Moving a point will automatically move the hole as well.

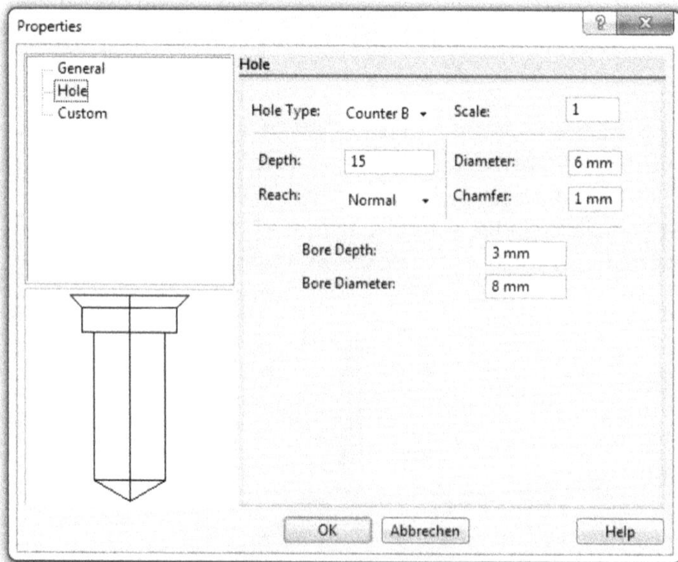

Figure 5-25 Hole properties menu

[1] Use of the "Add Holes" tool shown in the step by step exercise "Crane hook 3D"

Pins can be added with the hole type "Boss". Here length, diameter, draft and fillet can be specified.

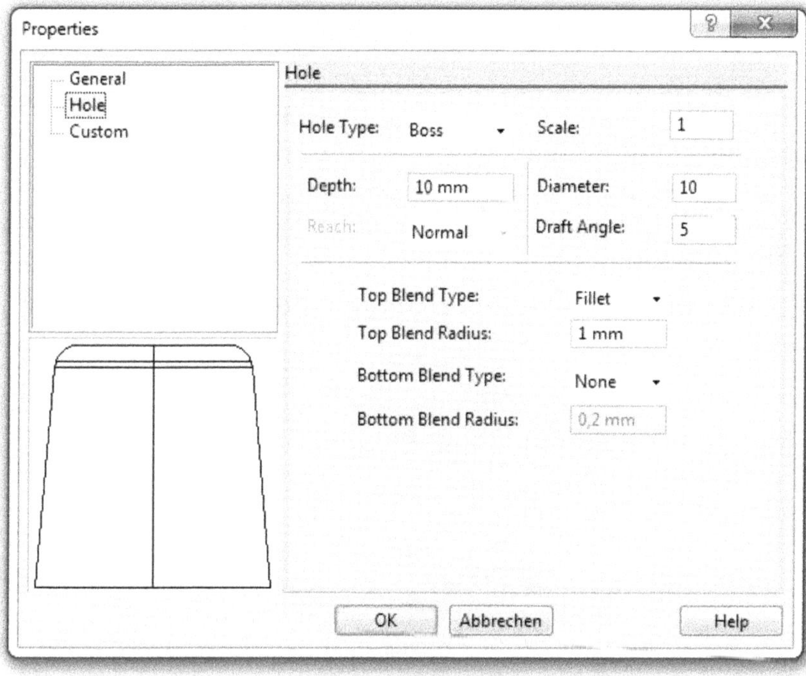

Figure 5-26 Hole properties menu – "Boss"

Figure 5-27 Example of the "Add Holes" tool

5.7 HISTORY-BASED MODELING

As mentioned earlier, the "Selection Info" palette offers a chronological overview of the drawing commands applied to a 3D part. These can be edited afterwards. Subsequent processing steps will then be updated automatically. Each processing step can be renamed to facilitate the ability to locate each one on complex parts.

Figure 5-28 shows an exemplary editing history of a 3D part in the "Selection Info" palette. In this example, several primitives have been merged (3D Add) and subtracted (3D Subtract). The chronological order of the individual steps can be seen below.

The "Properties" section contains information about each individual editing step.

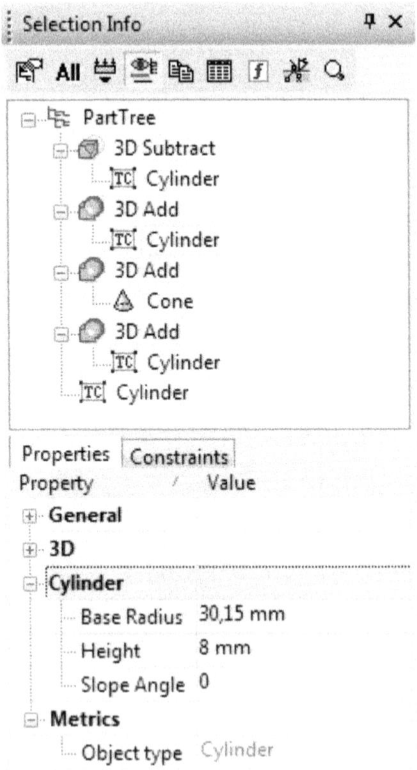

Figure 5-28 View of the editing history in the "Selection Info" palette

The 3D primitives used in the example given (cylinders and cones) can be changed in the properties of the “Selection Info” palette and influence the whole part structure, and thus the created component. Individual steps can be suppressed, or the automatic update deactivated. Moving single steps in time to change the order is not possible.

The "Edit Content" command in the upper menu area opens a selected 3D object and hides the rest of the part structure.

Parts created in TurboCAD® can be loaded along with the editing history which allow you to customize each individual editing step. In this case one speaks of an "intelligent part". When exporting to exchange formats to import the file into other CAD programs, this information is lost.

The same applies to the opposite way. If drawing files that have been created with other CAD programs are to be loaded, there isn’t usually an editing history. However, these models can still be edited using the editing tools and Boolean operations.

After installing TurboCAD®, and when using 3D editing tools for the first time, the program notification appears asking whether the editing history should be deactivated. In order to enable history-based modeling, the editing history must be activated. This setting is managed in the menu "Options/ Drawing Setup/ ACIS" (Figure 3-19) and can be subsequently changed there.

For some tools, caution is required when working with the editing history. By way of example, the tools "Mirror Copy" and "3D Subtract" should be mentioned here. This occurs especially in older versions of the program.

When mirroring or subtracting with the option "Don’t remove the subtrahend" activated, an “ACIS” solid, i.e. a solid without any editing history, may be created from the part originally containing an editing history.

This part can then no longer be edited in the further process the way it could be with the editing history still intact.

Regular check of the “Selection Info” palette is therefore urgently necessary.

> If you explode a part structure, you automatically create an “ACIS” solid and remove the editing history.

5.8 WORK PLANE

2D objects as well as sketches for creating 3D objects can only be created on the work plane. This plane is always located on the XY plane of the "User coordinate system" (see chapter 5.4) and can therefore be moved and aligned as required.

The most important commands for moving the work plane are listed here:

Table 9 Command overview for changing and displaying the work plane

Symbol	Command	Description
	"Show/Hide WorkPlane"	Show and hide the work plane. The work plane is always active.
	"By Facet"	To set a UCS or work plane on any surface.
	"Plane by World"	The work plane is again based on the "World coordinate system" (UCS and WCS are again aligned identically).
	"WorkPlane by 3 Points"	The UCS can be arbitrarily aligned by specifying three points.

For example, if objects are to be applied to different sides of a cube, they can either be created and subsequently positioned, or created directly on the target surface. For this, the work plane is placed on the respective cube side with the command "By Facet" and the desired object (in Figure 5-29 labels were chosen) is created directly on the cube face.

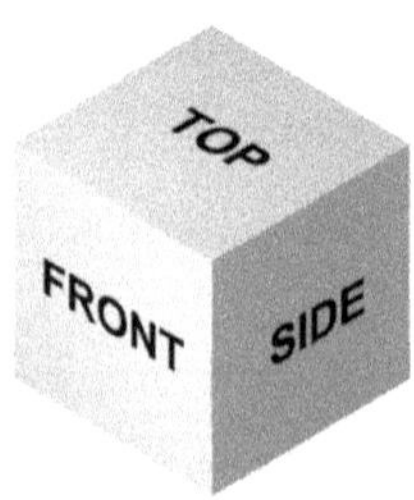

Figure 5-29 Sample cube with labels

The "Plane by World" command automatically places the work plane back on the XY plane of the "World coordinate system".

Work planes can also be saved and recalled. In the "Design Director", there is an area for this, in which work planes can be saved. If you then need one of these saved work planes in order to place a sketch on it, it can be activated by double-clicking on the name. Each work plane is defined by the origin as well as the X and Z vector.

Name	✓		Origin	X Vector	Z Vector
Front			x=0 y=0 z=0	x=1 y=0 z=0	x=0 y=-1 z=0
Side			x=0 y=0 z=0	x=0 y=0 z=1	x=1 y=0 z=0
Top	✓		x=0 y=0 z=0	x=0 y=1 z=0	x=0 y=0 z=1

Figure 5-30 Named work planes

If an object is offset or skewed to the work plane, the "Place on WorkPlane" command in the "Modify" menu lays it down flat on the activated work plane. The "Entity coordinate system" of the object is aligned with the currently set "User coordinate system" and both XY planes are superimposed. This applies to both 2D and 3D objects.

An exemplary application of this command is shown in Figure 5-31.

Also helpful in this matter are the commands in the standard "Assembly" toolbar. By using these, the faces, or defining points, of two different objects can be connected.

Step 1:

Creation of the wedge and the cuboid on the work plane shown.

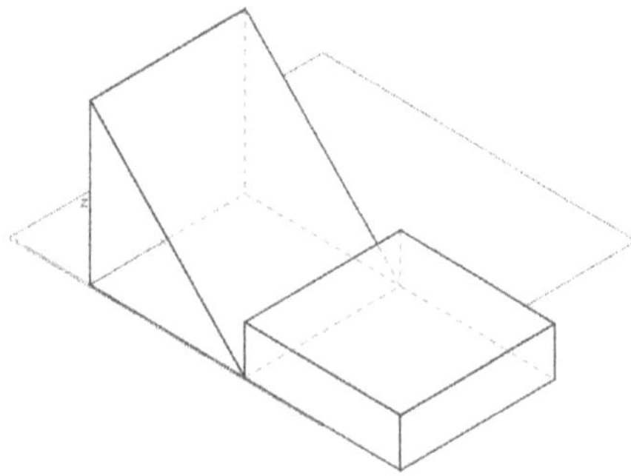

Step 2:

Move the work plane to the sloping surface of the wedge with the "By Facet" command.

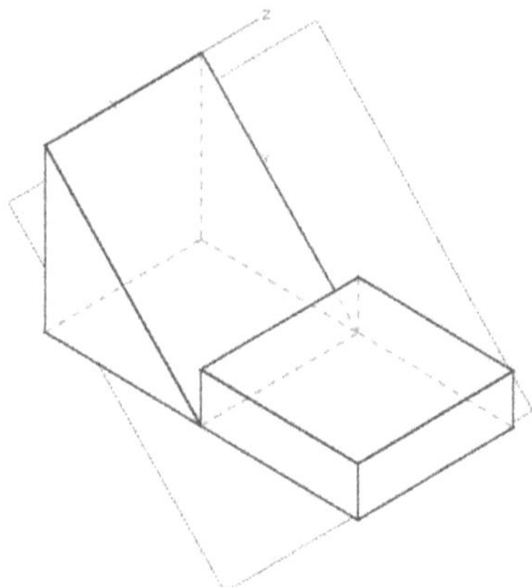

Step 3:

Select the cuboid and run the "Place on WorkPlane" command.

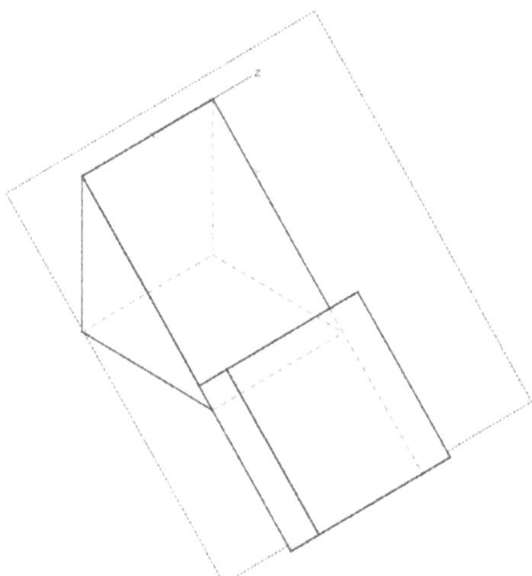

Figure 5-31 Using the "Place on WorkPlane" command

5.9 CONCEPTUAL SELECTOR

The "Conceptual Selector" provides immediate access to movement, rotation and scaling. It also provides the ability to deform 3D objects by selecting faces.

The TurboCAD® Help contains a listing of all the features of the conceptual selector. This is only available in the model space with 3D mode enabled (chapter 5.3) and in conjunction with the "Redsdk" rendering engine.

The "Conceptual selector" can be activated and edited in the menu "Selector Properties/ Selector 3D". There are settings options for visual presentation and operation of the "Conceptual selector".

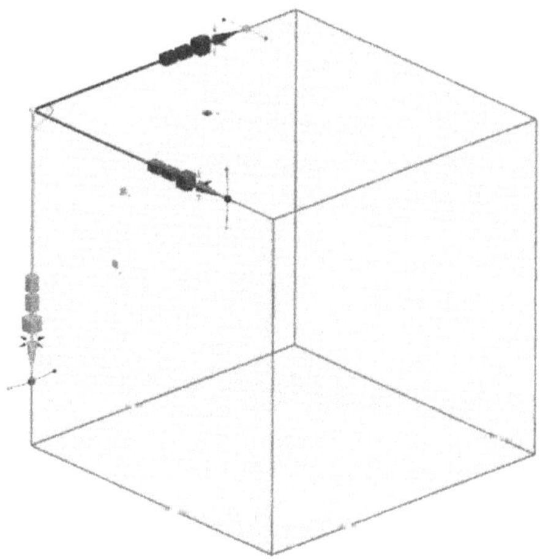

Figure 5-32 "Conceptual selector"

For conceptual work with 3D primitives (chapter 5.5), this tool is helpful because objects can be flexibly moved or deformed.

However, a general recommendation over the conventional selection tool cannot be given.

5.10 Pipe modeling

For modeling pipes, TurboCAD® provides useful features, such as the symbol library for managing standard parts, or commands for sweep pipe profiles from a guideline.

In the further course of this chapter, two different methods are shown for modeling pipes. Here, a distinction is made between a simplified and a detailed method. For this purpose, two techniques are applied analogously to the methods described in chapter 5.5 for the creation of 3D objects (extruding sketches vs. 3D primitives).

These methods follow different approaches. If in one method the true-to-scale figure of the pipe and the output of parts lists are in the foreground, the other should enable a rapid conceptual representation of pipe routes.

The following figure shows a pipe segment, which subsequently serves as a template for the description of the two methods.

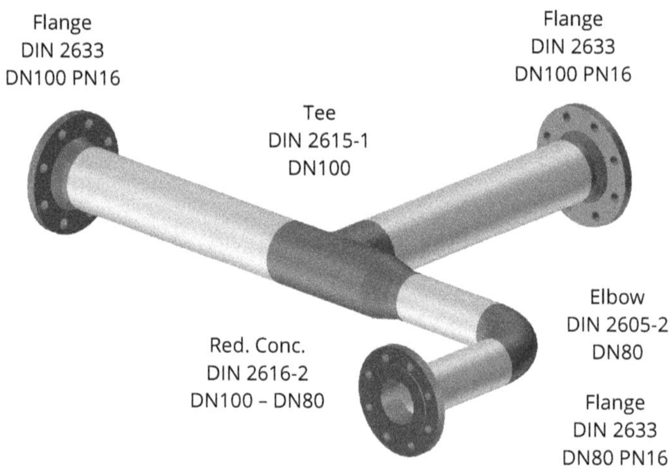

Figure 5-33 Exemplary pipe segment

5.10.1 Detailed method

In this method, all piping parts such as flanges or elbows are inserted into the drawing, after which they are positioned and connected by hollow cylinders as pipes. The advantage of this is the possibility to output an exact parts list (chapter 7.4 & 7.5) and to provide a true-to-life image of the pipe along with installed components.

By default, TurboCAD® does not have corresponding datasets for the piping standard parts shown here. The additional package "CADsymbols" contains ready-made standard parts for the mechanical engineering, electrical engineering and architecture sectors. This parts library contains fittings, seals, flanges and P&ID symbols especially for plant design.

Following is the modeling of the piping example with the detailed method shown:

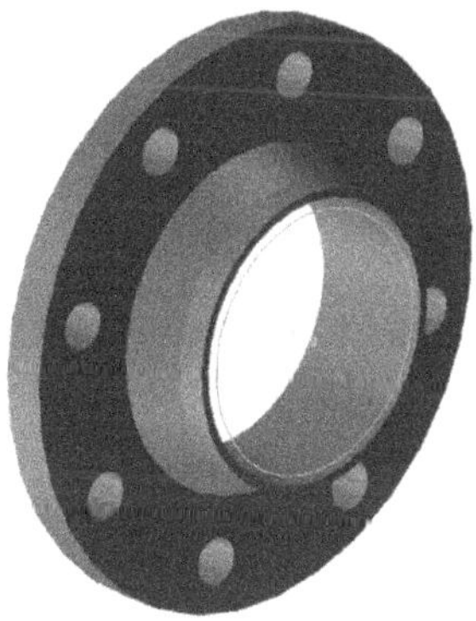

First a starting flange is inserted (previously created or loaded from a standard library). Thereafter, a cylinder is drawn at the welding end of the flange. If the base circle of the cylinder does not lie on the corresponding work plane, then the work plane can be placed on a flat surface of the flange by the command "By Facet".

The cylinder is now defined by the diameter and the height. The created cylinder is filled. With the command "Shell solid" it can be hollowed out, the desired wall thickness can be defined and the cylinder ends can be opened.

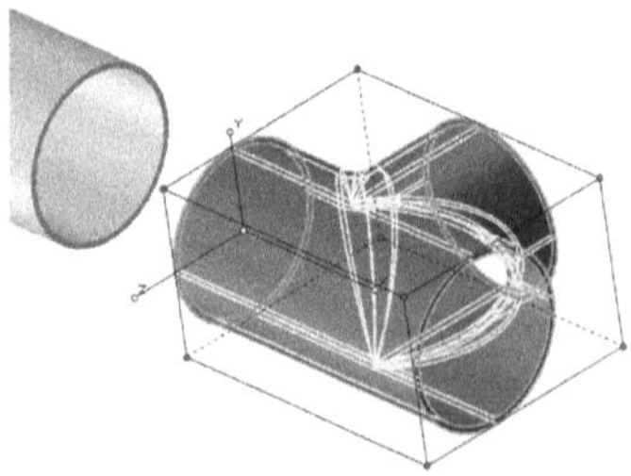

Further standard parts can now be inserted from the library and joined together. Here, the displacement of the reference point is essential (chapter 4.3). By moving the reference point into the center of the circle and then snapping the other center of the circle, the piping components can simply be lined up.

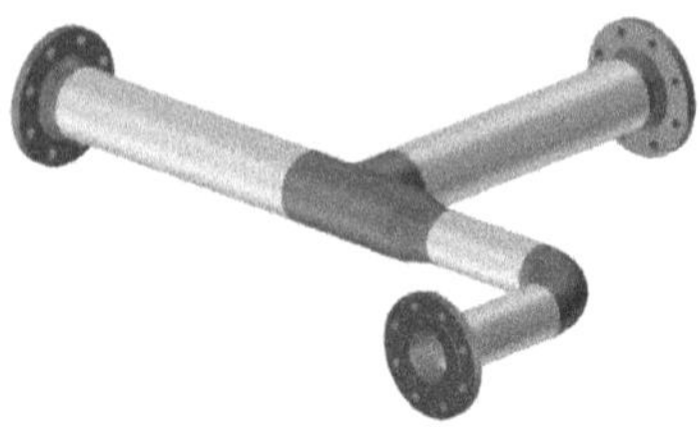

If further pipe pieces are required, a previously created one can be copied and repositioned to save working steps.

5.10.2 Simplified method

This method dispenses with the insertion of standard parts. Flanges are modeled as simple cylindrical bodies if desired. The pipe is discharged as a circular profile along a center line, which indicates the course of the pipe. The commands "Sweep" or "Rail Sweep" can be used to extrude a circular profile along a drawn 2D or 3D curve. Alternatively, the "Pipe" command provides a similar functionality. The procedure and the differences between the two mentioned commands are discussed below.

The simplified method is particularly suitable for the rough presentation of pipe routings in rooms, where it is not primarily about keeping accurate dimensions, but rather about the rapid visualization or coarse coordination of the piping. To what extent dimensions such as pipe diameter or radius of arc are estimated or correctly taken over is up to the user.

The modeling of the piping example with the simplified method is shown below. First the command "Sweep" (chapter 5.5) is used. Subsequently, the command "Pipe" is explicitly described.

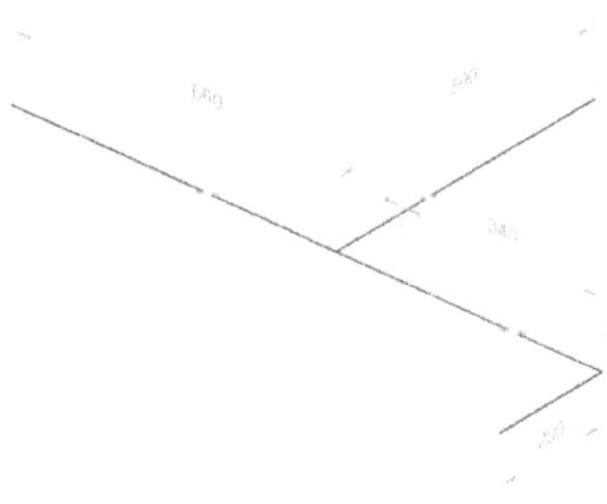

First, a guide line is created, which specifies the course of the pipe. This should be on its own layer to be able to show and hide it. It makes sense to emphasize this guide line in color and by using a thicker line width. Depending on the application, it can be created with the normal line command or, if it is a pipe that spans all three axes, also with the "3D Polyline" command.

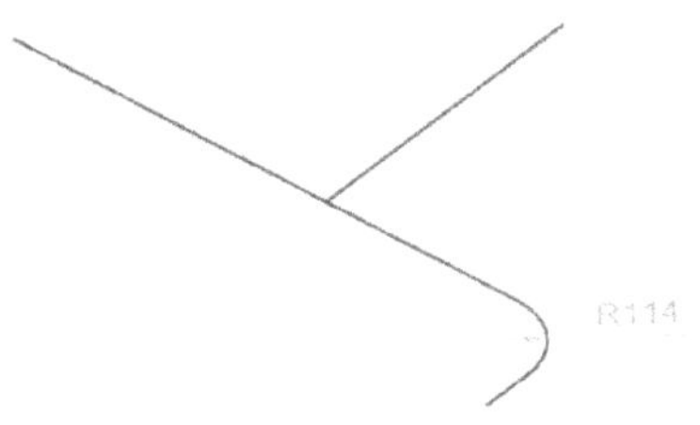

To represent the pipe elbows, the corners are now provided with the appropriate radius. The commands "2D Rounding" and "Fillet3D" are available for this purpose. If the command is activated, the "Inspector Bar" can be set to "Fillet all".

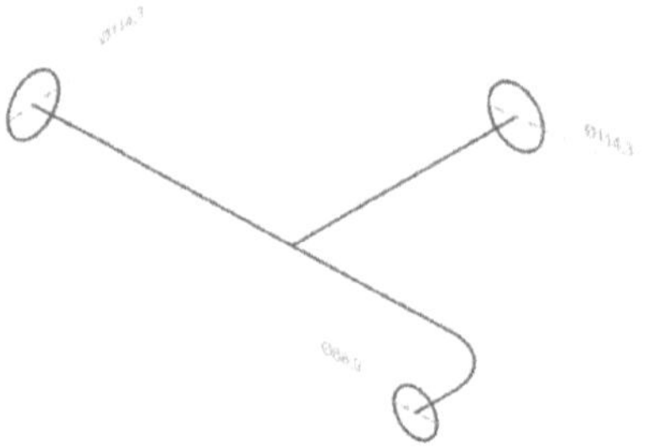

In order to extrude a pipe at the guide lines, circles with the desired outside diameter must be positioned perpendicular to the line at their ends.

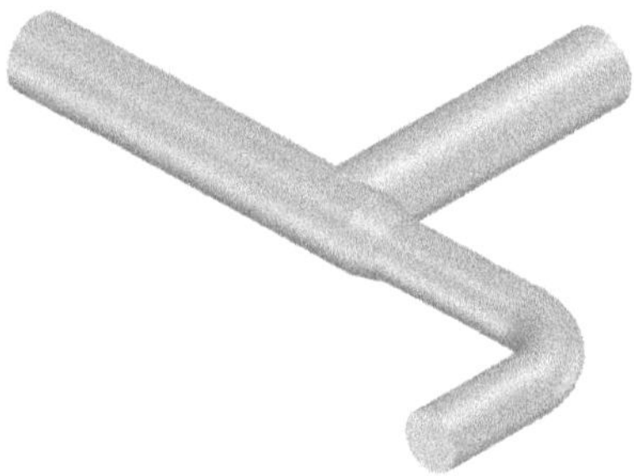

With the command "Sweep" these circles can now be carried out on the guide lines and the pipes are formed as solid bodies. The option "Use Compound Profile" must be activated in order to maintain a connection between the guideline, the circle profile and the extrusion. As a result, the route of the pipe and the outer diameter can be subsequently changed. In the example, the command "Chamfer Edges" is used to indicate the concentric reducer piece.

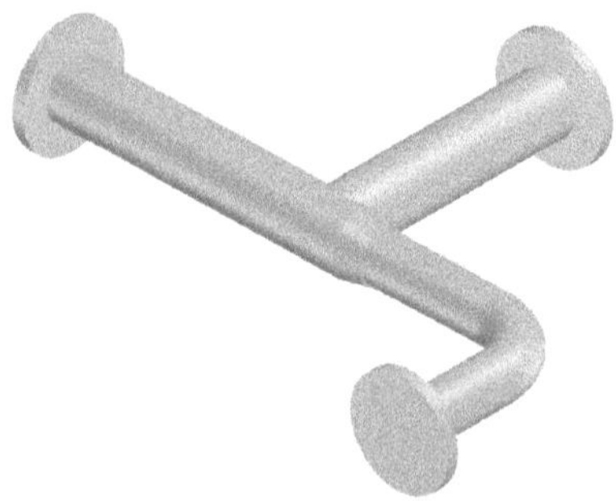

The pipe can now optionally be hollowed out using the "Shell solid" command. Simple cylinders are used to represent flanges.

The “Pipe” command 

By default, TurboCAD® brings along the command "Pipe" for pipe modelling based on a guideline. It is also a kind of "Sweep" tool where a round and solid 3D profile is created by specifying the outside diameter and a guiding line. However, unlike the “Sweep” command, there is no need to place a circular object. In the example shown before, for modeling the pipe with the simplified method, both the commands "Sweep" and "Pipe" can be used due to the similar function mode. The “Pipe” command and the differences to the “Sweep” command are explained below.

To apply the “Pipe” command, you must first create a 2D or 3D polyline. This indicates the course of the pipe. To round off the corners of the polyline, use the “Round corners of 3D polyline” command 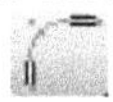. This is located in the "Special Tools" standard toolbar. Although the command name suggests otherwise, this command can also be used with 2D polylines.

The commands "Fillet2D" and "Fillet3D" are not accepted by the "Pipe" command and result in an error message.

The following figure (Figure 5-34) shows a pipe created with the "Pipe" command on a rounded and non-rounded polyline.

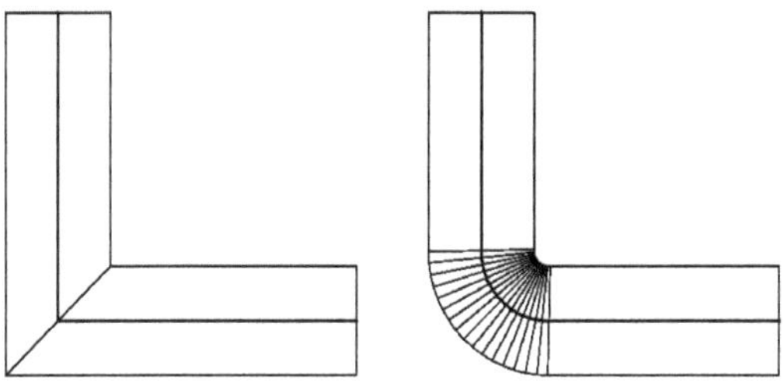

Figure 5-34 "Pipe" command on a rounded and not rounded polyline

If the created polyline is selected with the "Pipe" command activated, the following menu appears:

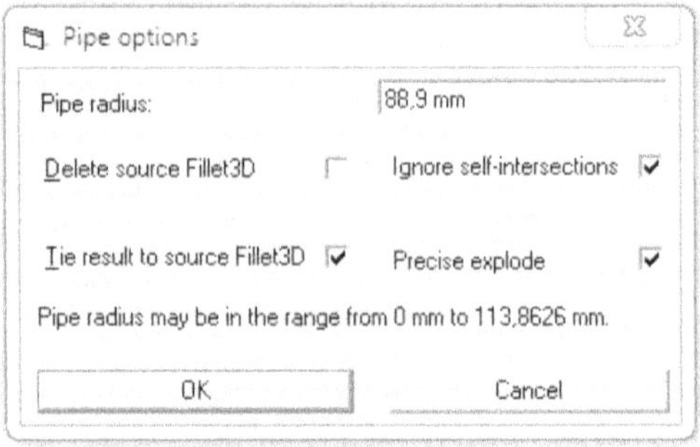

Figure 5-35 "Pipe options" menu

The option "Tie result to source Fillet3D" must be activated if the pipe model is to keep its connection to the guideline. This allows subsequent changes to the pipe run. The pipe outside diameter cannot be changed afterwards.

Based on the radii of the guide line, the menu gives a valid range for the pipe outside diameter. So, if you cannot enter the desired diameter, then most likely the radii of the pipe isn't large enough.

Initially, the created pipe model is a "TC Surface" (chapter 2.8).

If modify tools such as "Fillet Edges", "Chamfer Edges" or "Shell solid" are to be used on the created pipe model, the model type must be changed to "Solid" in its object properties under "Properties/ 3D". The mentioned modify tools cannot be used on a "TC Surface" model.

Changing the routing

A subsequent change in the course of a pipe, which was created by a "Sweep" or the "Pipe" command, is conditionally possible. The polyline used to create the pipe is still related to the 3D model resulting from the extrusion. So, changing the polyline also changes the pipe model.

In the example shown below, the pipe is extended in front of the elbow. For this, the corresponding nodes of the polyline and the circle used for the "Sweep" must be moved evenly so that the 3D model can then be rebuilt correctly.

The command "Stretch" (chapter 4.5) is suitable for this. The following Figure 5-36 shows, by way of example, the application of the "Stretch" command. First a selection frame is drawn around the corresponding area to be moved. All of the nodes of the guide line located therein, as well as the profile circle, are marked and can now be moved by specifying an offset and angle.

This initially requires a little practice. If the wrong nodes are selected or omitted, the model cannot be set up correctly.

With the standard command "Undo" , wrong steps can be undone, starting with the mostly recently undertaken step.

> If a non-rounded polyline is used to create the pipe (Figure 5-34 left), the subsequent change is easier because fewer nodes have to be moved.

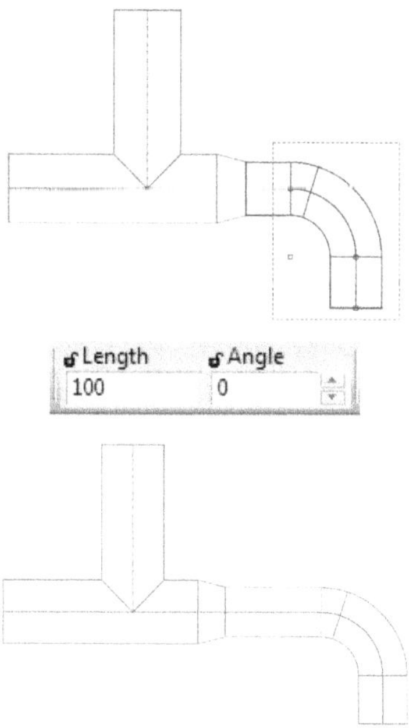

Figure 5-36 Changing a pipe run with the 2D command "Stretch"

Since the "Stretch" command is actually a 2D command, it can only be executed parallel to the work plane. Therefore, in the case of a three-dimensional pipe run the work plane may need to be consequently moved (chapter 5.8).

In order to subsequently change the outside diameter of the pipe, the circle used to extrude the pipe can be marked and, by changing the size in the "Inspector Bar" or in the object properties, the extrusion can be adjusted accordingly.

5.10.3 Comparison of methods

The detailed method using stored library parts has the big advantage that parts lists can be output.

In the case of systems where many pipes are routed in confined spaces with many piping components, the use of already existing standard parts offers the welcome advantage that not every flange or radian measure has to be read and entered during design in order to comply with the real dimensions. Of course, a well-maintained standard parts library is the prerequisite.

A disadvantage is the labor of this method. All parts must be aligned and moved to the correct positions. Nothing is done automatically. If the pipe run changes, the individual parts or parts groups must be subsequently moved and repositioned. Even the connection of components via constraints is not possible in 3D mode.

An advantage of the simplified method lies in the rapid creation of pipe runs, ideal in the conceptual phase of a project. Furthermore, the created guidelines can be used to create an isometric drawing.

To create pipe routes according to the simplified method, the commands "Sweep" and "Pipe" can be used. The "Pipe" command has the advantage that no extra circular profile has to be therefore created and aligned for extrusion (the outside diameter is entered in the command menu). Subsequent changes in the pipe course by changing the polyline are thus simplified. However, the pipe outside diameter cannot subsequently be changed with the "Pipe" command. This is possible with the "Sweep" command by the size change of the circle used for the extrusion.

A combination of the two methods (simplified and detailed) is conceivable, for example, when it comes to bended pipes.

5.11 Sheet Metal Design

Ever since the 2016 version, TurboCAD® has offered tools for the design of sheet metal components.

Sheets can be bent at a defined bending edge, plates added and components then unbent and dimensioned. Some of these features are described and shown below.

"Bend Sheet"

The "Bend Sheet" command allows objects to be bent around an axis by specifying the bend radius, angle, and neutral depth. You can choose whether the center of the bend lies in front of, on or behind the bending axis. Material is then added accordingly.

A part can be provided with any number of bends.

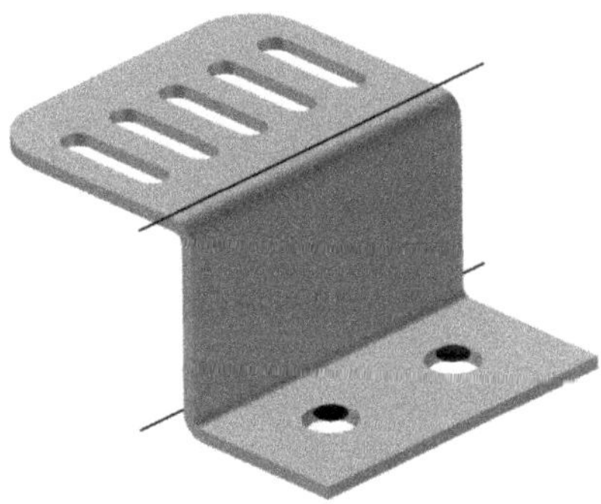

Figure 5-37 Bending a sheet metal

"Flange Sheet" 

On an existing flat sheet part, additional flanges can be added and provided with the desired bending radius, angle and length. The attached sheet metal can run over the entire edge length or be defined by the distances to the edge corners in its width.

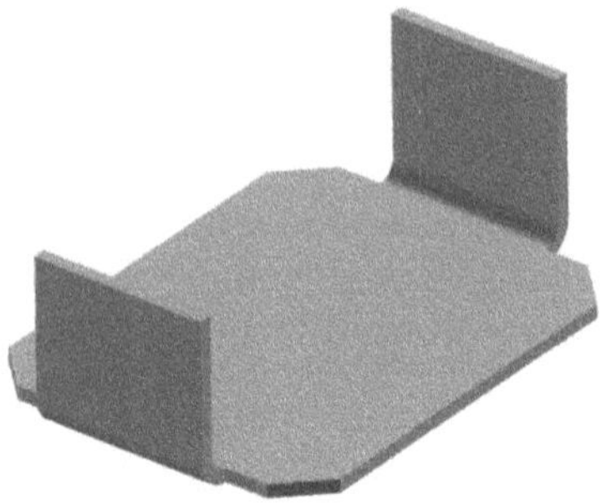

Figure 5-38 Adding flanges to a sheet metal part

"Bend by Sketch" 

This command extends a flat sheet metal part along a polyline. Here, several sides of the base plate can be selected. The entire edge length or only a certain length thereof. If adjacent sides are selected, a miter joint will be created automatically. Bend radius, miter width, corner cut and bending offset can be selected here.

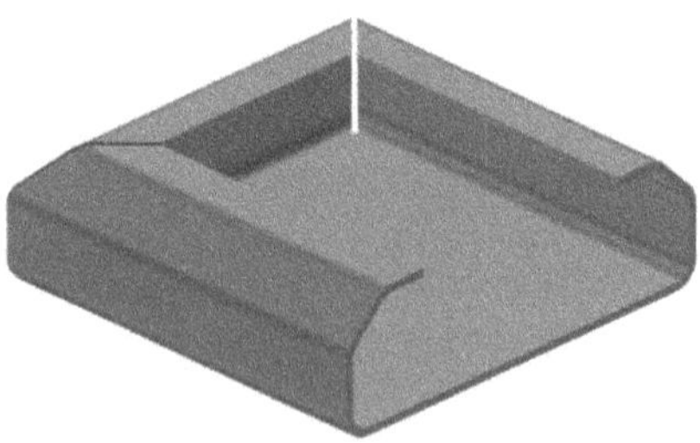

Figure 5-39 "Bend by Sketch" command

"Gusset"

Two mutually perpendicular surfaces, which have a uniform wall thickness in the bend, can be provided with a gusset or a stiffening rib. On the surfaces perpendicular to each other, 2D points must first be placed. These are then selected to create the gusset or rib. In the next step, width, rounding and, for the gusset, a draft can be selected. Unbending of the sheet metal part is no longer possible after adding a gusset / rib. To unbend, these features must be suppressed.

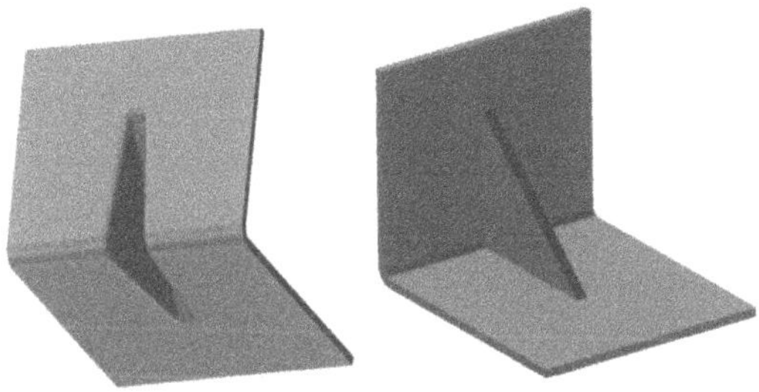

Figure 5-40 Gusset / Stiffening rib

"Unbend Sheet"

A sheet metal construction created with the above tools can be unbent on any reference surface using the "Unbend Sheet" command. By default, a transaction is added to the original body. This can be suppressed by deselecting the "Leave source copy" option. Bend edges and angles can be inserted as labels if required.

Figure 5-41 "Unbend Sheet" command

5.12 Drafting palette

With the "Drafting" palette (Tools/ Palettes/ Drafting...) sectional views, fragmental views, and break views of 3D objects or assemblies can be created.

In contrast to the simple viewport (chapter 6.1), which transfers a selected area of the model space into the paper space, the "Drafting Palette" picks up the geometric data of single or multiple 3D objects and displays them in the desired view type.

It is a powerful tool for drawing derivation. The following describes the handling of the palette and draws attention to its limits.

The following table shows the differences between the classic viewport and the drafting view.

Table 10 Differences between the viewport and the drafting view

Viewport	Drafting view
• Firmly defined view area; if the object shown is moved, the viewport must be realigned • Shows both 2D and 3D objects • Allows different rendering modes like "Hidden Line" or "Draft" • Sectional views not possible • Components which are added after the viewport was created will be displayed	• Only 3D objects can be transferred • Allows section views • Rendering modes limited to line view (similar to "Hidden Line") • Objects can be moved in model space without affecting the view in paper space • May lose the relationship between the 3D object and the drafting view if the 3D object is modified too much • Components which are added after the drafting view was saved in the palette are not included.

To create a view with the "Drafting Palette", the 3D object must be selected, and the desired view type must be chosen in the palette menu (Figure 5-42). All standard views and sectional views are available. A preview is shown. By clicking the "Add" button  the view is stored inside the "Drafting Palette".

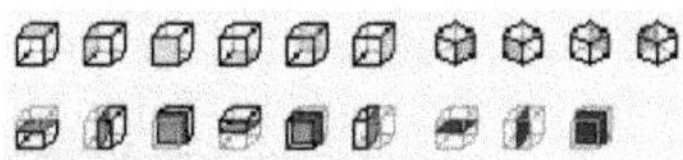

Figure 5-42 Default views of the drafting palette

The added view is listed in the upper display window of the "Drafting Palette" and can then be dragged to the paper space and scaled as desired. All views of a 3D object are grouped in a subfolder and can be renamed to ensure a clearer and less confusing list overview.

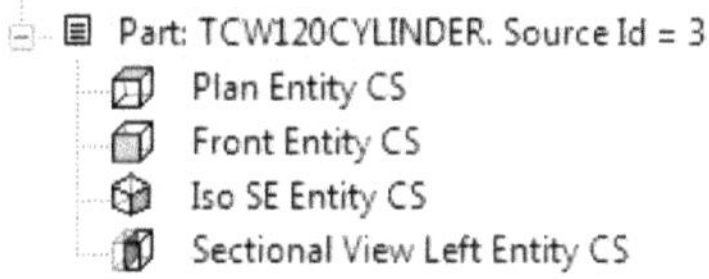

Figure 5-43 An example of a list of added views in the "Drafting Palette"

In style properties , line styles or section brushes can be edited. Settings made can be set for the whole "Drafting" palette or separately for each drafting view.

If a listed view is dragged out of the palette and it is moved over an existing one already in the paper space without releasing the mouse button, the scale, and if necessary the orientation of the new view, is adjusted automatically.

Sections based on a selected guide line, detail and fracture views require an already inserted drafting view.

> If a view is only needed to create further drafting views but isn't required to be shown on the print itself, it can be placed outside the print area.

Several objects can also be included in the "Drafting" palette as an assembly. They only have to be selected together when creating the drafting views.

Brushes can be set separately for each individual object, which is particularly useful for sectional views, for example to represent different materials. The brushes can be edited in the object properties of the respective drafting view under "Properties/ Section Brush/ Part of projection".

The names of each body listed in the "Part of projection" selecting box can be changed in order to have a better overview because the names given by default (example "TCW120CYLINDER.SourceId=3" sometimes make it difficult to differentiate between the parts. Entries in the "Info" box inside the "Selection Info" palette or in the "Attribute" box inside the parts object properties are picked up by the drafting view.

Different colors are also displayed in the drafting view when "By block" is chosen in the drafting view's properties under "Properties/ Pen visible/ Color".

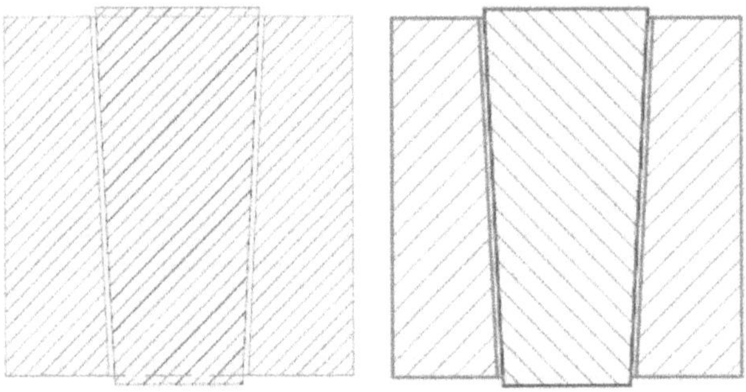

Figure 5-44 Multibody drafting view (left by default, right with settings adjustments)

If the 3D object is significantly changed in the model space, the drafting views may lose their connection to it and thus become unusable.

Drafting views should therefore be inserted, if possible, at a later stage in the design process.

If a design view loses the reference to the 3D object, it will be deleted along with any derived section or detail views. It is helpful to group the 3D objects before adding them to the "Drafting Palette". Working with groups and editing grouped objects are described in chapter 7.2. This way, the drafting view becomes less susceptible to reference loss to the 3D model.

When dimensioning drafting views that are not in scale 1:1, extreme caution is advised. Generally, dimensions match the scale of a drafting view and show the real dimension of the part. However, this only happens if both dimension points touch the edges of the component shown in the drafting view. If, for example, an axis of symmetry is added to the paper space and it is dimensioned to an edge of the component, the scale may not be adapted and thus an incorrect value is output.

> All dimensions should always be checked to make sure that the shown value matches the value of the measured object.

"Create by ViewLine"  (Section view)

The "Create by View Line" command allows the use of a line or polyline as a cutting path. These are first placed on an existing drafting view and selected as the cutting path when the command is applied. The cutting direction and the cutting path can be changed afterwards. The resulting section view adapts automatically.

For cutting paths as shown in Figure 5-45, the option "Aligned View" should be deactivated in the line or polyline's object properties which is being used as a cutting path ("Properties/ Format/ ViewLine"). If this option is activated, the cut line is first unwound, and the section view adjusted accordingly (Figure 5-46).

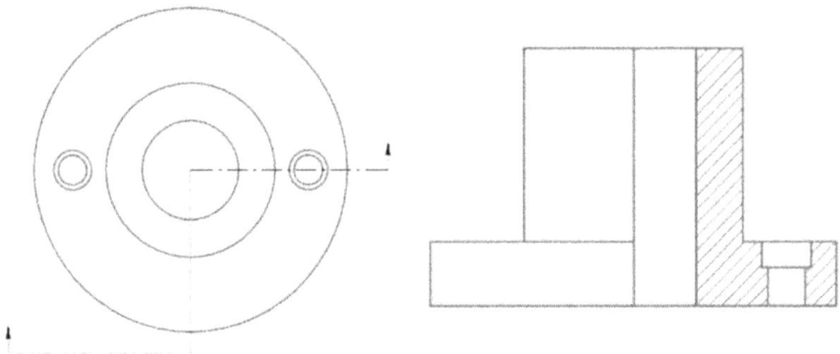

Figure 5-45 Cutting through a component

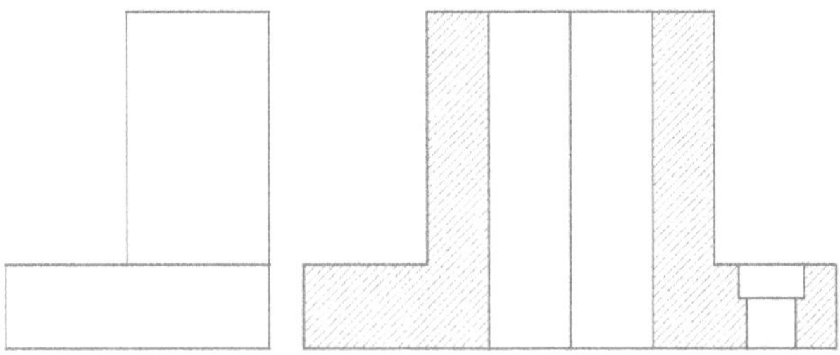

Figure 5-46 Cutting with activated "Aligned View" option

"Create Fragmental View" (Detailed view)

To create a detailed view, you must first lay a circular or closed line profile on an existing drafting view. This specifies the area shown in detail and remains linked to the drafting view. The change in size or position affects the detail view. For the detail view, an arbitrary scale can be set in its object settings.

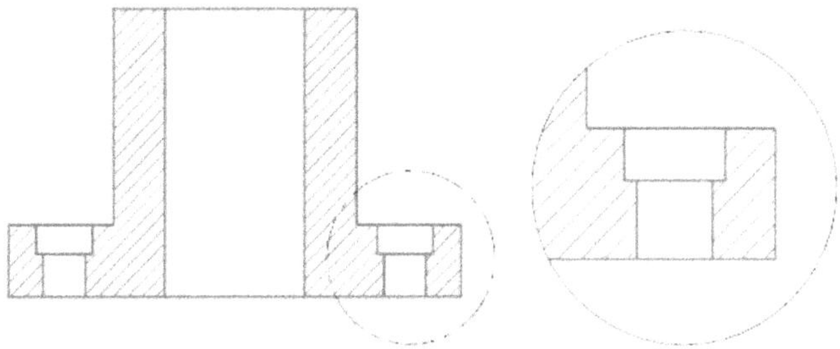

Figure 5-47 Detailed view ("Drafting Palette")

"Drafting Break" (Break view)

With the break view, long components can be shortened to find space on the drawing sheet. This allows you to trim previously placed drafting views by specifying the break position and width. It should be noted that a dimension over the length of the component does not show the real length, but rather the length of the break view. This must be taken into account when creating the drawing derivation. However, to specify the correct value, it is only possible to manually override the dimension value. However, this no longer responds to changes in the model. Therefore, it is important to identify such measures that have lost their associativity. A possibility for this is described in chapter 6.2.

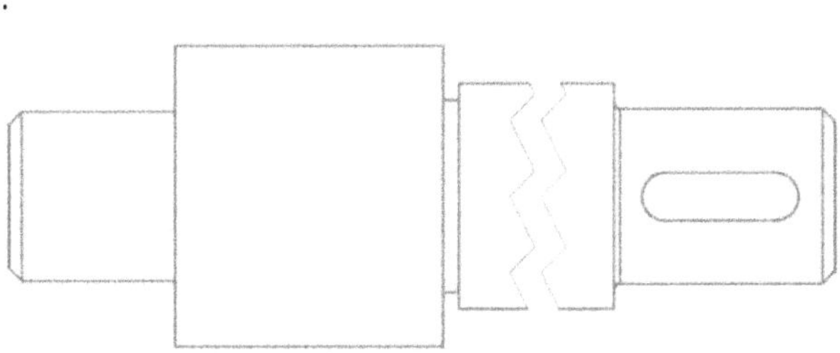

Figure 5-48 Break view ("Drafting Palette")

5.13 VISUALIZE / RENDERING

The lighting is essential for the visualization and conceptual rendering of 3D objects. Different types of light are offered.

In the menu "View/ Lights ..." or in the "Design Director" the lighting can be managed. New light sources can be added and edited in terms of light intensity, color, type, and position. In the menu column "On" lights can be switched on and off. If a lamp symbol is set, the corresponding light source is activated. In the "Visible" column, light sources in the model space can be made visible. These are hidden by default. The visibility of light sources has no effect on luminosity.

The most common light sources include:

The "**POINT**" which radiates from a given position evenly in all directions.

The "**SPOT**" which has a start point and a destination point where the spot is pointed. The spotlight is useful for lightening certain dark areas.

The "**AMBIENT**" which illuminates the 3D space evenly.

By using these three types of light in combination with different object colors or materials, you can already visualize models in a largely natural and realistic way.

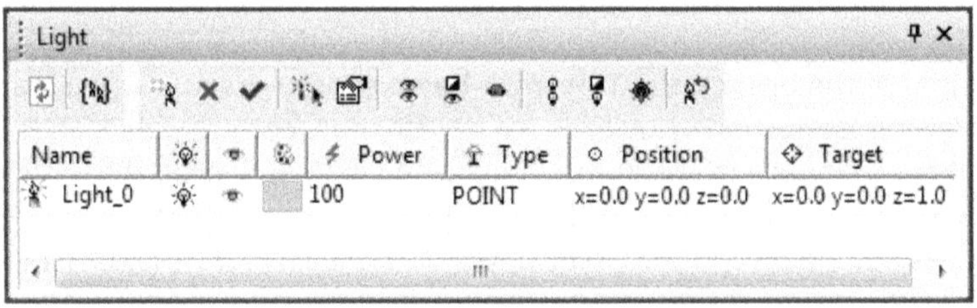

Figure 5-49 "Light" menu

If a light source is visible, it can be selected in the model space, duplicated by the conventional copy tools ("Copy Stamp", "Make Copy" or Copy & Paste) and positioned with the "Inspector Bar", such as by entering position or an offset.

The lighting properties can also be edited in the "Selection Info" palette. This facilitates the adaptation of the lighting. Lights can then be moved while a rendering mode is activated to adapt the illumination to your own ideas.

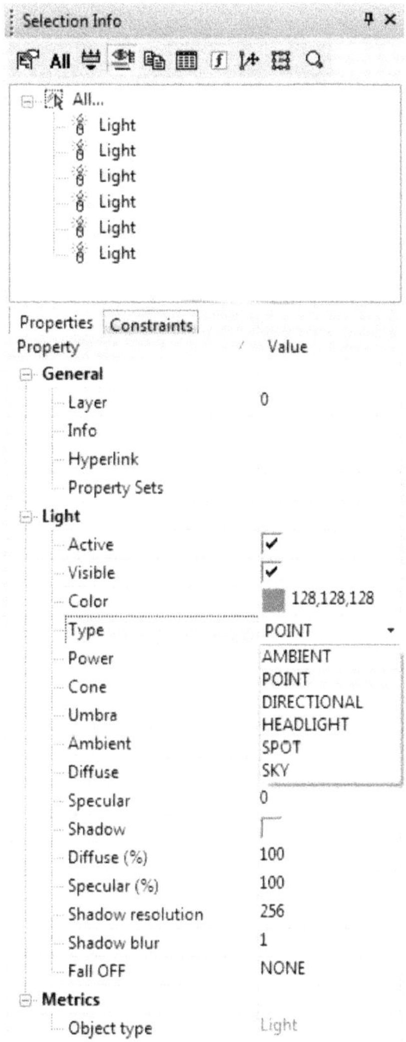

Figure 5-50 Light properties inside the "Selection Info" palette

Figure 5-51 Conceptual rendering using standard colors and materials

Another type of lighting is luminance. This makes it possible to provide 3D objects with a luminosity. This can be used to imitate the appearance of a lamp.

The luminance can be set in the object properties of any type of 3D object ("Properties/ Luminance").

Figure 5-52 Example luminance for the representation of a ceiling lamp

In the "Properties" menu shown below, the luminosity of the object can be adjusted. Here you can define different light sources (for example spot or point light), their light colors and intensities.

If you do not want to display the luminance object itself, but only use its luminosity, you can hide it by selecting the “Load to render luminance only” option.

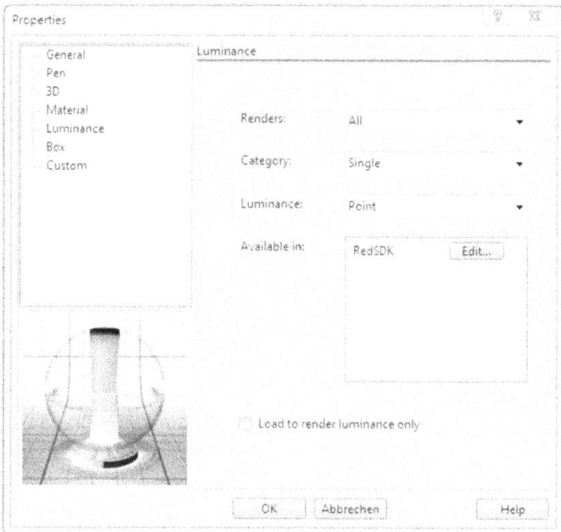

Figure 5-53 "Luminance" menu for adjusting the luminosity of an object

For visualization, 3D objects can also be assigned materials. The object properties contain the menu item "Material". This can be chosen from a material database.

Existing appearances can be edited, or new ones can be added.

Materials, luminance, wallpapers and render options can be managed in the “Render Manager”.

It can be opened under “Options/ Rendering Styles/ Edit RedSDK Rendering Styles...”.

The rendering tools usually have sufficient visualization capabilities for a coarse but natural rendering of 3D parts. If rendering is an area of focus in the own area of activity and high demands are placed on it, IMSI Design offers a separately available render engine called “LightWorks”.

LightWorks Plug-In

LightWorks offers more options in terms of material settings, surface finish, realistic shadows, and luminance, beyond the conceptual render modes already available in TurboCAD®.

The LightWorks plug-in is sold separately for the various TurboCAD® versions.

Below is a comparison of two render settings. Neither the default settings nor the default light sources were edited in either example.

Figure 5-54 Left: Render mode "Draft" with RedSDK, Right: Enhanced rendering mode with LightWorks plug-in

6 DRAWING DERIVATION

6.1 VIEWPORTS

In addition to the drafting views described in chapter 5.12, viewports also provide the ability to translate 2D or 3D objects created in the model space, into the paper space for viewing and dimensioning.

Viewports can be scaled and then dimensioned or annotated. They create a permanent link between the model space and the view on the drawing sheet. If a change is made in the model space, it is automatically transferred to the drawing sheet.

This technique has already been shown in the tutorial "Crane hook drawing derivation" in chapter 1.4.

The drawn object in the model space must first be entered in the desired view with the command "Create View" . For this purpose, the command is activated, and a selection frame is to be set, which initially represent the outer dimensions of the viewport. Only the selected area is initially shown in the viewport in the paper space.

If the selection frame is set, a name for the viewport must be entered. This option should be used as the named views must be selected when later inserting a viewport in the paper space. If no meaningful names are chosen, the overview will be quickly lost as it will be increasingly difficult to differentiate between the views.

All created views are listed under "View/ Named Views/ Named Views ...". This menu shows the views as well as the information needed for full definition, such as position, boundaries or rendering status.

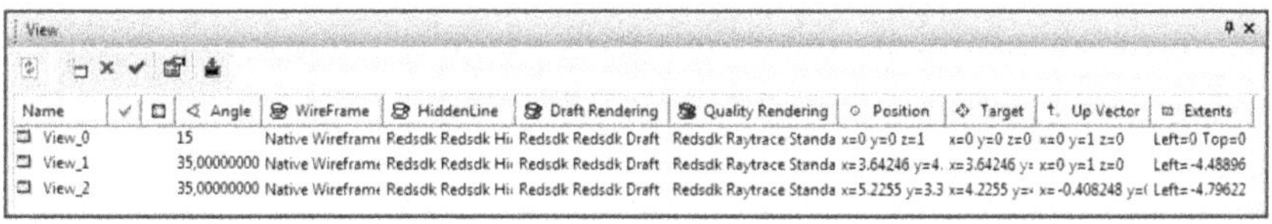

Figure 6-1 "View" list

Once the desired viewport has been created, it can now be inserted into the paper space anywhere on the drawing sheet. The command "Insert Viewport" is used for this purpose. When the command is activated, a selection frame is again drawn at the desired position. If the size is determined by the second click, you must now select a view from the list of already named views (Figure 6-1).

The following has to be noted:

After pasting, the viewport is inserted without a fixed scale. The size of the displayed part automatically adapts to the size of the selection frame that was created when the viewport was inserted in the paper space. If the size of the viewport is changed by dragging on one of the corner nodes, size and scale of the displayed part change accordingly. A fixed scale can then be set in the properties of the viewport. The properties menu opens by double-clicking on the viewport or by selecting the viewport and then right-clicking in the "Properties" menu item. Double-clicking or selecting the viewport will only work by clicking on the outer border of the viewport, or on a line or edge of the drawing shown within it. However, clicking on the free area does nothing.

If the "Fixed" option is checked in the "Properties/ Viewport/ Scale" submenu, a fixed scale can be selected or entered manually. If you confirm with “OK”, the specified scale is transferred, and the drawing object shown is displayed in it (only if it has been drawn on a scale of 1:1 in the model space). The scale now remains independent of the position or size of the viewport.

By default, the viewport has a visible border frame. It can be hidden in the viewport properties under "Properties/ Viewport/ Box". This can be also preset in the “Insert Viewport” command (chapter 3.3).

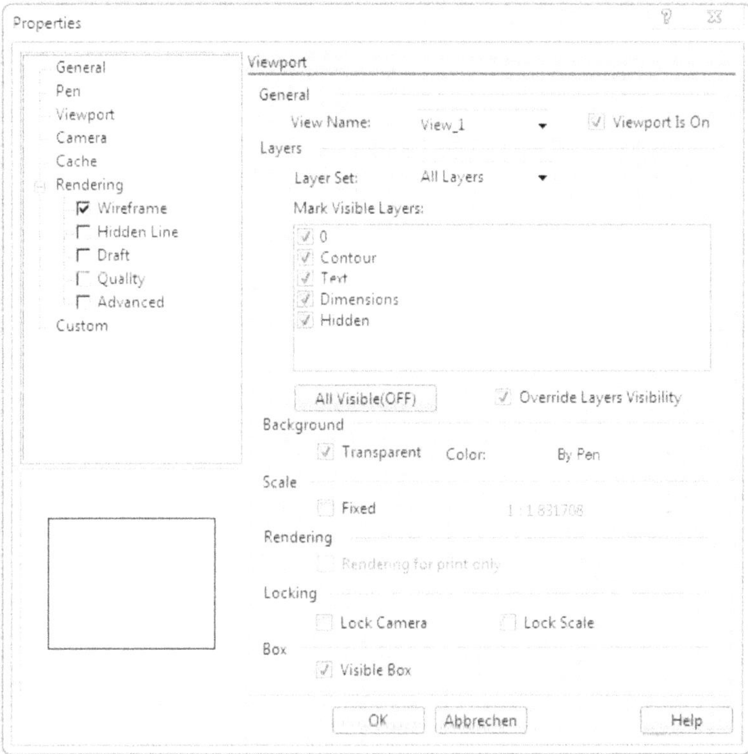

Figure 6-2 Viewport properties

The line properties of the border frame are managed in the menu item "Pen". Color, line type or width can be adjusted.

In a viewport, certain layers can be enabled or disabled. In the properties menu under "Properties/ Viewport/ Layers/ Mark Visible Layers" all available layers in the drawing are listed. All existing layers when creating the viewport are automatically activated and thus visible. If a layer is added later when the model is edited in the model space, it will appear in the list, but it will be disabled. Therefore, any drawing objects that are on this new layer are not displayed by the viewport and must be subsequently activated.

If layer sets (chapter 7.7) are defined, they can also be assigned to viewports. To do this, the desired layer set has to be selected in the drop-down list in "Properties/ Viewport/ Layers/ Layer Set".

6.2 DIMENSIONS AND ANNOTATIONS

For dimensioning and annotating of drawing objects, various tools such as orthogonal, parallel, angular or baseline dimensions are available.

Figure 6-3 Standard toolbar "Dimension"

With dimension properties, the dimensions can be adapted to each person's own ideas or company standards. Different arrowheads, fonts, tolerances, limits, line types, prefix, and suffix as well as alternating units are available.

It is possible to save different dimension styles and load them on demand. By doing this, as many dimension styles as liked can be added in the "Style Manager" under "Tools/ Palettes/ Style Manager ...". Each of them can be provided with the desired settings. These dimension styles can then be selected in the dimension properties, as shown in Figure 6-5.

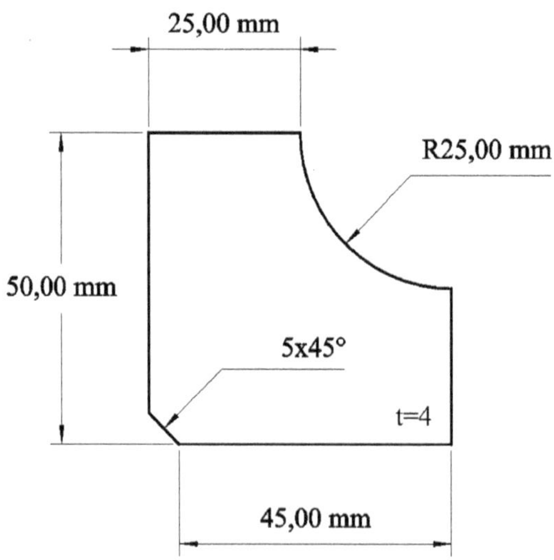

Figure 6-4 Example of different dimensions and notes

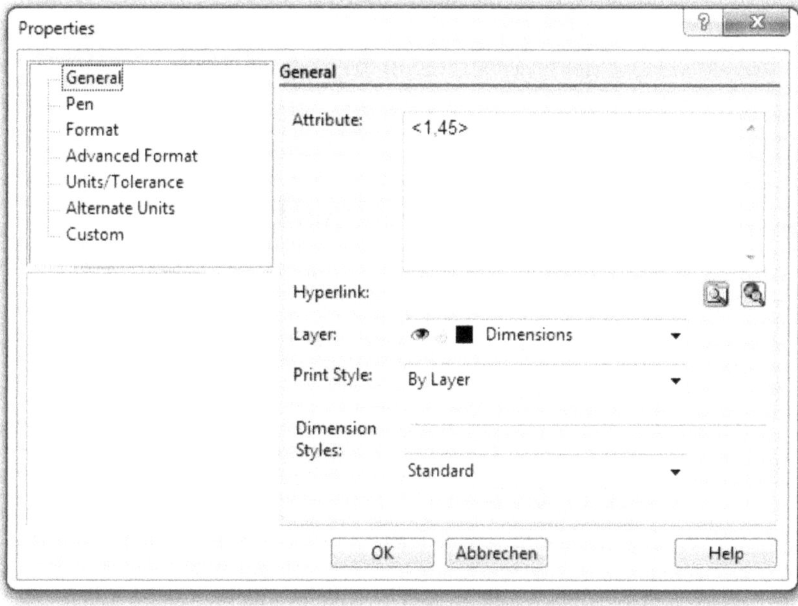

Figure 6-5 Dimension properties "General"

Once a dimension is created, the dimension value is shown in the dimension properties under “Properties/ General/ Attributes”.

A dimension number, which is controlled by the length, diameter or angle of the dimensioned object, is surrounded by small and greater characters (example: <50>). If this number is manually overwritten, it loses its associativity with the object. Length and size changes are then no longer recorded. The dimension is therefore no longer intelligently connected to the geometry.

If the manually entered number is deleted and <> is put in the attribute field, the dimensioning number will be automatically determined and output again.

Overwritten dimensions should be indicated. In practice, the dimension is underlined in this case. Unfortunately, the dimension properties do not offer this option. Alternatively, the measure can be indicated by manually placing a line to underline the number or by changing the color.

When dimensioning, it is to be noted that the default offset between the objects edge and the dimension extension lines may result in false snap points of other dimensions. This is illustrated in the following figure.

When placing the dimensions, it is important to ensure that the correct points will be snapped.

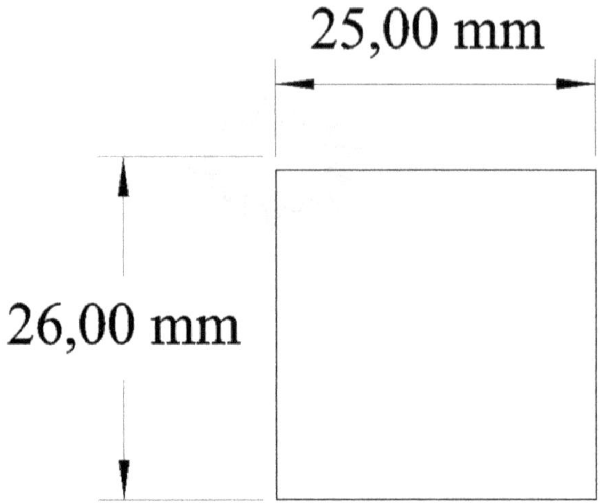

Figure 6-6 Dimension extension lines – Offset

The offset, i.e. the gap between the edge and the dimension extension line, can be changed in the dimension properties under "Properties/ Advanced Format /Extension Lines". Sometimes, zero cannot be entered in the "Extension" and "Offset" input fields. It won't be recognized and is subsequently replaced with the previously entered value.

> If this happens, a very small value (for example, 0,000001) can be entered. Once this value is below the unit precision set in the drawing options (Figure 3-16), the value is automatically set to zero and the offset disappears.

The decimal places used can be set under "Options/ Drawing Setup/ Space Units/ Units in workspace/ Precision".

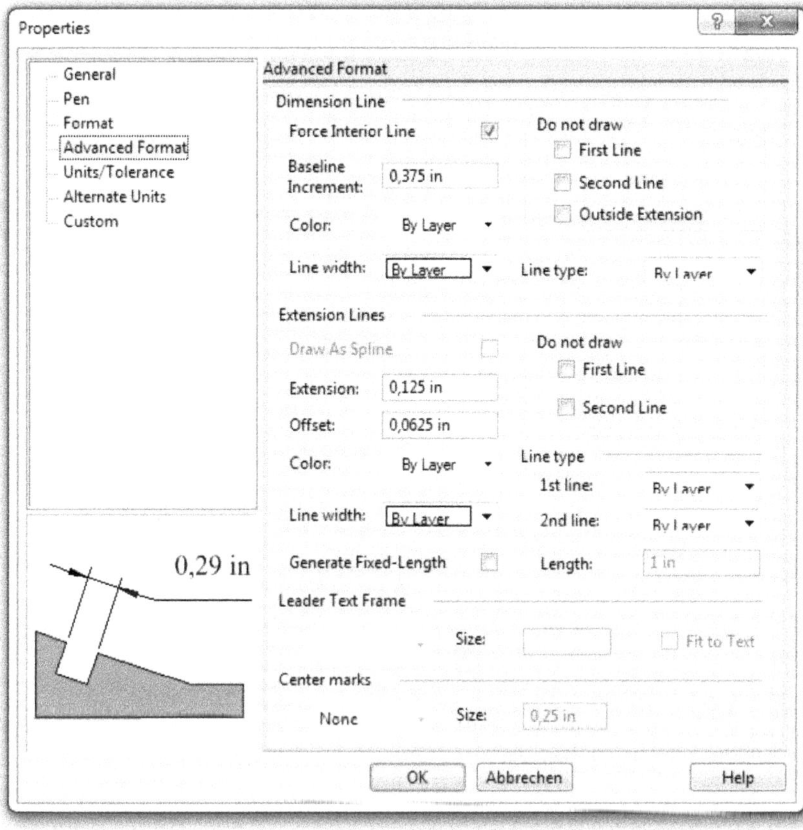

Figure 6-7 Dimension properties "Advanced Format"

In the following, some of the existing dimension types are listed, which are mostly used:

"Orthogonal" 

If the "Orthogonal" command is used, two points must first be defined. Between these two points the distance is then automatically dimensioned either vertically or horizontally. The third click then determines the position of the text and automatically determines the lengths of the extension lines.

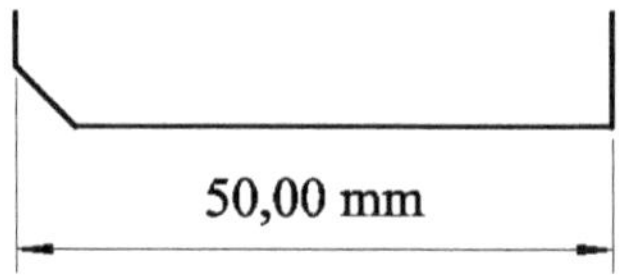

"Smart" 

This dimensioning tool creates the dimension between the endpoints of a line by just clicking on the line. Before dropping the dimension text, the position of the mouse cursor determines whether the dimension is placed parallel to the line or horizontally / vertically.

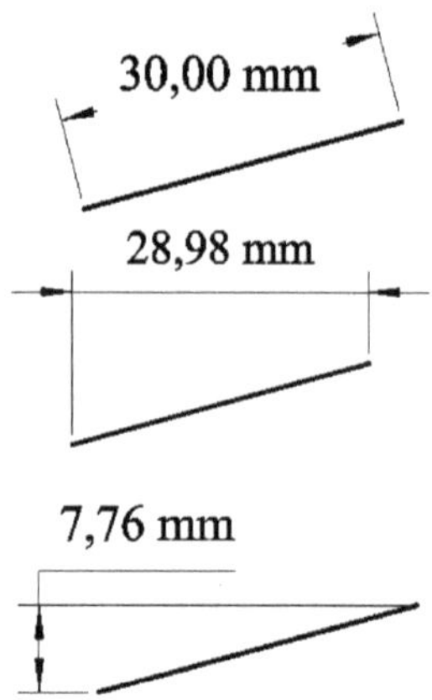

"Parallel" 

The dimension is set parallel to the line by defining the start and end point.

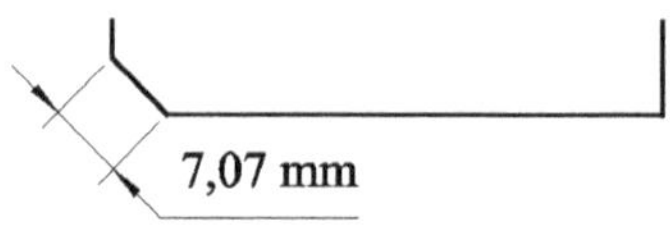

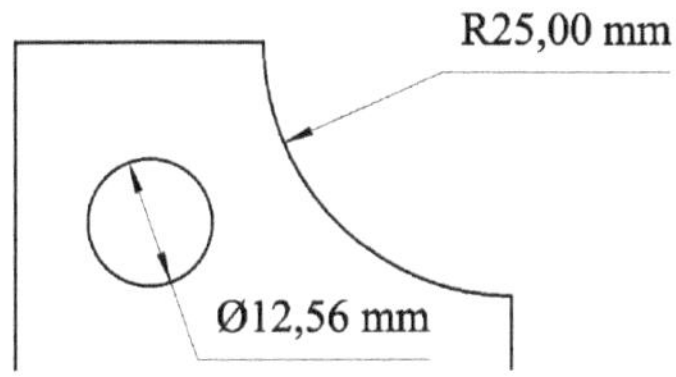

"Radius"  / "Diameter" 

Both radius and diameter dimensions are defined by clicking on the arc or circle. The second click drops the dimension altogether.

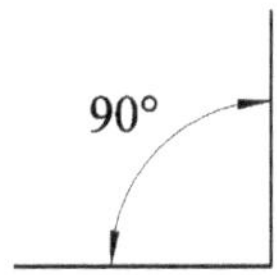

"Angular" 

The angular dimension is created by clicking on the lines to be measured in any order.

"Baseline" 

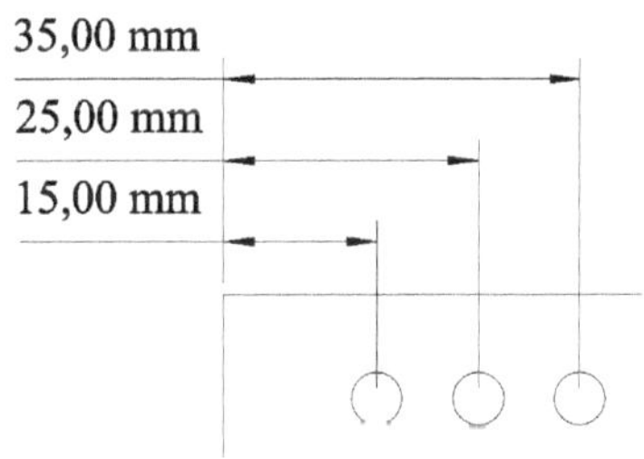

To reference multiple points to a baseline, first a dimension (e.g., "Orthogonal" dimension) must be created between the first two points. If you now activate the "Baseline" command and click on the desired extension line connecting to the edge which is to be referenced, further reference points can be added.

"Leader" 

The "Leader" command allows annotation with a reference arrow. The first click defines the point to which the reference arrow points. The second defines the transition from the reference line to the horizontal text line. The desired text and its orientation are entered via the "Inspector Bar".

By double-clicking on a dimension or right-clicking on it and selecting the properties, dimension properties such as text, arrowheads, extension lines, etc. can be edited.

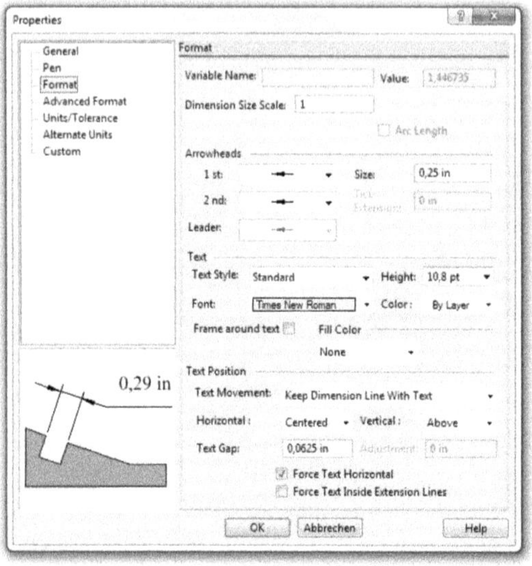

Figure 6-8 Dimension properties "Format"

Pen: Line width, color, scaling, pattern

Format: Dimension Size Scale, Arrowheads, Text Style

Advanced Format: Settings of dimension and extension lines

Units / Tolerance: Dimension units, Precision, Tolerances / Limits

Alternate Units: Multiplier, Prefix & Suffix, Tolerances

To change the position of the dimensions, you can use the "Edit tool" (chapter 4.6),

"Tolerance"

In addition to dimensions and simple text annotations, there are other useful marking commands. The "Tolerance" command allows the specification of geometrical tolerances for shape, profile, alignment and position of the workpiece.

The command is located under "Draw/ Tolerance".

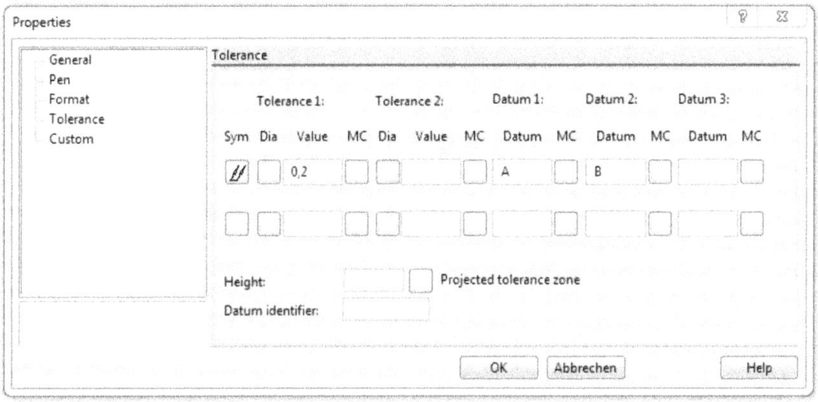

Figure 6-9 Tolerances properties menu

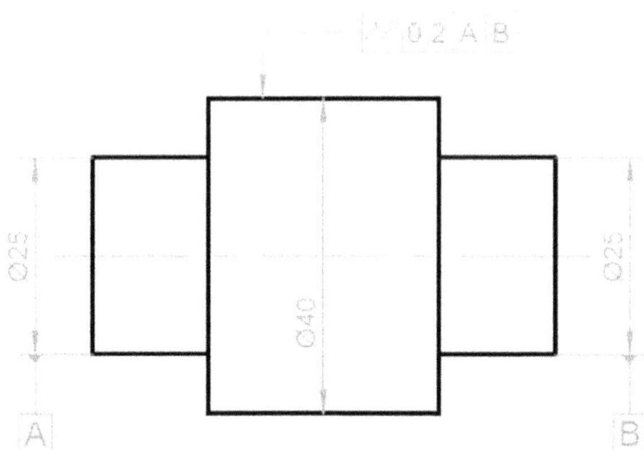

Figure 6-10 Application example for geometrical tolerances

"Surface Roughness" 

The "Surface Roughness" command allows the placement of symbols to determine the allowable surface finish of a workpiece.

The command is located under "Draw/ Surface Roughness".

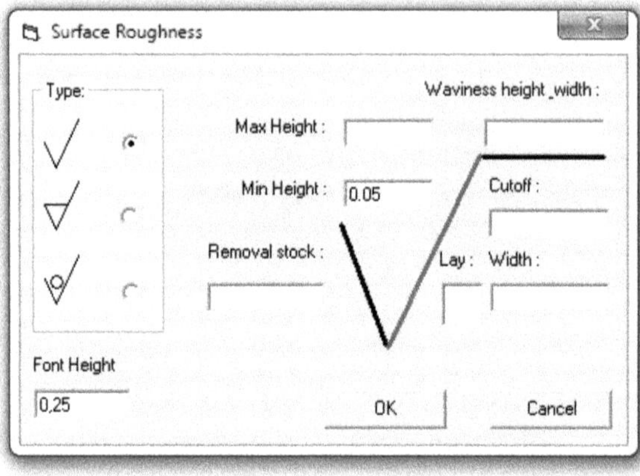

Figure 6-11 "Surface Roughness" menu

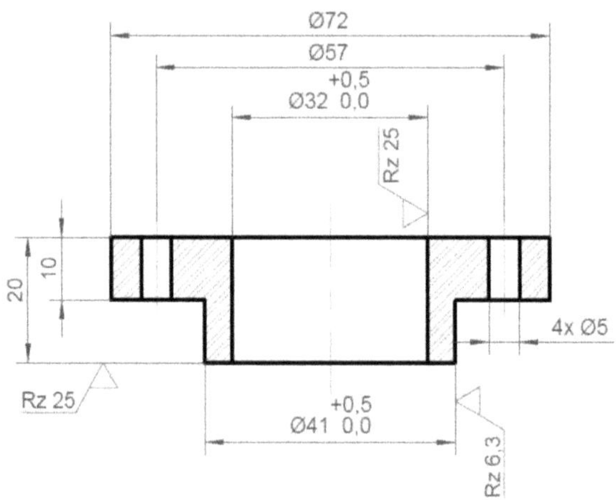

Figure 6-12 Application example for the "Surface Roughness" command

"Weld symbol" 

With the "Weld symbol" command, welded joints can be marked and defined.

The command is located under "Draw/ Weld symbol".

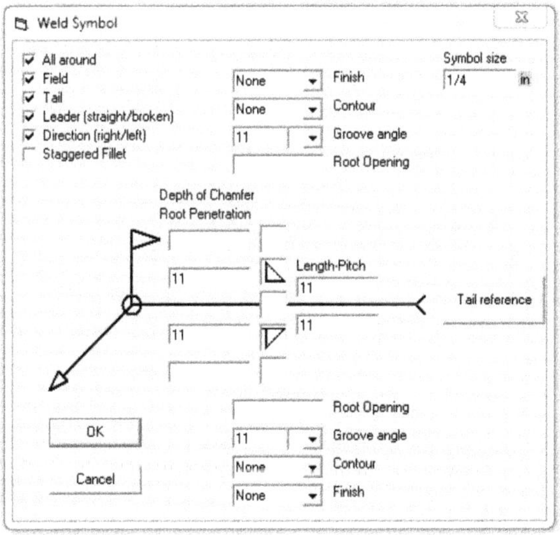

Figure 6-13 "Weld Symbol" menu

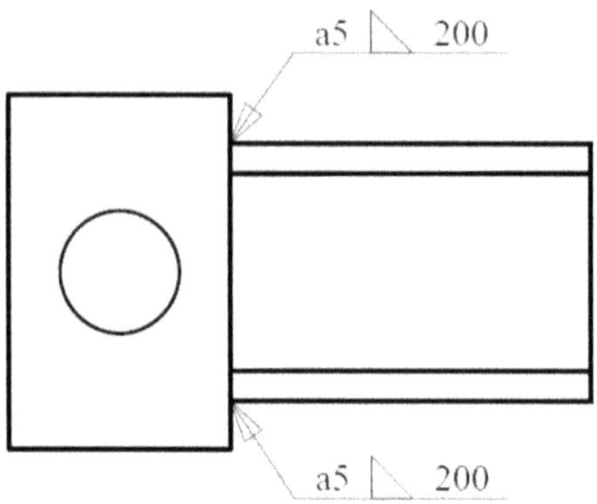

Figure 6-14 Application example for the "Weld symbol" command

6.3 PAGE / PRINTER SETUP

Sheet formats, margins and printing scales can be set under "File/ Page Setup...". A distinction is made between printer paper and drawing sheet.

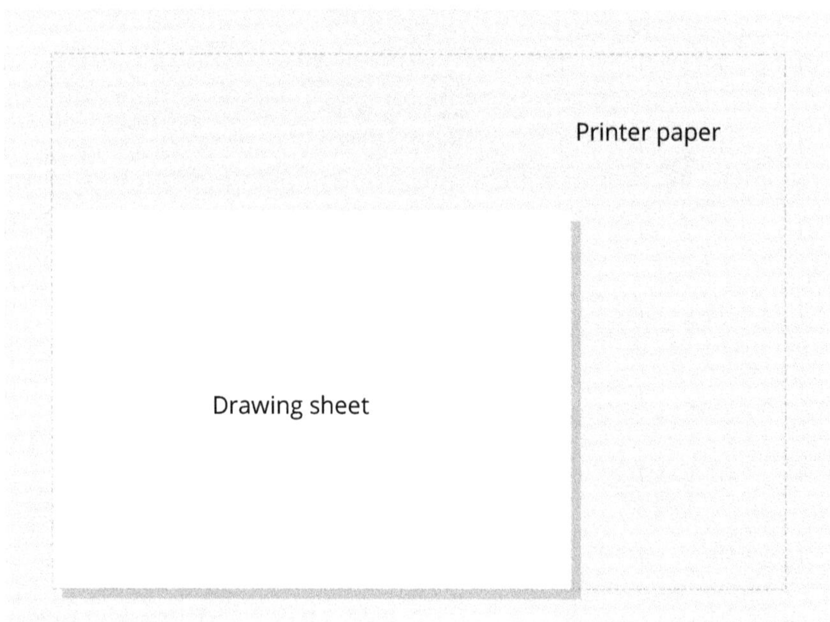

Figure 6-15 Printer paper and drawing sheet

The format of the printer paper and the drawing sheet format can be set individually in the "Page Setup" menu (Figure 6-16). The "Keep Centered" option centers everything located in the paper space around the paper space's central point. This does not affect the scale. The scale can be set under "Paper Space Printing Scale".

If there are drawing objects or viewports in the paper space that have been drawn on a certain scale, and if this should also be retained for later printing, the scale of the drawing sheet must be 1:1 (full size).

If no scale is required, but the drawings needs to be displayed as large as possible on the set drawing sheet, the scale can be adjusted by the "Fit" button accordingly.

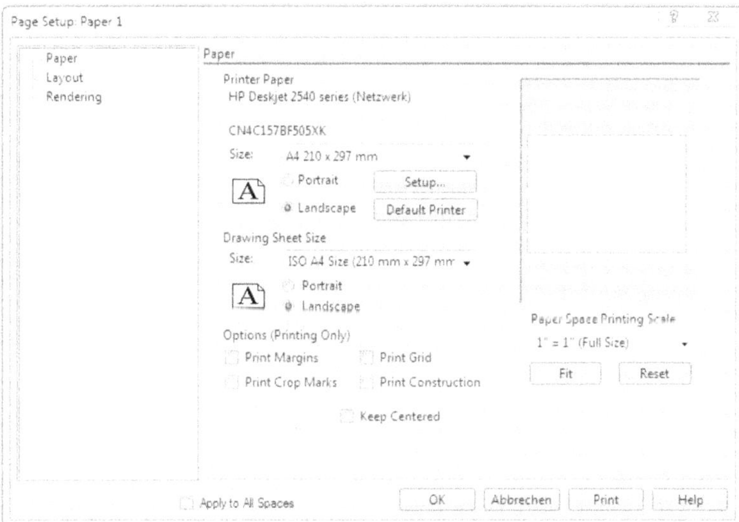

Figure 6-16 "Page Setup" menu – "Paper"

The "Layout" menu can be used to set page margins and split the printout into several pages. For example, a DIN A2 sheet can be spread over four A4 sheets as shown below.

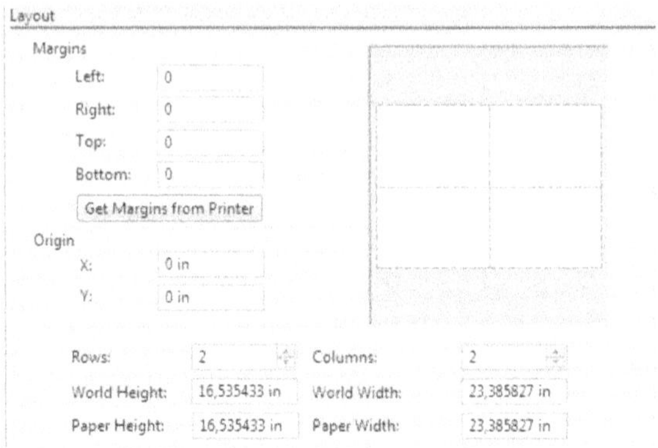

Figure 6-17 Rows and columns example

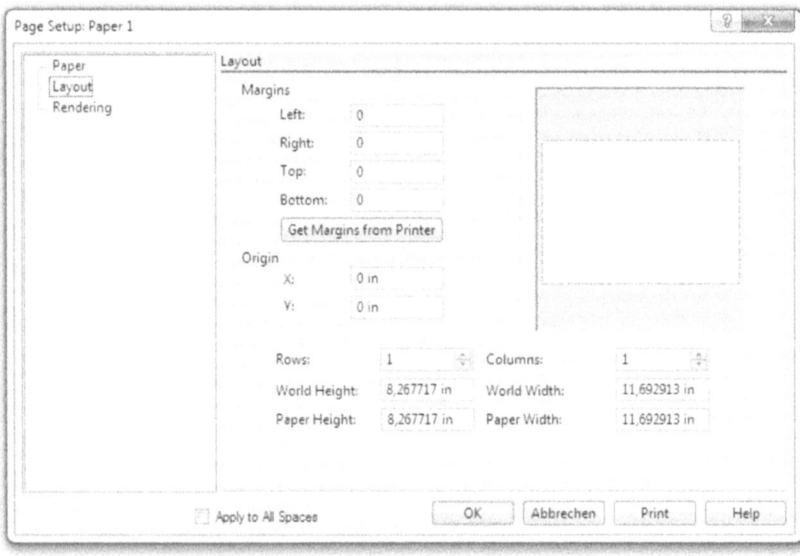

Figure 6-18 "Page Setup" menu – "Layout"

The origin refers to the lower left corner of the drawing sheet.

7 2D/3D OVERALL FUNCTIONS

7.1 TABLES AND BILL OF MATERIALS

TurboCAD® includes basic tools for creating and editing tables. A table can be created within TurboCAD® or imported from Excel®. In the standard "Text" toolbar or in the "Draw" menu, all necessary commands are collected.

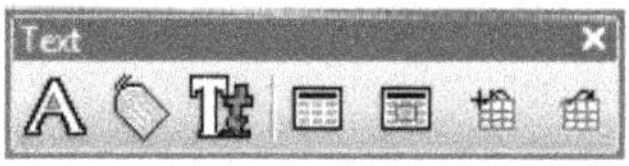

Figure 7-1 Standard toolbar "Text"

Different table styles can be created before inserting. This is done in the "Style Manager" ("Tools/ Palettes/ Style Manager ...") under "Table Style". Here font, text size, font and cell color as well as the text alignment can be determined. If a table is inserted, it can be chosen from the created table styles in the "Properties" menu. For example, this may be convenient for pre-defined ready-to-use table styles for bill of material lists.

If the command "Insert New Table" is activated, the table size and the number of cells can be set via the "Inspector Bar".

Texts can be edited with the "Modify Table" command. When the command is activated, a table must first be selected. By just clicking on a cell, the text can be entered in the "Selection Info" palette. By double-clicking, it can be written directly into the cell. The table style controls text properties.

However, each cell can be formatted individually using the "Selection Info" palette.

For adding, removing, or changing rows and columns the "Edit Tool" can be used. With this enabled and the table selected, clicking and holding down the "Shift" key activates formatting options in the "Inspector Bar" that can be used to further refine the table. If the "Shift" key is held down and two fields are selected, they can be merged into one. Created tables can be saved as Excel® files on the PC with the command "Insert Table to Excel".

Separately created Excel® tables can be inserted with the command "Insert Table from Excel" and be converted to a TurboCAD® internal table or pasted into the opened drawing by "Copy & Paste". This table can then be opened and edited within TurboCAD® in the familiar Excel® environment.

The following things should be noted.

> There is no connection between the inserted Excel® table and the source file. Changes to one of the tables are not reflected in the other.

If a table from Excel® is imported into the model or paper space, it can be resized by dragging the margins. If a uniform font size is to be adhered to, this should be avoided given the fact that scaling the table also changes the font size.

Depending on the graphics card and its settings, an inserted Excel® table may appear blurry, and in some cases unreadable. By pressing the "F5" key to update the drawings or activate the command in the menu "View/ Redraw", the table should be displayed normally again. Printing or exporting to PDF is not affected by this graphic problem.

BOMs[1] can be output as TurboCAD® self-generated reports directly as a table in the model or paper space. The database function can use groups or block names to create BOMs as well as the custom part information shown in chapter 7.5.

> It should be noted that the inserted BOMs merely represent snapshots and do not automatically adapt to the drawing. If parts are added or removed, the BOM does not change.

[1] Bill of materials

7.2 GROUPS, BLOCKS, AND EXTERNAL BLOCK REFERENCES

In the distinction between groups and blocks, the following explanation of these elements should help.

Groups

Multiple drawn objects can be grouped by the "Create Group" command. With the "Explode" command, the grouping can be broken up. A nested grouping (group in group) is possible.

The group can be edited in the "Selection Info" palette by the command "Edit Content" without having to explode it first. This also applies to nested groups. The view changes in such a way that only the group to be edited remains on the screen.

Multiple "Edit Content" can be reached in deeper group levels. Each group level must then be closed with "Finish Edit Content" before it can be further processed in the actual drawing.

> Furthermore, a group can be marked and edited by selecting the "Edit Tool" in the drop-down menu by right-clicking. The advantage of this method is that the rest of the drawing remains visible when editing the group and is not hidden. Also snaps to objects outside of the group are possible.

Blocks

Blocks are useful when drawing objects need to be reused many times in a current drawing. Blocks are stored in the internal block library of the drawing. Block references are then inserted into the drawing instead of the original object.

Any 2D or 3D drawing objects can be added to the "Blocks" palette. For this purpose, the corresponding object at the reference point is dragged and dropped into the dark gray area of the "Blocks" palette. In the window which then appears (Figure 7-2), an individual block name can be assigned under which the block is consequently also listed in the palette. The names of all previously created blocks are listed in the box below the name that has been entered for the new block, making it easy to see which names are already in use. If the option "Insert at current location" is activated, the added drawing object (now as a block) remains in the same position.

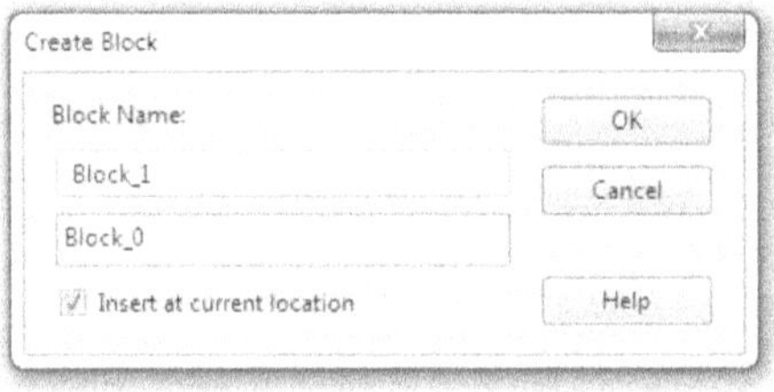

Figure 7-2 Adding an object to the "Blocks" palette

Blocks can then be inserted as often as desired from the "Blocks" palette by simply dragging & dropping into the current drawing.

When a block is edited, all instances of that block in the drawing are updated. The advantage of this lies in the smaller file size. Since the corresponding objects are not present multiple times, but rather only once in the drawing, they are therefore only present once in the computer memory. If a block is to be processed, for example when editing texts or layers, this can be done in the "Blocks" palette with the "Edit Content" command.

> Exploding a block breaks the connection between the block and the inserted block reference.

External References

An external block reference ("Xref") is a standalone 2D or 3D drawing that is inserted as a block into the "Blocks" library of the current drawing. Unlike normal blocks, the objects associated with an "Xref" definition are not stored in the drawing that is currently open. Only a reference to another drawing file is inserted.

If an external reference has been inserted, the entire contents of the other file will be displayed, even though it is not actually present in the drawing. This is similar to the principle of a Windows® shortcut.

Inserted external block references can be opened from within the main drawing file. This is done by right-clicking on the corresponding reference in the "External References" list in the "Blocks" palette and by selecting the command "Open". This opens the drawing, which was inserted as a reference, separately. After it has been edited and closed, the main drawing file must be updated. The changes will not be applied automatically. The "Reload" command is in the same drop-down menu as the "Open" command described above.

It is not possible to modify the inserted block references in the main drawing file with commands such as the "Boolean subtraction" of other bodies. Here only scaling is possible by entering new values into the "Inspector Bar".

It is useful to use external block references if:

- several complex drawings with large data volumes are to be put together as it reduces the loading times in a file, or

- there are standard parts, which should be stored centrally and not copied into every new drawing. It should be noted that if you change this centrally stored file, it will be copied into all drawings into which the part has been inserted as an external block reference.

To add an external block reference to the currently open drawing, first click on "External References"  in the "Blocks" palette. The menu window "External References" opens. Initially, this menu window only displays the drawing that is currently open. By right-clicking on the name of the drawing, another drawing file can now be selected and added as a block reference. Whether the drawing is inserted at the midpoint of the XREF extent (the frame surrounding all the contained drawing objects) or at a previously defined XREF insert base point, can be chosen by each individual user.

Any quantity of block references can be added. All block references are listed in the "External References" menu window in the "Blocks" palette. By right-clicking on the listed references, the functions "Open", "Reload", "Detach" and "Bind" are available. The "Bind" function first breaks the reference to the external drawing and imports all of its drawing objects into the active drawing as a local block. The file size will increase accordingly.

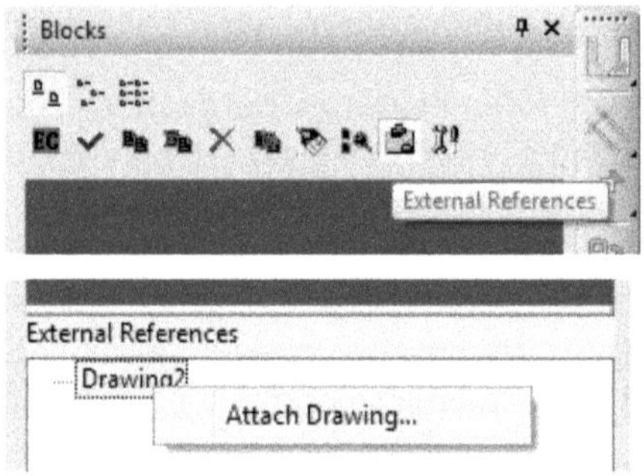

Figure 7-3 "Blocks" menu – External References

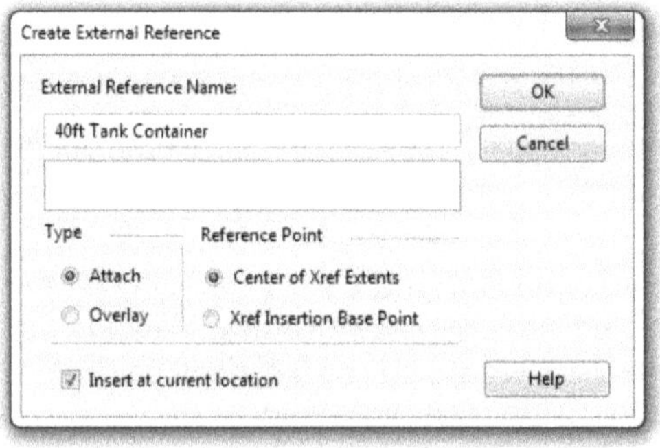

Figure 7-4 Create External Reference

> When using external block references, it is crucial that the path to the external block references are monitored. If, for example, a revision number is changed in the file name, errors will automatically occur in the assignment.

The path assignment can be viewed and edited in the "Blocks" palette under "Edit Content". This may be useful, for example, if the drawing file inserted as an external block reference has been moved or renamed. The correct assignment can then be restored by specifying the new path.

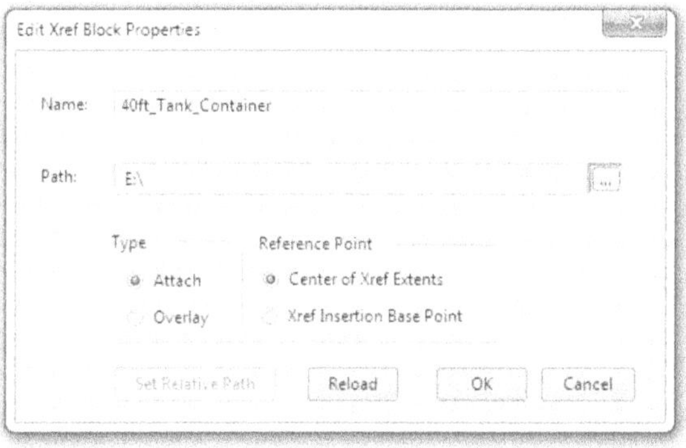

Figure 7-5 "Edit Xref Block Properties" menu

7.3 LIBRARY

The library enables central storage of both 2D drawing objects and 3D parts. There are stored objects that are likely to be used multiple times (P&ID symbols, title blocks, 3D objects such as flanges, pipe bends, screws, etc.). If, for example, a standard component is needed in the current drawing and it is likely to occur several times in the drawing, it can first be inserted from the symbol library and then converted into a block (chapter 7.2) to be duplicated.

If a part has been inserted from the library, it loses the reference to the file, which has been stored centrally in the library. Changing the library file will not affect the inserted part. If the relationship between the inserted part and the part stored on the server is required, the external block reference must be used.

The symbol library is stored locally on the computer after installation of TurboCAD® but can be centrally located on a network server so that several users can access the same library. However, setting up and updating the symbol library must be done on each computer. Only the data to be used is stored centrally in the network.

> The symbol library does not automatically match its content with the data on the server.

Therefore, before each use of the library, it should be reloaded to ensure that the most up-to-date data is used or, alternatively, changes to the library content should be communicated to all users.

7.3.1 Using the symbol library

The symbols can be imported into the drawing by dragging & dropping at the reference point from the "Library" palette.

The palette can be activated under "Tools/ Palettes/ Library ..." and attached to any screen edge.

All symbols imported from the symbol library are automatically grouped. This is to be considered during further processing. This applies to individual as well as multiple objects.

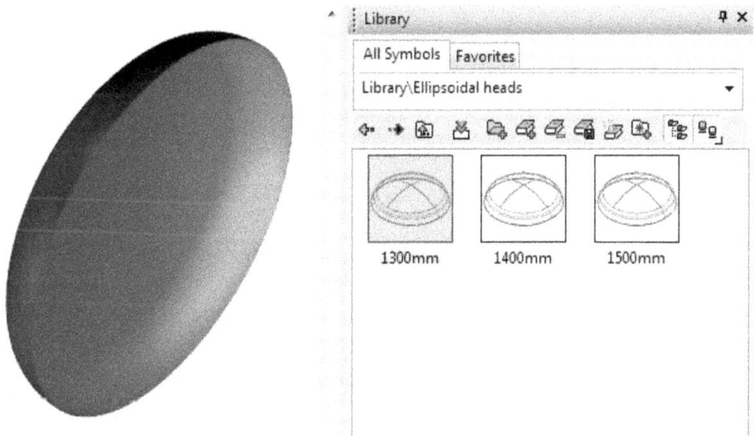

Figure 7-6 "Library" palette

7.3.2 Saving a file as a symbol

Saving parts into the symbol library is shown here using an example of 3D pipe elbows in various dimensions. First, a new drawing is opened and a pipe elbow in a certain dimension is modeled. This will be copied several times after completion in the same drawing and changed into the other dimensions. The individual copies have to be adjusted manually, but this is made easier by using the "Selection Info" palette. To model a pipe elbow, there are different ways. The following example uses the 3D primitive "Torus".

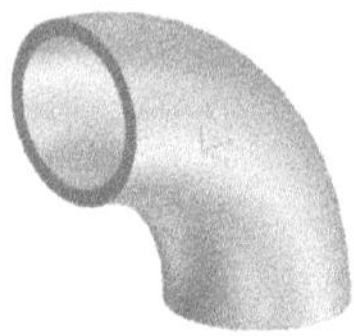

Figure 7-7 Creation of a pipe elbow with the 3D primitive "Torus"

The command entries "Base rad." and "Tube rad." correspond to the outer radius of the elbow and the radius of the elbow centerline. The pipe elbow can then be hollowed out with the "Shell solid" command (chapter 5.6). The created elbow can now be copied and brought into the respective dimension by changing the values (wall thickness, radius of the centerline base and outer radius).

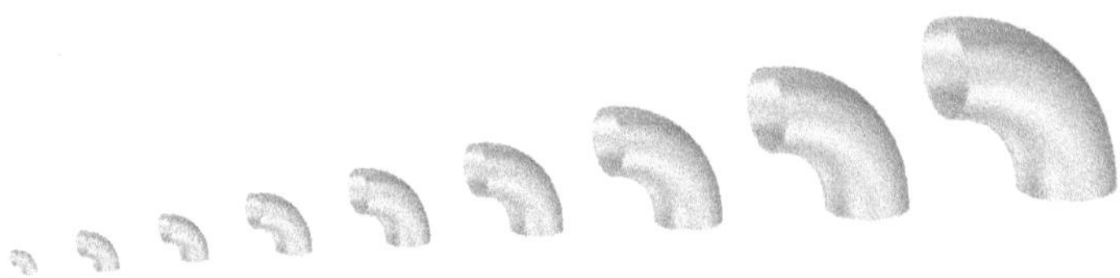

Figure 7-8 Pipe elbow in all dimensions

Now the "Library" palette is opened, and each elbow is moved individually into the pallet by dragging & dropping it at the reference point. First, a name must be entered. Then the location needs to be set.

In this case, it is helpful to consider a suitable folder structure before placing the parts. For example, instead of saving all elbows to one folder which would make the search more difficult, subfolders for type or material can be created.

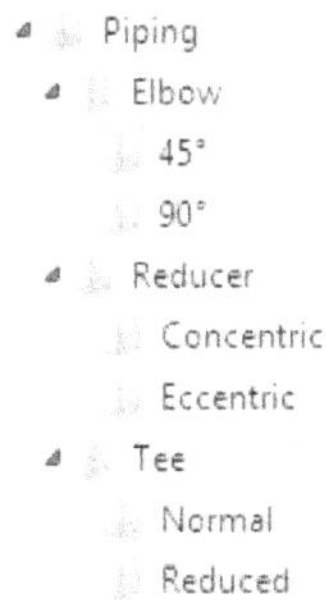

Figure 7-9 Exemplary folder structure to save library symbols

When an object is inserted into the symbol library, an external drawing file is automatically created and saved in the specified path. After adding all the pipe elbows, the drawing file, which was used only to create and add the elbows, can be closed without saving, since all elbows have been saved as separate drawing files by adding them to the symbol library.

The next time the library is loaded (chapter 7.3.3), the parts are included and can be used.

> In some cases, it may be useful to keep an overview drawing or parent drawing, in which all configurations of a component are stored so that they can be changed if necessary. They can then be exchanged for the individual files of the symbol library.

As mentioned earlier, all objects are grouped as they are inserted from the library. If possible, grouping several parts together before adding them to the library should therefore be avoided, as this results in a double grouping.

Sometimes when inserting a symbol into the drawing, there is an offset between the symbol and the mouse pointer. This can be caused by an incorrectly set reference point (chapter 4.3) or "User coordinate system" (chapter 5.4) when the symbol was created.

To rectify this afterwards, the drawing file of the symbol must first be opened. The symbol must be placed with its desired insertion point, which is defined by the reference point, onto the drawing origin (X=Y= Z=0).

7.3.3 Load and update the library

In order to update the library, it must first be unloaded and then reloaded. The necessary steps are explained below.

Step 1: First check if a library is already loaded. If so, the edit bar in the "Library" palette looks like as shown below in Figure 7-10. If no library is loaded, the "Unload Libraries..."  button is greyed out

Figure 7-10 Editing bar inside the "Library" palette

Step 2:

If old libraries are loaded, they have to be removed via the button "Unload Libraries ..." .

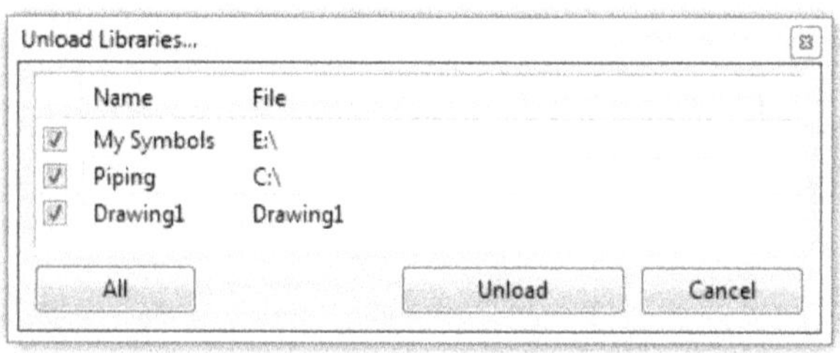

Figure 7-11 "Unload Libraries..." window

Step 3:

If no library is available, the centrally stored library can be loaded via the button "Load Folder ..." . All that needs to be done is to specify the path of the library.

In order for all symbols to be displayed correctly, the item "Update Thumbnails ..." can be selected by right-clicking on any symbol preview in the palette (Figure 7-12).

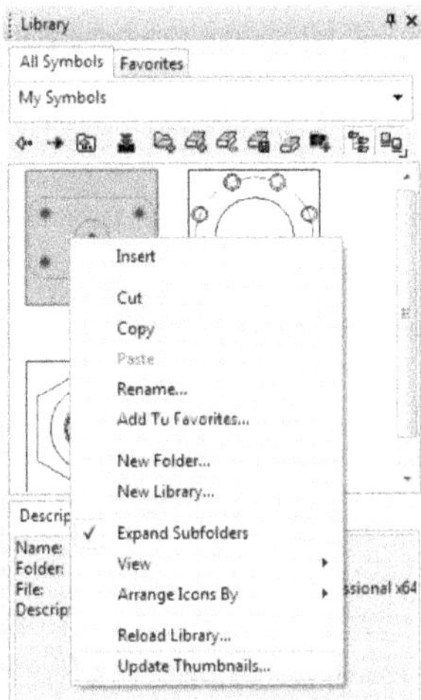

Figure 7-12 Library symbols thumbnails

In the next window the symbol thumbnail can be adjusted. Figure 7-13 shows a possible representation of the symbols.

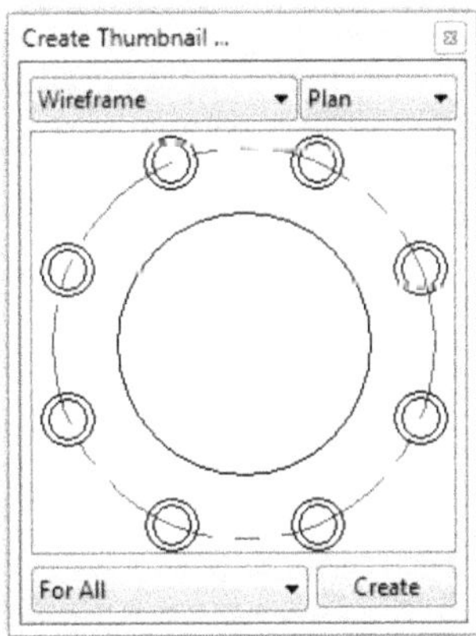

Figure 7-13 "Create Thumbnail" window

Click "Create" to update the icon preview. If the setting "For All" is selected, this will be done throughout the whole library. Depending on the size of the library, this may take slightly longer.

7.4 CUSTOM PROPERTIES

2D or 3D objects can be provided with user-defined part information, which can be read from report templates (chapter 7.5) and output as reports. Objects in the symbol library can already be provided with this information.

With the help of the custom properties it is easy to generate BOMs with all the information required by the company. This will be shown below by way of example on a valve list.

First, the desired field information must be defined. This is the information that will later be added to the object and taken up by the report.

The valve list should contain, for example, the manufacturer, dimension, nominal pressure, and a description. These properties can be created under "Tools/ Database/ Define Fields ..." (Figure 7-14).

The checkboxes "V" (Visible) and "E." (Editable) are initially activated. If the visibility is deactivated, the created fields can be assigned to an object and read from a list but are not visible to the user later. If partial information has been added to an object, deactivating the editable option can prevent this information from being subsequently changed by the user.

In the column "Description", comments can be made. The entered text will not appear on the later list and should only help with the administration of the lists.

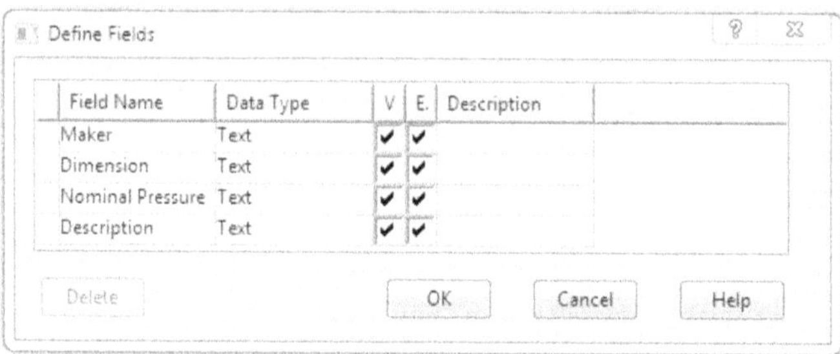

Figure 7-14 "Define Fields" window

Now, if a valve symbol is drawn, which usually consists of grouped single lines, the previously defined field names can now be added to this group in the group properties ("Properties/ Custom/ Attach ..."). The desired properties are to be selected and the window confirmed with "OK".

The custom properties can be attached to every kind of 2D or 3D object.

> If the order of the displayed field names is not the desired one, the properties can also be added one after another.

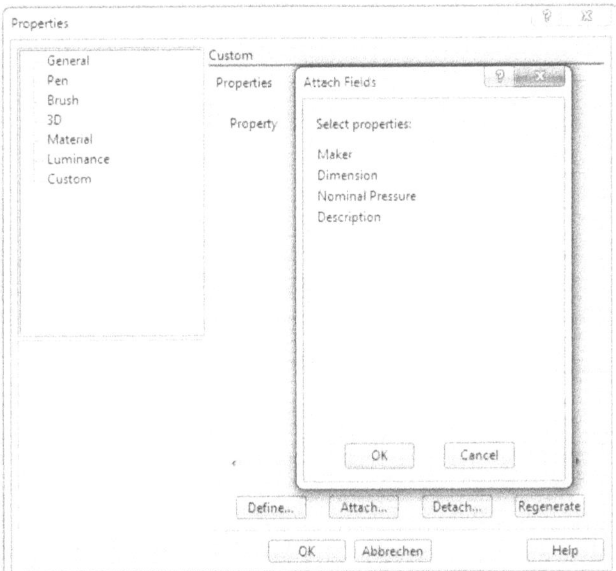

Figure 7-15 "Attach Fields" window

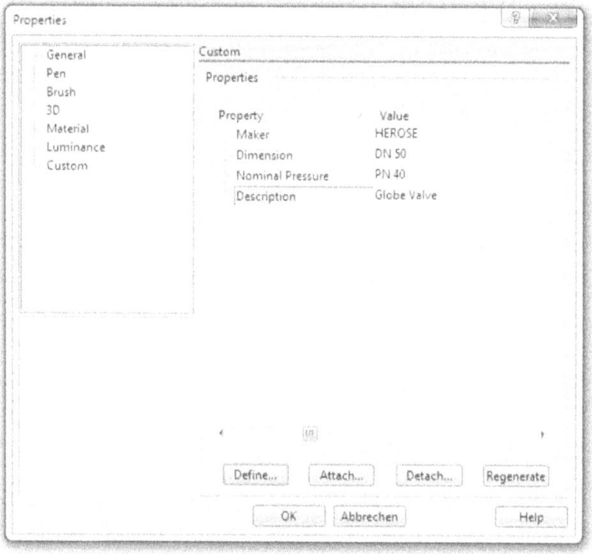

Figure 7-16 Custom properties

Now, when selecting the valve, the part information is shown in the "Selection Info" palette (Figure 7-17) and allows easy control during the creation of a drawing, such as a piping and instrumentation diagram.

The group name of the valve, which is displayed in the upper area of the "Selection Info" palette, can be renamed for the sake of clarity.

When naming the group, the following should be noted. Symbols are always grouped when they are taken from the symbol library and inserted into the current drawing. Since the valve symbols for attaching the custom properties are already grouped as described above, a nested grouping occurs here. A single explode resolves the double grouping so that the desired group name is displayed again in the "Selection Info" palette.

> The lowest group level of the valve (which can then be recognized by the valve name in the group name) must not be exploded, as this would automatically remove all contained custom properties. These are not available again after re-grouping. The valve must then be reloaded and inserted from the symbol library.

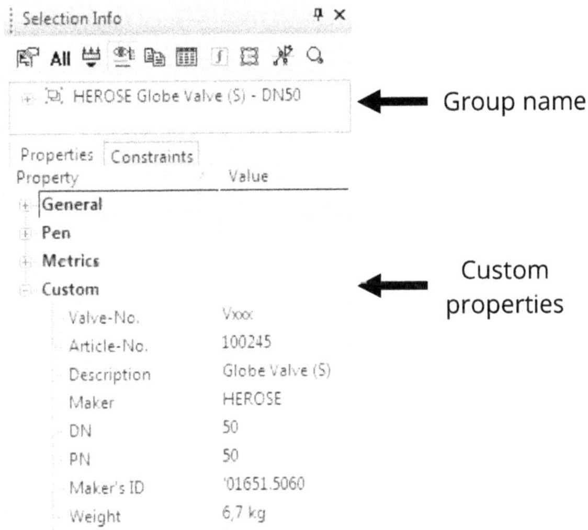

Figure 7-17 Custom properties listed inside the "Selection Info" palette

7.5 DATABASE AND REPORTS

If you need an overview of all objects contained in the current drawing (for example, a BOM), quantities or custom part information, the report function can be used create these lists. With this, all text objects can be read out and displayed in a list, which can also be exported as an Excel® file.

The creation of a predefined report query is shown below. Here, existing texts, object types or custom properties are captured and output.

Before a report can be created, it is first necessary to define the criteria which will be searched for. The report menu is located under "Tools/ Database/ Report ...".

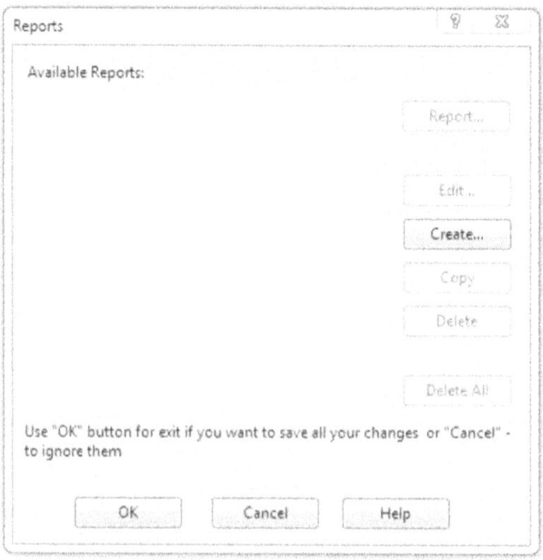

Figure 7-18 "Reports" menu

The "Create..." button opens the "Report Create" menu in which the desired search criteria can be chosen. The available fields that can be output in the report query are in the left selection menu and can be transferred to the right menu.

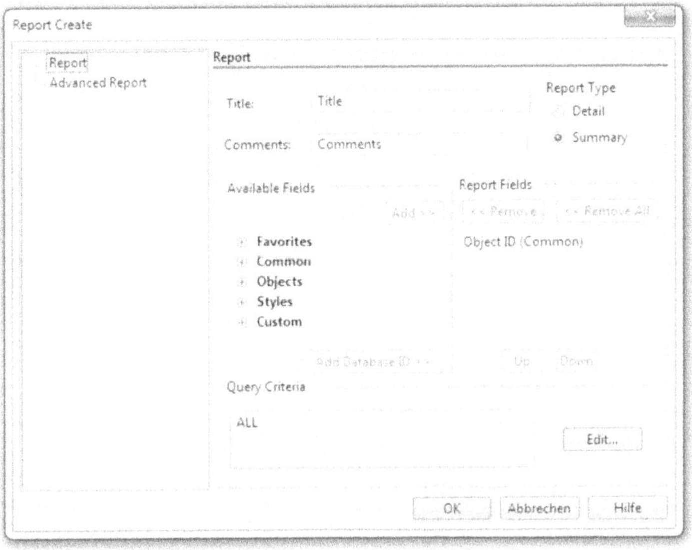

Figure 7-19 "Report Create" menu

The section "Custom" inside the “Available Fields” window lists all self-added custom properties for attaching part information (chapter 7.4). These can also be added to the report and output from It.

In the menu item "Advanced Report" the search limits can be defined.

If "Summary" is selected as the report type, the "Object ID" is automatically added. In the later report, this will summarize all objects with the same information in one row and list the quantity in a column named "Quantity". This is ideal to create bill of materials.

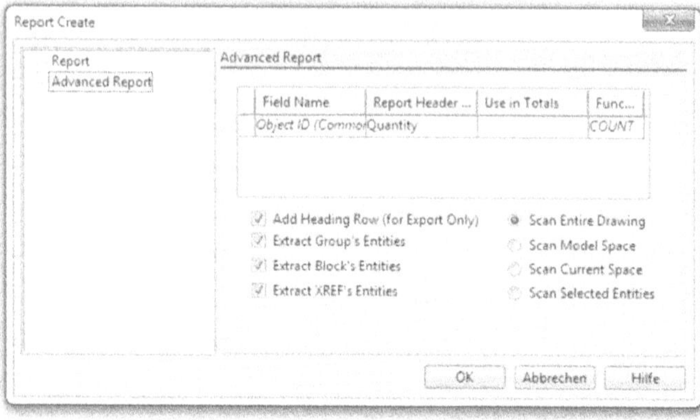

Figure 7-20 "Report Create" menu ("Advanced Report")

> As previously mentioned, a created report is just a snapshot. If changes have been made in the drawing, a new report must be created to make them visible. Only objects that are currently in the drawing when the report is created are displayed.

If you close the report window with "OK", the created report template is saved and is available again when the database report function is opened once more. This facilitates the regular querying and updating of the list.

The report can now be printed, saved and further edited as an Excel® spreadsheet, or stored internally as a table in the model or paper space.

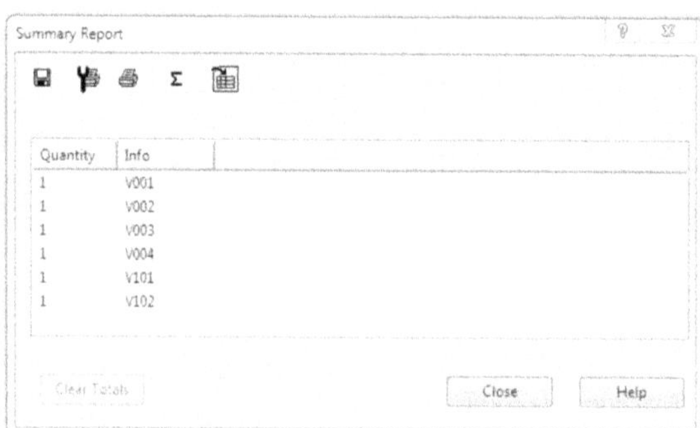

Figure 7-21 Exemplary summary report

7.6 Searching and Measuring

The "Select By" tool allows the searching and automatic selection of objects. For example it can search for attributes, object types or layers.

If all lines or objects of a particular layer need to be selected, the "Select By" function is a helpful tool. It is located in the "Edit" menu. After selecting "Layer..." inside the "Select By" menu, only the layers that appear in the drawing are listed in the selection list (Figure 7-22).

> It should be noted that the search applies only to the currently active window (model or paper space). Layers from the unopened space or spaces are not listed.

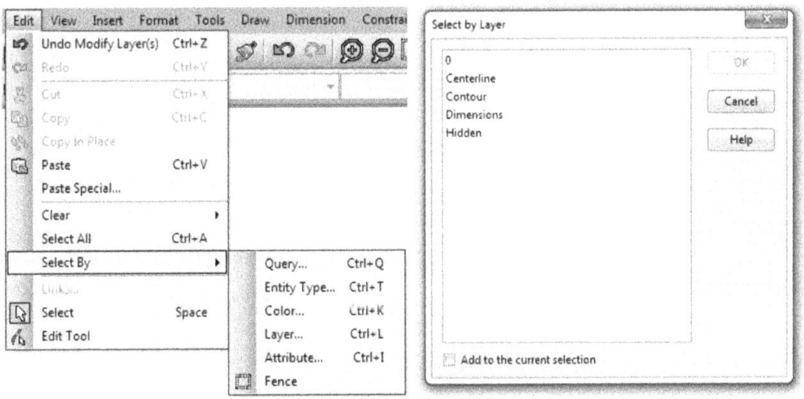

Figure 7-22 Example of a selection by layer

To search for a specific text or number, the menu item "Attribute..." can be used. The window shown in Figure 7-23 opens.

When entering the text, the following must be noted:

If, as in the example, the number V001 is searched for, the search text must exactly match the number. If the search is successful, the searched text will be marked, so it is clearly recognizable in the model or paper space by its selection frame.

Should not be searched for a specific number, but e.g. after all texts beginning with "V", "V*" can be entered in the "Attribute:" box. So, all text boxes are added to a selection starting with a "V".

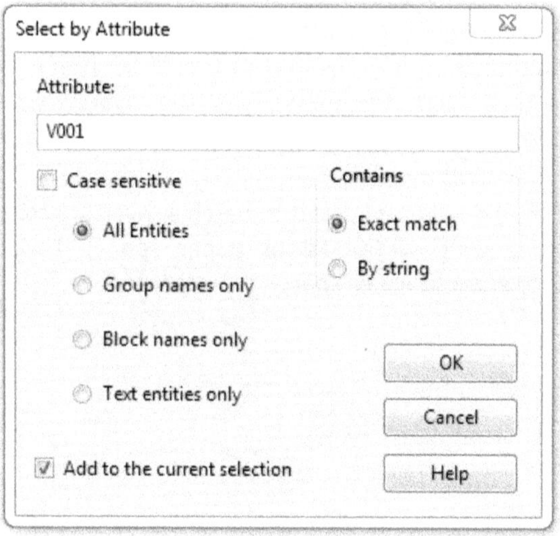

Figure 7-23 Search window "Select by Attribute"

TurboCAD® offers tools to measure the distance, area, angle, volume and surface area. These tools are located inside the standard tool bar "Measurements", or under "Tools/ Inquiry".

Figure 7-24 Standard toolbar „Measurement"

> To measure a distance between two points in the 3D space, the "3D Polyline" can be used. Once the two points are connected, the length of the polyline between the points can be read inside the "Selection Info" palette under "Property/ Metrics/ Length".

7.7 LAYER SETS

A layer set can be used to control several single layers, for example to show or hide them at the same time. This offers the user the opportunity to highlight different operating states or aspects of a drawing, or to hide them if necessary. The creation and use of layer sets is described below.

First, a layer group must be created or defined. In the "Design Director" the corresponding menu (Figure 7-25) can be opened by right-clicking on "Layer" and choosing the item "Edit LayerSets". Here, a new layer set can be added and named, and in the following step the individual layers can be set so that they are visible or hidden. Any number of group sets can be added.

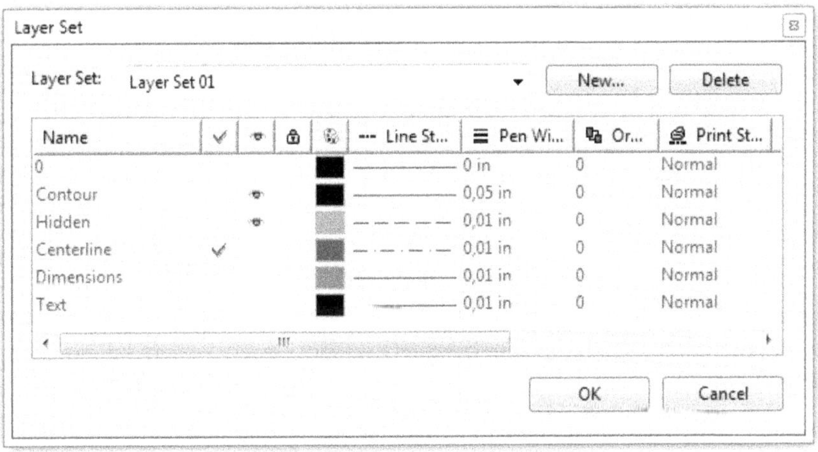

Figure 7-25 "Layer Set" menu

When the desired layer groups have been added, the menu can be closed. The created sets can now be selected under "Format" in the upper menu bar. The "All Layers" set is always available by default and represents the original layer structure set in the "Design Director".

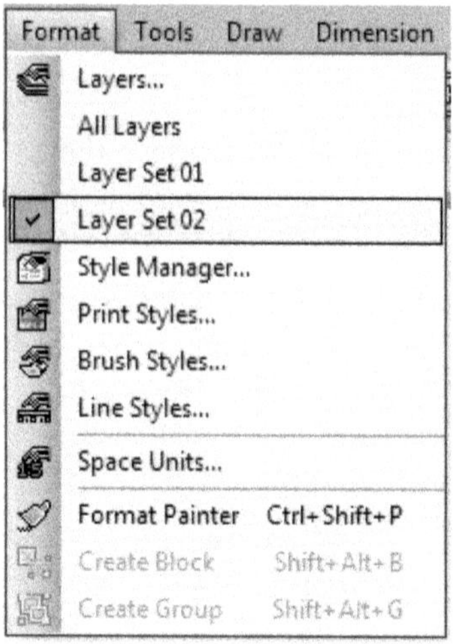

Figure 7-26 Selection of layer sets

The layer groups can also be set in the viewports in the paper space (Figure 6-2). As a result, different operating states or configurations of a part or a drawing can be shown in separate viewports. How to manage layers and layer sets of the viewport has already been discussed in chapter 6.1.

The visibility of layers within a layer set can be set separately in viewports in the paper space. Settings in the "Design Director" have no direct influence on the visibility in the viewports.

7.8 PDF Underlay

With the underlay function, PDF files can be imported into the drawing to serve as a drawing reference. This is ideal for modeling over hand drawn sketches or drawings that are only available in paper format. Only a PDF format can be loaded.

Similar to an inserted image or an Excel® table, the drawing view has to be updated by pressing the "F5" key ("Redraw") depending on the degree of zoom being used.

Figure 7-27 Standard toolbar "Underlay"

Before inserting an underlay, a PDF must first be selected, loaded, and named in the "Underlay Manager"  ("Tools/ Underlay Manager"). It will then be listed in the "Underlay Manager" as shown below. If the path or the name of the source file changes, it must be modified under "Edit".

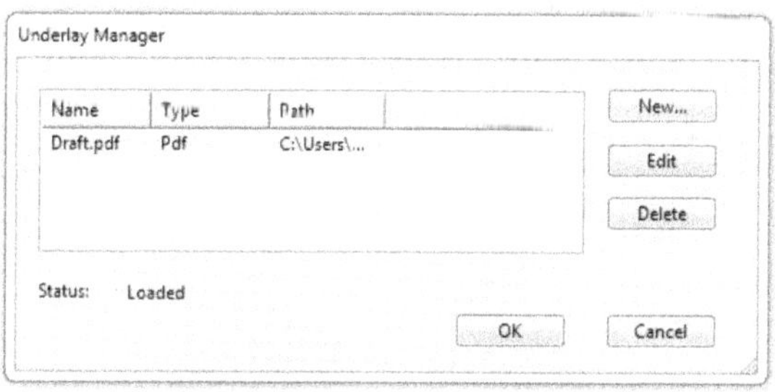

Figure 7-28 Underlay Manager

It is advisable to place the underlays on a separate layer in order to be able to lay it all the way back in the draw order, so that drawn geometries lie above the contours of the underlay. In addition, the layer can be locked, so that unintentional shifting of the underlay is prevented. The underlay can also be faded out easily if so required.

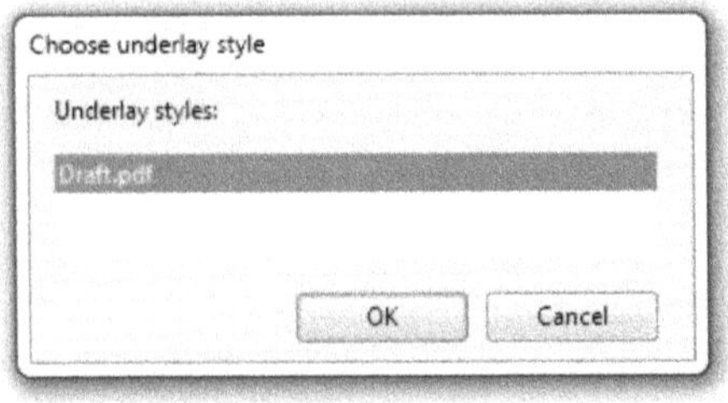

Figure 7-29 "Choose underlay style" window

For inserting, the command "Underlay" is activated , and the corresponding file is selected from the list shown above. The underlay is inserted by opening a frame. Then the underlay can be resized to its desired size by pulling on the frame. Dimensions or edges with known lengths can be used to determine a scaling factor.

In the object properties (double-clicking on the underlay or selecting the properties option in the "Inspector Bar") contrast, transparency and a black and white mode can be determined.

> If the PDF file being used as an underlay has vector data, snap points are available. This allows a more accurate setting of the scale.

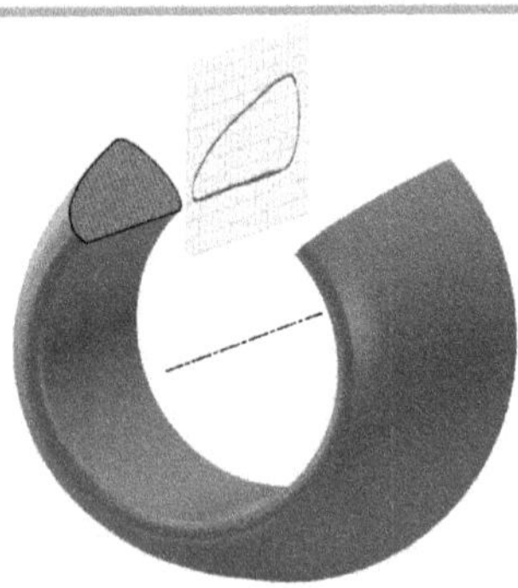

Figure 7-30 Underlay to create a rotation profile using a hand drawn sketch

SUMMARY

The program's structure, all two and three-dimensional drafting and modeling tools as well as the drawing derivation tools which are necessary for the use of TurboCAD® in technical professions have been shown and explained. Light has been shone on the different ways of working with these tools and where necessary assistance has been offered.

In many areas, TurboCAD® can achieve the same results as established, but usually much more expensive CAD software. But it also reaches its own limits. To be aware of this limits, and not to confuse a lack of knowledge in dealing with the program with program weaknesses, is initially the first step on the way to choosing the perfect construction software for your own tasks and demands.

The clear strengths of TurboCAD® lie in a broad range of 2D and 3D commands, the use of blocks and symbol libraries, the custom part information to create bills of materials, high file compatibility and, last but not least, the good price to performance ratio.

The ability to create 3D primitives such as cuboids and cylinders, or by the extrusion of 2D sketches with subsequent editing using individual processing steps in a part structure, allows the creation and processing of complex components.

In the next step, they can be drawn to scale on a drawing sheet as a drawing derivation. There they can be provided with dimensions, sectional and detailed views, at the same time as being visualized.

These strengths of the software are contrasted by an initially non-intuitive User Interface and in some cases under-developed commands.

If you note these weaknesses, learn to deal with the small issues and how to circumvent them with sometimes unusual but expedient ways, you can use TurboCAD® for the creation of professional drawings and 3D designs, as well as for conceptual or even photorealistic visualizations.

Since the manufacturer IMSI/Design, LLC is always working on new commands and functions by using existing developments and taking into account the experience and recommendations of the users, it is expected that TurboCAD®, in terms of performance and versatility, will continue to catch up and find its place on the market as a professional CAD system.

For most common CAD tasks, a satisfactory solution is usually offered. The purpose of this book is to help the user to find the appropriate commands, to adapt their own working methods, often characterized by years of use of other programs, to TurboCAD® and thus get the maximum commercial benefit out of the software.

INDEX

Matthias Bosse

Using TurboCAD® in technical professions

Lightning Source UK Ltd.
Milton Keynes UK
UKHW020640190820
368484UK00015B/1009

9 783746 098708

Instagram Marketing 2020

The Playbook for Increasing Your Following and Generating Profits

Jaimason Bixley

Table of Contents

Book Description

Instagram Marketing 2020: The Playbook for Increasing Your Following And Generating Profits

Social media is all the rage in our modern, tech-savvy society. Today more than ever, social media marketing is a crucial step in the growth of your business or personal brand, and guess where all the top influencers and businesses hang out the most? That's right, you guessed it! Instagram!

A multi-feature platform that prides itself on connecting its users with each other, Instagram, when used strategically and intentionally, is a surefire recipe to boost profitability along with an increase in followers. *Instagram Marketing 2020: The Playbook for Increasing Your Following And Generating Profits* is your comprehensive guide to all things Instagram, content creation, and marketing strategy. It teaches you how to identify your niche, generate a unique and creative Instagram handle, and provides you with a wealth of resources on hashtag creation and generation. It discusses the 4 pillars of online branding: Brand messaging and positioning, Brand value, Consistency, Brand personality. It discusses the importance of creating quality content consistently — what to post, when to post it, how to identify content creation strategies within your niche. It also teaches you how to use the various features offered in Instagram such as posts, Instagram Stories, direct messages, and shows you how to analyze and track your brand performance by taking you through an in-depth review of Instagram insights. Additionally, you will walk away with tangible, helpful tips to optimize your reach and grow your following while boosting your brand's engagement through strategic posting times and content planning.

If you are new to Instagram as part of your personal brand or business growth strategy, stress no more, this book will teach you all that you need to know to start growing your brand and monetizing it sooner rather than never. Instagram is an evergreen, every growing platform that can change the trajectory of your business forever when used correctly! So come and play with the 'gram and grow your brand while increasing your profitability!

Introduction

I want to thank you for choosing my book, "Instagram Marketing 2020: The Playbook for Increasing Your Following And Generating Profits."

The way brands communicate with their existing and target audience has undoubtedly transformed. One of the main reasons for this transformation is the increase in the popularity of social networking platforms. These days, an increasing number of brands are using visual media for communicating their brand's message. Social media has certainly revolutionized our lives.

Gone are the days when Facebook used to be the only social networking site. As time passes by, newer platforms keep rolling out. However, Instagram has stood the test of time and is now one of the most popular social networking platforms today. So, if your brand isn't already on Instagram, then there is no time like the present to get started. Instagram has been around for a while, but not a lot of people know how to make the most of its features. The creators of this platform keep introducing new features along with changes to the algorithm. So, it is quintessential that you stay on top of all the updates.

In this book, you will learn about the things you need to increase your following on Instagram so you can maximize your profits. You will be given information about the different benefits you can reap by using Instagram. You will learn about various tips for choosing the perfect Instagram name and tricks to optimize your brand's Instagram profile. Apart from this, you will also learn about specific strategies for building your niche on Instagram and thoroughly engage your audience. Marketing on Instagram and how you can increase your following are also discussed in detail in this book. A combination of all these factors will ensure that your brand makes the most of all that Instagram has to offer.

So, if you are ready to learn more, then let us get started immediately!

Chapter One
Reasons Why Instagram Dominates Every Social Media Platform

Unless you've been living under a rock, it is quite unlikely that you haven't heard of Instagram. Instagram is an incredible platform that enables you to create and share visual content. Instagram is being used as a marketing tool by several brands and businesses. If you thought that Instagram was only about sharing visual content, then there is so much more to it than just that. Instagram boasts of over one billion active followers and users. Therefore, it is no wonder that brands and businesses alike are eager to jump onto the Instagram bandwagon. Before you start learning about how you can optimize and capitalize on this platform, it is quite essential to understand the different benefits your brand stands to gain from Instagram. If you want to know whether it will be worth your while to invest your time and resources on Instagram or not, then read on.

Connecting With Customers

The most obvious platforms that anyone thinks about when it comes to connecting and engaging with customers and potential customers alike are Facebook or Twitter. Yes, these platforms certainly help you engage with your customers online, but you must not overlook Instagram. Over 60% of people between the age groups of 18 to 29 years are active users on Instagram. It has one of the most diverse user bases a social media networking platform can have. If you're interested in targeting millennials, as well as Gen Z users, then

Instagram is an excellent place to start. In 2014, Forrester research came across a startling statistic. It was discovered that the engagement rate provided by Instagram to brands was 58 times more than the engagement provided by Facebook and 120 times more than the engagement provided by Twitter.

Therefore, Instagram is the place to be if you want to interact with your audience. This is an excellent way to not only connect with your customers but also obtain feedback and establish better relationships. There are different ways you can increase your engagement with customers on Instagram, which you will learn about in the subsequent chapters.

Better Access To The Audience

Instagram makes it rather easy to discover new people, businesses, and brands too. One of the most common ways users discover new content on Instagram is by using hashtags. Whenever someone includes a specific hashtag while posting something on Instagram, it automatically creates a link on the platform. So, if someone else uses the same hashtag, all the pictures and posts associated with that hashtag will pop up. This is a great way to find any users who are interested in the same kind of content that your brand posts.

The ever-growing network offered by Instagram is quite helpful because brands can start leveraging visual content to provide a better description of the products or services you offer. Since the audience base is growing rapidly, it gives you more extensive access to the same. As this network keeps increasing, potential shoppers understand that Instagram is not only great for visuals, but it also becomes a reliable source for information about brands and businesses. So, even if you don't realize it, your target audience is pretty much primed to see the kind of content you will post. Instagram has certainly become quite business-friendly in the last couple of years.

Targeting And Retargeting

If you want to use Instagram for marketing or promoting your brand, then it is quintessential to produce certain advertisements. If you want your advertising campaign to be successful, then you need to target the right audience. Are you wondering how Instagram will help you reach your target audience? There are various targeting features available on Instagram, such as location, demographics, behavior, lookalike audience, and interests. By using the location feature available, it allows you to target a specific geographical location. You can target an entire country, a particular city, or even a neighborhood locality. By identifying the different demographics of your target audience, you can target your ads toward them. For instance, if your business caters explicitly to middle-aged women who speak Spanish, then you can select the related demographics on Instagram and create well-targeted ads. According to the interest of your followers, you can create ads which will appeal to them. By doing this, you increase your chances of success. While on Instagram, you can accurately define the audience for your ads based on their action. For instance, you can quickly target any potential customers who've visited your business website but haven't ever made a purchase. Instagram allows you to target lookalike audiences as well. It essentially means that the ads on Instagram will be directed towards all those people who share similarities with your existing audience. By targeting and retargeting your ads or marketing efforts on Instagram, you can quickly improve your online visibility. This, in turn, increases your number of followers and encourages the rate of engagement as well.

Learn What The Audience Likes

You might not have realized it, but your target audience might already be talking about your brand or even sharing photos about it on Instagram. If you have a brick and mortar location that is accessible to customers, then this might already be happening. For instance, a lot of people visit restaurants and post about their experiences on Instagram. In a global culture dominated by social media and networking sites, people have become more and more interested in sharing their lives and experiences with others. So, don't be surprised if you notice any photos of your personal brand or business shared by other users of your brand using your physical location. It isn't just about restaurants, but people tend to share a variety of images from various sites. Not only to tag your location, but your business too. Whenever a post like this pops up on Instagram, it increases your online visibility.

A great thing about Instagram is that you can gain an understanding of what your audience likes. As you start posting content, you will notice that certain material has a higher engagement rate than others. If a specific post of yours gains more likes, reposts or comments, it means that your audience is enjoying that content. Once you carefully analyze the kind of content you are creating and sharing, it provides you with better insight into what your audience likes and dislikes. Additionally, when you scope out the Instagram profiles of your competitors or any other businesses brands in the same industry, you will also get an idea about the type of content that works well. Once you know what your audience likes, it becomes easier to create content. This also comes in handy whenever you're developing any marketing strategies. Not only will you reach a wider audience, but you can start creating targeted marketing campaigns.

Chapter Two
Steps To Creating The Perfect Instagram Name

The Instagram handle that you select needs to be simple. If you have a business website or domain name, then make sure that your Instagram handle is similar to the domain name. It makes it quite easy for others to recognize your Instagram profile. The username must not be vague or obscure. If that is the case, it will be difficult for others to recognize your brand on Instagram. Before you start brainstorming for the perfect username, take some time to learn about all those brands and businesses that failed at growing on Instagram even before they began. Business and brands typically hinder their growth on Instagram when their audience (target and nontarget) are confused and don't know what the brand stands for, identify a lack of cohesiveness throughout the brand messaging and content. Simply put, they realize that the username or profile name doesn't match the content posted on the account.

So, take your time and don't be in a rush when selecting your Instagram handle. It is a great idea to do some research and consult others when brainstorming ideas for your Instagram account. You can ask your family members, friends, colleagues or anyone else to help you along the way. Pick a name that not only suits your brand's objectives, but is also in sync with the marketing strategy of your brand. In fact, you can conduct a quick survey to understand whether or not the Instagram handle you like is the right choice. Why don't you tell a few people about the potential handles and see their first reaction? The initial response is often natural. If they react favorably to it, then maybe you actually have a good Instagram handle in hand.

If you want to use Instagram as a promotional tool, then it is absolutely vital that your Instagram bio is attractive and inviting. Your bio is what will compel visitors to interact with your brand on Instagram. Perhaps, one of the essential aspects of the bio is your brand's username. After all, this is the first thing that your audience will see on your Instagram profile. You must start thinking of ideas that will make it easier for others to find your Instagram profile. Also, you must ensure that the Instagram handle of your brand helps convey your brand's message. The name you choose will depend on the kind of audience you wish to target. It becomes easier to attract your audience's attention when the Instagram handle is unique. If you want to increase your engagement rate on Instagram, a good starting point would be to get creative with your Instagram handle. In this section, you will be given a couple of tips that you can follow for creating the perfect Instagram username.

Think About Your Hobbies

A good Instagram handle usually tells the visitor something about the brand other than its name. This comes in handy, especially if your brand is associated with any form of hobby. By doing this, you're making it easier for your audience to associate themselves with your brand. It also increases the chances of acquiring more followers. For instance, let's assume that you are a brilliant chef named Danielle. There are bound to be several people named Danielle in the world, so you need to come up with an Instagram moniker that will set you apart from the rest. Don't just think about displaying your regular name, instead think of ways in which you can directly associate it with what your page is about. If your Instagram page consists of posts about recipes, the food you cook, and so on, then the username must convey the same. Maybe you can try something along the lines of @crazychefdanielle, or @danisdeliciousfood. You can get as creative as you want with the username.

A Name Generator Tool

You can undoubtedly sit around and brainstorm until you get a perfect idea. However, this isn't always easy, and it can be rather time-consuming. Also, you might not even come up with a good idea after hours of brainstorming. The good news is that there are various online name generating tools that you can use to get started. Even if you get a little idea by using these tools, it will give you some momentum. There are various online username tools like The Cool Name Generator, Spinxo, Screenname Generator, or even Rum and Monkey. In fact, a quick Google search will help you with this. Even if you don't like any of the suggestions given by these tools, you will certainly get some ideas along the way. Most of these online tools require you to enter a couple of keywords along with specific personal characteristics for generating different usernames. Once you make a list of all viable options, the selection process becomes easier.

Use Your Name

You can create a unique Instagram handle by combining different words. At times, having an uncommon name might work in your favor. You can play around with your name and come up with a unique handle. You can try combining your first name and your last name and use it as your Instagram handle. It may or may not work, but spend some time and try rearranging the letters in your name to form a unique handle. For instance, the famous tennis player Serena Williams launched her own clothing line Aneres. Aneres sounds quite exotic and inviting. The name of the clothing line is merely Serena spelled backward. You can do something like this too.

Think About Your Audience

When you're thinking about your Instagram handle, think about the audience your brand caters to. Create a name that will give your audience an idea about what your brand stands for. By doing this, it also enables you to stand apart from the rest of your competition and increases the rate of engagement. Additionally, it becomes easier for your audience to find you. Spend some time and research trending keywords or hashtags related to your brand industry. You can use the Instagram search feature to do the same. While selecting certain keywords, keep in mind that they are not being used by your competitors. You can choose keywords that are associated with the products or services your brand offers.

Unique Characters

You don't have to restrict yourself just to the letters of the alphabet and can also include other characters or numbers into the handle. There are various symbols which you can use like @, #, $, * and so on. However, don't go overboard with these unique characters. Remember that the handle must be easy to find and remember. If the handle is a complicated combination of various characters in letters along with numbers, you merely make it difficult for your audience to find you. You can also use characters for creating emerges which can be placed in your Instagram handle. Even a common name can be jazzed up with a couple of unique characters.

Location

If you have a local business, then it is a good idea to include your location in the handle. Your potential customers might be interested in looking for a specific product or a service in the given area. By adding your location to the Instagram handle, you're making it easier for your potential customers to identify your business or brand. It doesn't mean that you simply include the name of the city in the username. At times, it might even make sense to include the name of the country or even the state. For instance, the famous clothing brand Forever21 has different Instagram accounts for each of the countries it is present in. By doing this, Forever21 is making it easier for its customers to find the Instagram handle that's relevant to them.

Using A Title

If you have a professional title, then you can try adding it to your Instagram profile. Adding a title can certainly help distinguish your brand from others. Ever heard of Dr. Phil, Dr. John, or Dr. Dre? What is the one thing that all these people have in common? They all have a title added to the name. Regardless of whether they are real doctors or not, the title does help. If you are a professional, then try adding your title to the Instagram account. It not only makes the username seem more distinguished but also seems to have a nice ring to it. Don't use a professional title if you don't have one and don't try to trick your followers into believing that you're someone you are not.

Competitor's Profiles

Coming up with the perfect username will undoubtedly take some time and effort. However, if you feel like you hit a roadblock or need a little bit of inspiration, then start checking out the Instagram profiles of your competitors. Make a list of all the people who are popular in your industry or niche and check their profiles. A quick search on Instagram must help you do this. You cannot steal your competitor's profiles, but it will undoubtedly give you an idea or some motivation to come up with a different name for your own profile. At least it will provide you with a starting point.

Duplication Of Names

While creating an Instagram handle, a common problem that a lot of users come across is that after finding the perfect name, they realize that it's already taken. Given that there are billions of people in this world, it is quite likely that someone else might have had the same idea as you. If you come up with a seemingly perfect Instagram name firebrand, and it's already taken, don't worry about duplication of names. Anyway, Instagram will not allow two users to have the same username. So, it is time to get a little creative and modify the username such that it isn't a perfect replica of an existing username. Let us assume that the username you want to opt for is @clarklewis, but you realize that it is already taken. Now, you can try adding a couple of different characters to the basic username to make it different. For instance, you can try, @clarklewi$ or @clark.lewis.

Using Adjectives

Another creative way to create a good handle is to add a few adjectives. Maybe you can opt for a specific attribute, which perfectly describes your brand. For instance, if you are an Instagram blogger who offers relationship advice to women, then @sassysasha sounds better than @Sasha. So, take some time and come up with a couple of adjectives, which describe and lend character to your brand. Once you have a list of adjectives, come up with creative ways of adding to them to your Instagram username.

Additional Tips

The Instagram handle you choose must be easy to pronounce. A person must be able to repeat it without having to write it down. It must be easy to understand and must not be ambiguous. If any part of the name is confusing or is vague, it will merely hurt your reach on Instagram. Keep in mind that if your username is quite similar to an existing username, it can lead to copyright infringement issues. So, be careful while you're trying to imitate another username. Anything too close to an existing username well leads to unnecessary legal trouble.

Another thing that you must keep in mind is that the username must not be lengthy. Regardless of whether it's a profile for a brand or a personal profile, it needs to be short and specific. Adding a word like supercalifragilisticexpialidocious to your Instagram handle is not a good idea. If the name isn't easy to pronounce, how will anyone remember it? Also, a short name offers a certain degree of exclusivity.

Avoid using any names that are related to a specific gender, ethnicity, religion, or sex. If the name seems biased, once again, it will only land you in hot water. The username must not offend or be biased toward anyone. Also, don't make the handle too common or generic. You can certainly combine a common word with a unique word to come up with something exciting and appealing, but don't try to make a generic name your Instagram handle.

Initially, it might seem a little tricky to come up with the perfect handle. The first thing that you must do is stop stressing about it. By following these tips, you can undoubtedly come up with a unique and creative username.

Chapter Three
Tips For Every Brand

There is no time like the present to capitalize on the boom that Instagram is experiencing. Instagram has more than one billion users, and this number is steadily increasing. Different features, as well as functions, are regularly introduced by this platform. Any hype that you heard about Instagram is real. However, the algorithm of this platform keeps changing frequently, and this can prove to be a rather tricky part for a lot of brands that are trying to maximize their engagement rate. The changes in the Instagram's reach aren't as severe as the ones on Facebook because of the latest update. In your best interest, it is undoubtedly prudent to ensure that you are indeed following the best practices suitable for Instagram. Regardless of whether you're new to Instagram or are trying to optimize your reach on this platform, the tips given in this section are certainly worth going over. So, here are specific tips, which you must keep in mind while using Instagram.

Don't Ignore The Bio

A common mistake that a lot of brands make when using Instagram as their marketing platform is that their sole focus tends to be only on the photos and captions that they use. They concentrate so much on these two aspects of Instagram that they forget about another essential part of their Instagram profile: their bio. The bio of a brand is as important as the content posted on this platform. Instagram bio is an incredibly valuable space of real estate in the virtual world. The bio can be used as a call to action button, or it can also be used for directing visitors to any promotional campaigns you're running. There is a lot that you can do by using the bio space.

Here are a few things that you must include in your bio regardless of what your brand is about.

You must have a custom hashtags that other users, as well as your brand, can use for tagging and sharing. It creates relatability and boosts visibility and engagement on Instagram. You can also use the bio for adding a relevant link to your business website or homepage to direct any traffic. You can also use the bio to hide any Instagram-specific promotional links. Did you know that you could include a URL tracker in the bio to analyze your Instagram traffic? You must include a brief description, motto, or a slogan, which conveys your brand's objective to the visitors of the page.

Start Using Instagram Stories

Essentially, this tip will help optimize your content strategy for Instagram. One of the most popular features introduced on Instagram is their Story tab. The Instagram Stories feature is quite similar to the Snapchat Stories, which were quite popular a few years ago. Instagram stories are among the most popular type of content feature being used by brands these days. This feature is time-sensitive, and its self-destructive model of content is what attracts the users to use it.

Other features, like audience polls, along with Stories' ads, have become quite common on Instagram. All these things indicate that the platform is actively encouraging brands to use Instagram in their promotional activities. If you want to increase your engagement rate, then make it a point to update your Instagram Stories regularly. The best part about using this feature to promote your brand is that there is no expectation of perfection. Your Instagram Story does not need to be polished or professionally shot. It can be a combination of a small post, selfies, snapshots or anything else. It is an excellent way for a brand to connect with the audience. Typically, brands start using stories to provide a behind the scenes snippets to their followers.

Concentrate On Video Content

Instagram stories are certainly among the best techniques to market your content online. However, don't forget about producing videos along the way. All social networking platforms promote content in the form of videos, and Instagram is not an exception to this rule. Creating content in the form of videos is not difficult, especially because there are various video creation apps which you can use. The popularity of Instagram has given rise to several ancillary applications, which can be used to optimize the benefits provided by Instagram. Hyperlapse and Boomerang are two of the built-in options offered by Instagram, which allow for basic editing of a video within no time. In fact, various brands use these features as part of their video content strategy. The doughnut giant Krispy Kreme uses Boomerang videos and posts them on Instagram.

Instagram is essentially a platform used for promoting and sharing video content. So, don't forget about this essential thing while using Instagram. Videos are a great way to increase your rate of engagement and effectively communicate your brand's message.

The Publishing Frequency

Your publishing frequency is directly correlated to the engagement rate on Instagram. The best way to go about this is by analyzing how often you post and the time at which the content goes live on the platform. Check the frequency of your posting. Spend some time and review your posting history. Do you notice any patterns, or do you have a set schedule? Or do you simply post at random times? Even if your answer is no to both these questions, you don't have to worry about it. By carefully analyzing your brand's Instagram metrics, you can establish the best time for publishing your content and gauge the optimal number of posts you must publish in a week.

Using The Captions Wisely

If you use your captions wisely, you can certainly increase your rate of engagement. Just like the bio, there are a few ways you can use the captions strategically. Don't just think of a caption as a mere description of the post. You can use captions to show off your creative side and also increase engagement. Start including a call-to-action in the captions you post. For instance, you can increase or encourage engagement by asking open-ended, yet polarizing questions in the caption or encourage your audience to share your post by using hashtags or even reposting your content. If you want to trigger any conversations between your followers, then you can include a call to action like "tag a friend" in the caption. You can also use the captions for directing the users toward the link in your bio. When used wisely, not only can you display your brand's personality and voice in the caption, but you can also influence your followers to take action on whatever your call-to-action is.

Use Hashtags

One feature that differentiates Instagram from other platforms is the frequent use of hashtags. Seldom do you see an Instagram post without a hashtag. Every post can include up to 30 different hashtags. A lot of brands don't realize the importance of hashtags. Hashtags serve a dual purpose — they make it easier to search the content you post and also encourage other users to use your brand's hashtags. You can use branded hashtags along with community or generic hashtags. For instance, the reusable red cup that was introduced by Starbucks for the holiday season became widely popular. Starbucks used a combination of custom or branded #redcup along with the common #coffee for promoting its posts. Use the relevant hashtags for increasing the brand's visibility on Instagram.

Start To Repost

You must post content frequently if you want to keep your audience interested. At times, this can be somewhat overwhelming. So, why don't you allow your followers to do some of your work? You can gain new followers and increase engagement by posting user-generated content by using branded hashtags. You can, in turn, repost this content from your profile. When you reshare posts, it makes your audience feel valued, and it also gives you a constant supply of content. The popular shoe brand Vans started curating content by using the #myvans. You can use this tactic whenever you don't have any fresh ideas for posting content or just want to show your followers that their loyalty is appreciated. Reposts are a great way to increase your engagement rate on Instagram.

Thinking Beyond Instagram

It is great that you want to use Instagram for your business. However, are you certain that your existing users, as well as your target audience, are aware that your brand is on Instagram? You might have an incredible social media manager posting brilliant content, but it will do you no good if your audience is unaware of your Instagram presence. This might seem like an obvious thing to consider, but a lot of brands fail to consider this point. For instance, if you have accounts on various social media platforms, then it is a good idea to mention your Instagram profile once in a while on those platforms as well. If your brand has an official page on Facebook, then you can start referring your brand's Instagram pages. Start using social media buttons on your website. You can have their links embedded into your homepage to give the visitor a better idea of all the social media networks you are present on. If you have an existing email list, make a point to refer to your Instagram presence regularly while sending out emails. Apart from this, you can also include a social button in your email list as well.

Active Engagement

You must avoid one of the common mistakes made by a lot of people using Instagram. Instagram is not a platform to establish a monologue. You must not do all the talking but must encourage your audience to participate as well. You cannot engage with your audience if you don't give them a chance to engage with you. The simplest way in which you can engage with others is by replying to any questions and comments posted by other users or even tagging your followers. This not only is a great way of providing customer service, but it also boosts your engagement rate. You must respond to your followers and listen to what they have to say. Don't forget to reply to any mentions your brand gets. Make sure that you respond to the concerns or questions posted by the users as promptly as you can.

Human Touch

Actively engaging with other accounts is a great way to show that your account isn't an automatic bot. In addition to being responsive through comments on your posts or another brand's posts, there are many ways in which you can lend a human touch and humanize your brand's Instagram profile. So many brands are moving further away from just posting promotions about the brands or products and are working on creating people-centric content. You don't have to keep using Instagram as a place for hard selling. Remember, people use Instagram for networking, and if you fail to remember this, you will quickly lose followers. A couple of personal photos here and there and maybe behind-the-scenes snippets can help.

Use Analytics

If you want to improve your reach and your rate of engagement, then you must be aware of the kind of content that clicks with your audience. You must understand what your audience likes and dislikes. To do this, start monitoring your Instagram analytics. Instead of flying blindly and posting without a plan in place by using various analytical tools, it becomes easier to create well-targeted content. The best way to appease the audience is by providing them with content that they will appreciate.

Content Calendar

When it comes to content creation for your Instagram feed, the sky's the limit. You can post customer photos or product photos. You also have the option of choosing videos, selfies, snapshots, and even text overlays. There is no shortage of the type of content you can post on Instagram. If you want to track your posts and increase your Instagram presence, start using a content calendar. A content calendar helps establish a schedule for the content you wish to post. When you know what you have to post and the day and time it needs to be posted, it reduces a lot of your burden. Also, it makes marketing efforts quite easy on Instagram.

The increase in competition, coupled with Instagram's algorithm changes makes it non-negotiable for brands to make certain changes. By using the tips discussed in this section, a brand can optimize its presence on Instagram.

Chapter Four
How To Build A Niche

How To Find A Niche

In this section, you will learn how to identify your niche in a subsection or a small segment of a large market. Essentially, it is a piece of the pie. For instance, an example of a market demographic can be pet owners, while a niche in this market could be dog owners, cat owners, and so on. If you want, you can delve further into each of these niches. If you are looking at the niche of dog owners, then maybe you can start by thinking about the different dog breeds. You must define your niche if you want to be profitable on Instagram. When you set your niche, it helps you gain clarity on the kind of audience you wish to target. Once you know what you're selling, it becomes easier to understand what your audience needs and how you can deliver it to them. Targeting, marketing, and delivery become easy once you decide your niche. By doing this, you can save yourself a lot of unnecessary expenditure and can instead concentrate on those strategies which will be profitable.

Instagram is one of the fastest-growing social media platforms these days. Creating a niche-oriented Instagram account is a great advantage for any brand. It not only enables a business to connect with its target audience, but it also helps in establishing a large following. So, how do you niche yourself on Instagram? In this section, you will learn the answer to this question.

Make a note of your interests

If you want to create shape your personal brand or business brand on Instagram, then there are two questions you must ask yourself: What are your interests? Do any of your interests overlap with the interests of other users on Instagram? If you want to ensure that your motivation levels stay high, select a niche that you are passionate about. If your chosen niche doesn't interest you or reflect you, sooner or later you'll end up giving up on it.

If you're just getting started with Instagram, then it is a good idea to stick to one specific niche. It might be rather tempting to post other content, but if you stick to a niche, it makes it easier to build a following for yourself. After you build some momentum and gain plenty of followers, you can expand into other niches. If you are uncertain about the things that interest you, don't worry, there are a few ways you can uncover your niche. You can go to your Amazon profile and browse through your favorite categories of pages in the Amazon bestsellers list. It will help you come up with different ideas related to the bestselling products. This is a great way to go about, especially if you're interested in selling products. Additionally, it will help you identify your favorite subject matter as well, hence helping you come up with content creation ideas within your particular niche. For eg, if your Amazon favorite categories include things such as fitness, nutrition, wellness products, and health/wellbeing reading material, your niche is health and fitness. Within that category, you can focus on paleo meals and non-toxic health and wellness products, hence niching down furthermore.

Another simple method is searching your favorite keywords related to your niche. Use Google Trend to research the keywords, locations, and necessary time frames that interest you. If you notice that competition is low while the trend is increasing, then you have just found yourself a profitable niche. It is also a good idea to exploit the page about related topics that come up on the Google search.

Categories

While selecting a niche, keep in mind that there is a difference between a category and a niche. A lot of people tend to start their online businesses while targeting a specific category and start believing that category is said niche. This is a common mistake that a lot of beginners make, and you must avoid it. For instance, if you want to blog about food, remember that it is a category. A niche would be blogging about a specific kind of food or diet. A niche identifies those people who have a particular interest in a category.

The theme matters

Remember that your Instagram account is your personal brand. Your brand needs to convey a specific message about what you do and what you stand for to the onlooker. The best way to create a strong message about your brand is by establishing a cohesive theme. The picture size, the logo, the style of photography, or even the color effect on the pictures you post will help create a theme. A theme needs to be consistent. It can be something as simple as the style of the font you use. If you want to start posting poetry, then ensure that the styling of the poetry along with the font that you use is the same. So, whenever someone sees a similar post, they will know that it is you. A theme helps in creating a unique identity for your Instagram profile.

Consistency is important

If you want to establish yourself as a credible brand on Instagram, consistency is king. You cannot post four pictures on one day and then be inactive for a month. Instead, you can post one picture every week and maintain consistency. If you post inconsistently, you will quickly lose your following. If your followers know that you will be posting content consistently, they will continue to be interested and stick around. Remember that the idea is to gain followers and not lose some. So, create a content schedule for yourself and stick to it. If you want to post one picture per day, then make sure that you post a picture every day. At least during the initial phases, it is quite crucial to stick to a schedule.

Build A Niche Following

In this section, you'll learn about certain tips, which you can keep in mind if you want to build a niche following for yourself on Instagram.

Prepare the profile

The first step that you must follow is to create an Instagram profile. Ensure that your Instagram profile looks appealing and attractive. Other Instagram users must feel compelled to follow your profile upon viewing it. It needs to look professional and organized. It doesn't mean that you forget to keep it interesting, engaging, and entertaining. Spend some time and create a compelling bio which includes information about your brand and its objective or aim. Sum it all up in 150 characters or less. Once you do this, ensure that you provide a link to your official website, blog, YouTube channel or any other social media profile. Start posting content using all the different features offered by Instagram.

Define your audience

According to the niche you've chosen, it is time to decide who your potential audience is. If your niche is about fashion, then it doesn't make any sense to target those who are interested in business. If you need pets, then you must start looking for those users who are interested in pets. If your niche is about a specific hobby like networking, then you need to search for those users on Instagram who share the same interest. Spend some time and define your audience.

Find your audience

Now that you have successfully identified your target audience on Instagram, the next step is to start finding the audience. Since Instagram caters to a wide range of audience, you must concentrate on attracting the kind of audience you want. There are different methods you can use to make this happen.

The most popular way in which you can find users who are interested in the kind of content you wish to create is by using hashtags. Make a list of all the hashtags associated with your niche, and do a little research. Use the Instagram search feature to find specific hashtags. Once you do this, it will show all the different posts related to that hashtag. By using these posts, you can find individuals who are interested in the same subject. You might even come across different Instagram accounts which are dedicated to the subject of your niche. By doing this, you will certainly come across followers who will be interested in your Instagram profile too. They're different online programs that you can use to find the popular hashtags in your niches like Webstagram or Iconosquare. Even a simple Google search will be helpful. You will not only be able to understand your audience, but also have an idea of who your competitors are in the niche. By going through the Instagram profiles of your competitors, you will identify the type of content your potential audience likes.

As you look at your competitor's profiles and their followers along with the content they post, it gives you a better idea of your audience. Maybe you can even start interacting with these people and start gaining followers in the process. You can also use the hashtag along with the location tag about specific events that are linked to your niche. For instance, if your Instagram account is about traveling, then you can find plenty of activities related to traveling.

Interact with the audience

A significant part of your work is now done, which means you can now focus on the next step: interacting with your audience. If you don't interact with your audience, you will never create a loyal following for yourself on Instagram. There are different ways you can start interacting with your potential audience. The first step is to simply start following the profiles of those people who you think will be interested in your profile. By doing this, it gives the user an idea that you are interested in the content that they are posting. It is quite likely that the user might also extend the same courtesy to you. Whenever you start following someone, they get a notification about the same. Once you get the notification, they will be curious to see what your profile is about. If your profile interests them, then you will certainly gain a follower.

Another simple approach is to start commenting or liking posts of other users on Instagram. Not only is this extremely simple, it also shows your users that you appreciate their content. Even if a post has received several likes comments, it will certainly make the other users take note of you.

Most Profitable Niches On Instagram

Now that you know how to find a niche and know more about the different ways you can increase your following, let us look at the most profitable niche of an Instagram. So, how do you know if a specific niche is profitable or not? One simple thing you must keep in mind is that not all niches are created equally. You can end up choosing a niche that happens to be a little too niche. You can certainly pick a specific category but making it specific will not be profitable. For instance, it doesn't make any sense to start selling dog collars for Great Danes named Hachiko that are owned by people named Edward. A niche needs to have sufficient customers for it to be profitable. Here are a couple of questions that you must answer to another niche is profitable or not.

- Does the specific niche have sufficient people interested in it?
- Will the existing customers in a niche be interested in it for long enough that you start earning profits?
- Are the existing people spending any money on that specific niche?
- Do they have a specific need or want? If yes, will you be able to satisfy the same?
- Can you fill any existing gaps in the niche?

If the niche you've chosen is a profitable one, then your answer to all the questions as mentioned above will be yes.

You don't have to worry about selling a specific product to be profitable on Instagram. In fact, this is only one of many ways you can profit from Instagram. There are different ways in which you can make money on Instagram. You can sell ads, provide shoutouts for others, or even provide affiliate links. While selecting a niche for yourself, here are a couple of questions you must answer. Once you answer these questions, you'll get a good idea of the kind of niche you want to be a part of.

- What are your passions?
- Is there any niche that you love?
- What are your hobbies?
- What are your areas of expertise and do you think others will be interested in the same?

If you're still uncertain about the niche, then here are the most profitable niches on Instagram.

- Health and fitness
- Travel
- Business
- Beauty
- Fashion
- Lifestyle or luxury
- Animals
- Gaming
- Relationships

Chapter Five
How To Keep Your Audience Engaged

In addition to connecting with your audience on any social networking platform for that instance, you must ensure that your audience is engaged. If your audience is not involved, you will undoubtedly lose your following.

Before you learn about how you can increase your engagement on Instagram, it is quintessential that you learn what engagement means. Engagement rate is a means to measure the loyalty of your followers. It doesn't refer to the size of your following but refers to the degree of their involvement with your brand on Instagram. It helps measure your follower's interest and interaction with the content that you post. The key parameters that you must carefully follow to determine your engagement rates are followers, comments, likes, shares, and reposts.

A lot of people tend to believe that the only thing that matters on Instagram is the size of the following. It is vital to have a large following to increase your online visibility, but that's not the only parameter. It's not just about the number of followers that you have, but you must concentrate on the speed at which you are acquiring new followers. Another critical fundamental parameter is you must keep track of the likes that you receive on the post. It's a primary measure used to understand whether your Instagram posts are doing well or not. If the number of likes and reposts are high, it means that your audience finds your content engaging. The number of likes that you receive is a quantitative metric.

Another metric that you must keep track of to determine your Instagram engagement is the comments. If you carefully go through the comments that you receive on your Instagram posts, you can understand what your followers like. It essentially provides a qualitative analysis of whether your followers are enjoying your posts. The number of times your content is shared or reposted also matters. If a specific post is shared multiple times, it shows that does something about it which appeal to your audience. You can use all the information you derive from these metrics to create better and more audience-centric content.

If you're wondering how you can keep your audience engaged, then you are not alone! Given all the changes made to Instagram's algorithm combined with the fact that there are numerous brands which are competing for the user's attention, it has become a little tricky to increase engagement on Instagram. Don't let the competition disheartened you. Instagram is still one of the best platforms available for marketing your brand, creating a loyal following, and building a community which will help your brand. In this section, you will learn about different ways in which you can keep your target audience engaged.

Use Instagram Story Stickers

It is time to rethink your engagement strategy on Instagram. Engagement on Instagram is no longer confined to just likes and comments, but it also includes any engagement you can generate from IGTV views, branded hashtags, Instagram stories, and more. As people start following several accounts on Instagram, the organic reach may decrease. That said, the popularity of Instagram stories is steadily growing. Did you know that over 400 million people actively post as well as view stories on Instagram?

This is the main reason why Instagram has been coming up with innovative ways to enable brands to keep the audience engaged. Because of this, Instagram has come up with story stickers to increase the engagement from Instagram stories. Using story stickers is a brilliant strategy, which prompts your followers to share their opinions and experiences along with their comments on your non-negotiable. This, in turn, can help build a loyal and committed following for your brand. Here are a couple of ways in which you can start using Instagram story stickers to increase your rate of engagement. The two stickers that you must use are the question sticker and the poll and vote sticker. A brilliant way to start a conversation is by using the story sticker. A simple ask me anything story sticker can spark a conversation quite easily. The story stickers often used by people to get to know their audience. You can use the same tactic to encourage conversation about your brand.

This provides your followers with an opportunity to learn more about your business and get more information about your brand. Also, it encourages your followers to ask you questions. It's not all about your customers asking you questions, but you must also respond to them. If you don't reply, then there is no point in using this feature. So, by using Instagram story stickers, not only do you obtain customer feedback but you can also start conversations and building a movement. If your audience knows that you will promptly reply to them, they will be more interested in asking you questions.

If you want to know what your followers like and dislike, then you can use the poll and vote stickers on Instagram stories. So, by doing this, you can not only increase your engagement rate but also get the opinions of your followers. For instance, if you want to know whether your users like short videos more or Instagram stories, then you can conduct a poll about the same. It will enable you to come up with content, which will appeal to your audience. Also, it will make your followers feel like their opinion matters when they think that their opinion matters, their interest in your brand will increase. Everyone likes to know that their opinion matters. Even your followers think the same. So, why don't you capitalize on this?

Optimize The Captions

Don't be under any impression that a caption is merely a description of the video at the pictures you post on Instagram. A caption is so much more than this. You can use up to 2200 characters in a caption. This is prime space, and you must try to make the most of it. According to Instagram's new algorithm, the time that a user spends on a post influences the performance of your Instagram posts. So, what is the best way to increase the time that a person spends on your post? The most straightforward answer is to write lengthy captions. If there is more to read, then the user will stick around longer.

Well, this doesn't mean that every caption of yours must run into thousands of words. If you do this, you will quickly lose your audience's attention. Maybe you can try writing a couple of sentences and using emojis is every now and then. While doing this, keep in mind that Instagram is all about visual media. If you clutter your post with too much content, your audience will not be interested. So, you must strike a balance between visual media and textual content.

So, how can you write better captions? Here are three questions you must ask yourself whenever you write a caption on Instagram.

- Why is this post relevant?
- Does this post matter to me and only me, or will others find it useful too?
- What does this caption convey?

While answering these questions, remember that a caption is not about just a couple of objectives, which are placed together. A caption needs to provide some meaning to the post. It must trigger the viewer's curiosity and engage them. It needs to leave your audience eager and waiting for more. You can leverage the caption space, come up with detailed captions describing your brand, and can even continue your caption in the comment section. This is a lot of space that is available to you, and it can help you effectively deliver your brand's message. You can use the space to inform your followers about your brand, provide any descriptions or values about your brand, and also keep them informed about your business goals or objectives, etc,.

Writing a lengthy caption is not an easy feat. Reviewing or editing the content you want to include in the Instagram caption while using this app on your phone is not easy. To be fair, the editing box for the caption on Instagram is not user-friendly. A good practice is to start scheduling your Instagram post and creating all the captions at once. Instead of sitting and brainstorming every time you need to post a caption, you can set some time aside and come up with the content before you post anything. When you're scheduling your post on Instagram, it essentially means that you can write the captions ahead of time on your desktop or desktop apps such as Later or Planoly or Postfity. You can save it and then wait for the right time to post it. This is so much better than fidgeting with a small screen on your phone. For some inspiration, you can always go through the posts of influencers and auto brands in your niche.

Schedule The Instagram Stories

Instagram engagement can also come from the number of views you get on the stories you post. As mentioned earlier, this is a great way to create a loyal base of followers. If you post at the wrong time or if you don't post regularly, you are merely hurting your engagement rate. Also, if you have brilliant stories to post, but your audience isn't active at that time, then it doesn't make any sense. The self-destruct feature of stories is undoubtedly appealing, but it can also hurt your engagement rate if you aren't careful. If you don't want to limit your rate of engagement on Instagram, then it is quintessential that you start scheduling your Instagram Stories.

Before you can schedule the stories, you must spend some time and do the research relating to monitoring and tracking the Instagram analytics from your previous Stories. The simplest thing you can do is go to Instagram insights from your Instagram business account. The Instagram insights, as the name suggests, gives you data and analytics related to your Instagram account. In Instagram insights, go to the audience option. In this, you'll find a lot of information related to your followers. Under this tab, you can also find details about when your followers are most active on Instagram. The data can be sorted by days or even hours.

Once you are aware of the best time to post stories on Instagram, it makes your work easier. You can create multiple stories for the week and batch edit them all. After you have all the content that you need, you merely need to schedule it and post it later. By doing this, you not only save time and effort, but you are also able to optimize your engagement. Batching also helps you optimize the content you want to post. Instead of working in a hurry, you can work at a leisurely pace and come up with brilliant content. This will undoubtedly improve the quality of the content you're sharing.

If you don't want to spend any time going through the analytics, then a simple thing to do is ensure that you post the stories at the same time every day. The ideal time is to schedule your post between 3 to 5 pm.

Optimizing Every Story

Instagram stories are certainly a great way to share behind-the-scenes footage or even post something spontaneous. It doesn't mean that you don't concentrate on optimizing every story that you post. Putting in a little time and effort to create a perfect story will certainly help increase your engagement rate. There are three things, which you must include whenever you post a story, and they are the location, mention stick, and hashtags. By adding these three elements, you can significantly increase engagement on Instagram.

If you're collaborating with other brands or are reposting any user-generated content, then it is quintessential that you mention the same in the story you post. Whenever you do this, the other account will also be notified, and this comes in handy when you're trying to build a loyal following. When you repost any user-generated content, the other account might also respond by thanking you or even sharing this with their followers. This, in turn, increases your online visibility.

You must start tagging the appropriate locations if you want to boost your engagement and improve your exposure. The location sticker on Instagram makes this quite easy. So, whenever someone else searches for the same location and Instagram, even your posts and stories will show up. For instance, if you're posting from a specific restaurant in New York, don't forget to tag the location. When you tag the location, your story might also appear in the Instagram stories of that location.

Don't forget to add hashtags whenever you're posting something on Instagram. You might be adding hashtags to the Instagram post, but make sure to include them in your Instagram stories. With all the editing features available on Instagram, you can make the hashtags smaller, place a GIF or even a stick over them or do something along the lines to hide them if you think they ruin the aesthetic of the story. You're allowed to include up to 10 hashtags in your stories. So, carefully consider the relevant hashtags and used in the stories.

Share About Your Brand

As mentioned earlier, the way brands are interacting with the customers and audience has certainly changed with the advent of social networking sites. People no longer want to see just snapshots, but they're interested in getting to know more about the people behind the brand. They want to know about the behind-the-scenes activities, the brand's mission, and more details related to the brand. Instagram has become a great place to share all this information with a brands audience. When your audience gets to know more about your brand and if they like it, it helps increase your following. When your brand has a human touch to it, it becomes more appealing. So, start actively sharing your brand on Instagram.

Collaborating With Others

A great way to increase your online visibility is by collaborating with other similar brands or influences in your niche. Through collaborations, you get to access the followers of the influencers in your niche. Instagram influencers have a significant following, and by collaborating with them, you are introducing your brand to their followers. The age-old saying, "Two heads are better than one," is certainly true when it comes to Instagram marketing. This doesn't mean that you collaborate with anyone who comes along your way. You must collaborate with only those brands are influencers who are relevant to your niche. So, you will need to spend some time and effort to identify the right influencers and connect with them. There are three questions which you must answer before you decide to collaborate with someone else on Instagram.

1. Are there any similarities between your business goals and those of your collaborator's? You must ensure that your brand's objectives, as well as goals, are in sync with those you wish to collaborate with. If you share similar goals, it becomes easier to target your audience. The partnership you decide to make must be valuable not just you, but your audience as well. After all, you are trying to increase your reach and engagement on Instagram.

2. What is the duration of this collaboration? If you want the collaboration to be valuable, then it is essential to ensure that it is not

a short-term collaboration. If the influencer you are partnering with is willing to promote your brand all year long, it makes more sense. If the collaboration is only for a one-time post, it seems more like paid advertising. However, if the collaboration is for a more extended period, it makes the followers more inclined to trust the content that is shared. The more trust you can generate, the greater your chances of creating a valuable and loyal audience.

3. What will this collaboration offer to your audience? If you want the collaboration to be valuable, then you must offer something to your followers as well. It must be something that your followers will not be able to get somewhere else. It can be in the form of a physical product or even valuable information. Regardless of the project that you want to work together, ensure that it is unique. If the idea is unique and authentic, then the chances of success increase.

Must Be Fun

Don't make it all about business, instead add a little fun to the Instagram post you make. An Instagram Story certainly takes a little planning and effort to get right. By adding simple elements of pop culture, or even humor, you can make the content more engaging. Using pop culture references, memes, or even comic strips, you can make the content enjoyable. When the audience finds the content relevant, their willingness to stay on-board increases. Try to provide more information to your audience without making it seem too dull or technical.

Communicate

If you want to build engagement, then communicating with your audience is paramount. Reply to comments and reply to any direct messages you get. If you don't respond to your audience, they will quickly lose interest. You cannot build engagement if you aren't actively communicating with your audience. Remember that people on Instagram are there to connect and network with others. Don't just communicate, but also listen to all that your followers are saying. Ensure that you respond positively to positive as well as negative feedback that you get. You can build an online community for your brand if you show your followers that you are listening to them. Everyone likes to be heard, and when you can show the same to your customers, they will be more inclined to stick around.

By following the practical tips discussed in this section, you can effectively increase your engagement rate on Instagram.

Chapter Six
How To Get More Followers On Instagram

There are certain shortcuts that you can use to get more followers on Instagram, like purchasing followers or even using bots. Well, these tactics are defective in the long run. If you want to create a well-established brand on Instagram and get a large following, being authentic is crucial to your brand. Also, there have been different changes made to the Instagram algorithm that prevent inauthentic activity. The best way to go about doing this is to increase your number of followers organically.

Do you want to learn about ways in which you can increase your followers on Instagram without burning a hole in your pocket or by engaging in shady tactics? If yes, then read on to learn more.

A Good Instagram Strategy

If you want to ensure that your time, effort, energy, and resources are not wasted, then you need a good strategy. Without a clear plan, you cannot optimize the results from Instagram. So, the first step is to come up with clear goals. You need a goal to devise a plan of action. Since you're reading this book, your goal must be to increase your Instagram following and maximize your return on investment. This is certainly a good goal to start with, but you need a strategy, which connects your brand's objective to your marketing plan so you can attain your goals. Ask yourself why you want to increase your

Instagram following. There can be different reasons why you want to do this, but the most common reasons are as follows.

- To increase awareness about your brand.
- Maybe to increase the traffic to your website.
- To improve your sales (if you are interested in selling products or providing services).

Only when you have these goals, can you ensure that your Instagram profile stays consistent. If you have a goal, it becomes easier to create a compelling brand story for improving your following.

The Target Audience

Once you know what your goals are, you must define your target audience. This step has been mentioned a few times in this book. Here are a couple of questions you can answer to define your target audience.

- What is the age group of your target audience?
- Where do they live? What do they do for a living?
- How often do they use Instagram?
- Do they have any needs or wants that you can satisfy?

By answering these questions, you can come up with an active Instagram strategy to create the right content, which will appeal to them.

Photography And Editing

When it comes to Instagram, ensure that you focus on the quality of the posts. Quality matters a lot on this platform, more than it does on any other networking site. Your followers on Twitter might overlook a couple of bad tweets, but a lousy post on Instagram can cost you dearly. So, you must start concentrating on your photography as well as editing skills whenever you post something. You don't have to be a professional photographer or need any professional equipment to do so. Here are a couple of photography and editing tips which will undoubtedly come in handy to improve the quality of your posts.

Instagram is a mobile application, so it is quite likely that the photos you post on Instagram are also clicked on your phone. You can always use professional photography for your Instagram accounts. Whenever you're clicking a photograph or making a video for Instagram, make sure that you're only focusing on one specific subject at a time. Don't worry about the negative space and instead, start embracing it. Try experimenting with different perspectives. A simple change in perspective can make all the difference between a photograph which is clicked by an amateur versus a professional. Focus on symmetry and capture any small details. It might sound a little vain but editing your photographs before you post them can work wonders. It not only helps improve the quality and fix any flaws, but it also makes the pictures look better. It doesn't mean that you go overboard with editing and distort the image so much it doesn't represent the actual image anymore. There are various editing tools provided by Instagram that you can use. If you think this is not much, then you can always opt for other editing tools.

A Posting Schedule

Once you're happy with the profile you have created and optimized, you must start posting. Before you can start engaging with others on Instagram, make sure that your account has at least about 10 to 15 good quality posts. When you do this, anyone who visits your profile knows what it's about. If the content you posted is brilliant, you will immediately start gaining followers. Now that you know how to use Instagram, it is time to create a posting schedule for yourself. As you start using Instagram more frequently, you must ensure that you have a database of pictures, videos, and even written content that you can post. For instance, if you go on a vacation, make sure that you have a couple of backup photos or videos, which you can post later. While doing this, don't forget to keep in mind the preferences of your target audience.

Your posting schedule will primarily depend on your target audience. If you are targeting an audience which resides in a different time zone, then your posting schedule will differ. The timing, as well as the frequency of your post, will help you win or lose followers. If your audience is located in the US, the best time frame to post is between three to four in the afternoon during the weekdays, and around 11 am on the weekends.

Following Others

Did you ever notice that the top influencers on Instagram seldom follow several accounts? If an influencer has over 20,000 followers, it is quite likely that they don't follow more than 1000 accounts. While establishing your credibility on Instagram, your follower ratio matters. You can certainly increase your online visibility and the number of followers by following others. However, if you start following too many accounts and do so quickly, it will work against you.

Consistent Brand Story

The aesthetics that you use while posting on Instagram must be consistent. Maybe you want to display the human side of a business, or maybe share your experiences with others. Or perhaps you want to post something that can inspire others. Regardless of what you're trying to achieve, there needs to be consistency.

You must strive to maintain a consistent brand personality. It means that the stories you post, the pictures you use, all the content you share along with the visual look of your Instagram account needs to be consistent. The posts need to be relatable as well as easily recognizable. There needs to be consistency in the way you post and create content. So, whenever a user comes across your post while searching for something on Instagram, they must be able to identify your brand quickly. This is quite similar to the way branding works in general. Whenever you see a bright yellow and, with the first thing that comes to mind? It's quite likely that you end up thinking about McDonald's. Likewise, you must craft your Instagram content to make it recognizable.

An Exceptional Profile

Your Instagram bio provides lumbar support to the rest of your profile. So, making sure that your bio is well crafted will undoubtedly improve your chances of increasing your followers on Instagram. Did you know that more than two-thirds of the visits your profile gets are usually from non-followers? Therefore, it is extremely important that your bio is compelling and inviting. If your bio is incomplete or barely contains any useful information, then it is highly unlikely that the viewer will click on the follow button. There are four main things that you must include in your profile. These are your name, the username, bio, and link to your website. Follow the different tips that have been discussed in the previous chapters to create an exceptional bio for your Instagram profile.

Tagging Your Location

As mentioned earlier, tagging your location can work wonders for your Instagram following. Whenever you feel like you can tag a specific location, don't fail to do so. Any business with a physical location must use this feature and must also encourage their customers to do the same. Whenever a user clicks on the location tagged in a post on Instagram or searches for a specific location, all the content associated with the specific location that is tagged will show up.

Running Contests

Running an Instagram contest is an excellent method to get new followers. A simple idea is to ask your followers to comment on your photos by tagging one of their friends. You can also partner with other Instagram accounts or influencers in your niche and run contests together. You can ask the participants of the competition to follow both the accounts. You can also encourage the users to come up with innovative posts to increase your reach. Maybe you can run a contest whereby the follower who tags the maximum number of users in a specific post on your account wins a giveaway. Or maybe the user who shared the post the highest number of times wins something. Make sure that you offer a reward for the contest. There needs to be an incentive that motivates and encourages others to take part in the competition. Another great idea of running an Instagram contest is to encourage your followers to use a specific hashtag in their posts. The user who comes up with the most creative post will win. This is a great way not just to engage your audience, but also for curating user-generated content. You will learn more about creating high-quality content for Instagram in the subsequent chapters.

Engaging Content

Only if the users find the content to be engaging and exciting will they like, comment or share it. If your engagement rate is high, it gives your posts a boost in the Instagram algorithm. When this happens, Instagram increases the reach of your post. This, in turn, will enable you to garner new followers. While creating the content, make sure that you keep your target audience in mind. Even if you create exceptional content, it will not make much of a difference if it doesn't appeal to your target audience. Keep in mind that your goal is to entertain, engage, and connect with your target audience. Only when the content you create checks all these boxes can you gain more followers on Instagram.

Promotion On Other Social Networking Sites

It might sound obvious, but if you want to increase your followers on Instagram, then you must make sure that people can easily find you in. Simply put, ensure that your profile is easily discoverable, set it to public. If you have any existing accounts on other social networking sites, then inform your followers on those sites about your Instagram profile. Try to inform as many people about your Instagram account as you possibly can. If you're just creating an Instagram account, then make sure that you have a couple of posts on the profile before you start promoting your account on other platforms. If you want, you also have the option of promoting the content that you post on Instagram onto other social networking sites as well.

Apart from this, there are different online and off-line tools that you can use to ensure that people are directed towards your Instagram account. If you have a business website, be sure to include your Instagram account handle on the business website. You can also include it in your online newsletters along with any email signature that you have. Doing so ensures that others are aware of your Instagram presence. If you have an existing email list, then a great way to start promoting your Instagram account is by sending out an email blast.

Using Hashtags

Any content that you post on Instagram becomes easily discoverable whenever you use hashtags. Well, here are a couple of the do's and don’ts when it comes to using hashtags on Instagram. The first thing that you must do is make a list of all the relevant and popular hashtags. Once you do this, you can start using the same in relevant posts. You can also create your own hashtag. A branded hashtag is a great way to motivate the audience to share and engage with your content. Well, hashtags are useful, but that doesn’t mean you go overboard using them. If you use too many hashtags, it will take away the focus from the content you’re posting or sharing. Apart from this, too many hashtags can also flag your post as spam by the Instagram algorithm. As mentioned earlier, don’t forget to use the relevant hashtags on Instagram stories that you upload. Apart from this, there are certain hashtag gimmicks that you must not use. Using different hashtags like #likeforlike, #followme, #followforfollow, #tagsforlikes, or anything else along these lines is a bad idea. Steer clear of these hashtag gimmicks because it makes you seem rather desperate and spammy on Instagram. Instead, make an effort to come up with relevant hashtags and stick to those.

Using Nametag

Did you know that there's a scannable Instagram code that enables other users to follow you instantly? This is known as an Instagram nametag. As mentioned earlier, there are different off-line modes of increasing your followers on Instagram. You can effectively include this on any signage, packing slips, or even the backing of a product. The Instagram nametag certainly comes in handy when you're networking at any conferences or other events where you can get new followers.

Getting Featured

All those accounts that reshare and curate the content created by other users by using hashtags or tagging are known as featured accounts. Some of these accounts tend to have a rather large following, and if you can get featured on their account, it increases the likelihood of new users finding your account. Almost every possible niche has a feature account. As you start searching for hashtags, you will end up coming across some of the featured accounts. For instance, the Instagram account @discoverearth is an account that features travel photography. This account features photos related to travel and lifestyle. It has quite a large following, and any Instagrammer whose niche pertains to travel or lifestyle photography will certainly benefit from this account. Once you are aware of the niche you wish to target on Instagram, you must start searching for featured accounts in that niche.

Explore Tab On Instagram

Did you ever notice the icon, which resembles a magnifying glass towards the bottom of the Instagram app? This icon represents the Explore tab. The explore tab is a place where you can find videos or photos from other accounts which you aren't following but might interest you. Stories, Instagram posts, and IGTV videos are all available on the explore tab. The grid of content which is immediately visible when a user clicks on the explore tab is chosen by the Instagram algorithm. Instagram also provides various options for a user to choose from according to his or her needs. There are various topics or contends that any user can choose from. Over 200 million people use the explore tab every day. If you're trying to grow your audience, then you must try to get featured on the explore tab.

The content featured on the Explorer tab is based on an algorithm, which takes the following into consideration.

- Content with a high rate of engagement.
- Any similar content the user has previously engaged with.
- Content from different accounts that are similar to the ones that the user follows.

Instagram's algorithm is quite smart, and after a while, it analyzes the user's preferences and shows relevant content on the Explore tab. If you want your content to be featured here, then you must target the right audience, use the right hashtags, and increase your rate of engagement.

Bonus Hacks To Increase Followers

Apart from all the tips, which have been mentioned in this section, here are a couple of growth hacks that you can use to supercharge your follower count on Instagram. The first thing that you can do is start hosting giveaways. You can conduct giveaways on Instagram, which require a user to follow your account in order to participate. Who doesn't like free stuff? Everyone does. You can pretty much gain a bunch of followers overnight by holding giveaways. Also, don't forget to promote your giveaway if you want to attract your audience. One condition to enter the giveaway must be for the user to tag their friends. It is a great way to generate organic followers for your Instagram account. If you want to generate considerable results, then the best time to hold a giveaway is after you have at least 10,000 followers.

If you have a budget for Instagram ads, then start using them to reach your target audience and acquire new followers.

You can also create various fan pages and then use the same for directing traffic to your Instagram profile. You can create and manage multiple Instagram accounts now, so make the most of this feature. Use different tactics to create fan pages and leverage it to increase your followers.

Another simple strategy that you can use is the thunderclap strategy. Essentially, in the strategy, you must make several accounts share a post from your account at the same time. It is a great way to direct new users to your account. It is like a shout out not just from one account but from multiple accounts. The more accounts that can get on board with this strategy, the more effective it will be.

Chapter Seven
How To Market On Instagram

There are numerous influencers on Instagram, and they have a significant number of followers. Armed with the right plan, you can become a famous brand on Instagram. To do this, you must understand how to market your brand on Instagram. In this section, you will learn about some tips that will come in handy.

A Business Profile

If you don't, then it is time that you switch to a business profile. Merely go to the settings in your account and enable the "Switch to Business Profile option." Are you wondering why you must switch to a business profile? Here are a couple of benefits you stand to gain. Once you create a business profile, you no longer have to use the advertising tools provided by Facebook for publishing and creating ads on Instagram. An Instagram user can get in touch with you from your Instagram page by clicking on the contact button placed in your profile. It is quite similar to the way anyone can contact you from your official website. Apart from this, it also gives you access to Instagram's analytical tool known as Insights. As mentioned in the previous chapters, you can use Insights to track essential metrics like impressions and reach of your account. Once you have a business profile, we can examine all the other steps for successfully marketing your brand on Instagram.

Using Instagram Tools

The business profile is an Instagram are quite similar to those on Facebook. Using insights enables you to view various statistics related to your account and followers like engagement data, impressions, and so on. If you want, it also provides you a detailed breakdown of your follower's demographics. You can get a detailed analysis of demographics like age, gender, active hours, and location of your followers on Instagram. Insights don't have to be generalized, and you can make them as specific as you want them to be. In fact, if you wish, you can get accurate insights about any of your posts on Instagram. This tool comes in handy, especially when you're trying to understand the kind of content that your audience appreciates. The more information you have about your audience's preferences, it becomes easier to connect and interact with them.

Product Teasers

Do you ever watch teasers of any upcoming movies? Do you ever wonder why teasers are made? Well, it is to generate buzz and create curiosity about the movies. Likewise, you can also create product teasers to generate curiosity about products. One of the best places where you can start advertising about any products you offer for sale or services you provide is Instagram. If you understand the nuances of marketing, then you don't have to worry about wooing your potential customers by showing them advertisements about any upcoming products. You must be careful not to be too pushy. If you're too pushy, you will quickly lose your followers. A product is a simple post, which can generate a buzz about the products without making it seem like a hard sell. There is an Instagram account known as the Gilt Man, which is essentially a shopping destination for men. While advertising, they didn't mention anything that might make it seem like they were trying hard to sell. Instead, they came up with a promotional offer wherein customers could download the app and avail amazing discounts. Their Instagram posts consisted of product photos and their captions mentioned the promotional offer. Each of their posts received tens of thousands of likes. Their Instagram advertisements worked because it didn't come across as being too pushy. Likewise, whenever Starbucks comes up with a seasonal drink, they post pictures on Instagram and provide product teasers without trying to force their followers to make any purchases.

By using product teasers, you don't have to force your audience to take any action. Instead, you are gently coaxing them to take an action you want without making it seem like a hard sell. Since you know that your audience is interested in what you are offering, you are merely trying to tip the scales in your favor. If you keep forcing your audience to do something you want and come on a little too strong, you will merely lose your followers. Posting product photos is a great way to create interest.

Partnering With Influencers

The fastest way to reach potential customers is by partnering with influencers in your niche. Influencers already have an established base of followers. Influencers have become rather popular on Instagram these days. A lot of people are buying products or availing services based on the reviews given by influencers. This happens because an influencer often has the trust of his or her followers. If you manage to partner with the right influencer in your niche, you can certainly generate more publicity about your brand. So, the first step is to identify the most popular influencers in your niche industry. Don't merely concentrate on short-term gains whenever you're working with an influencer. Instead, start thinking about all the long-term benefits this relationship can offer. You not only gain access to an influencer's existing base of followers, but you also get a chance to network and establish a strong relationship with someone who can help you attain your brand's goals.

Never Over-Post

While using Instagram, keep in mind that you must not over post. You might be tempted to start posting several pictures at once. Don't do this. If you start clogging up your follower's feeds with multiple posts on a single day, you will lose their interest. If you do want to post multiple pictures in one go, use the album feature wherein you can create a carousel gram, which includes multiple pictures that are displayed in the format of a slideshow. In this manner, you will not clog up their post or lose their interest. Not only is it important to be mindful of posting content at the right time frames, you also need to ensure you don't post an excessive amount. After all, you are trying to build a brand and not come across as spam page. If you start overwhelming your audience with an excess of content regardless of how wonderful the content is, you will not be able to get more followers. For instance, if you have an Instagram account where you post motivational quotes or life philosophy, it is a good idea to stick to just one post per day. No one is really in the mood to read more than one or two inspirational posts at once. So, keep this in mind whenever you're creating your content schedule.

Sponsored Ads Can Work

Instagram ads have become quite popular these days and rightly so.

One of the great things about these ads is that you have complete control over the amount you want to spend on these arts. Essentially, you can budget your ads and stick to the budget. Apart from this, it also gives you the option of selecting the format of the ad. It can be one ad in the form of a sponsored ad or multiple ads in the form of carousel advertising. It not only gives brands a chance to target their customers, but it also curates such advertisements which will prompt customers to take a specific action you desire. Before the concept of sponsored posts was introduced on Instagram, only those users who were following your account will be unable to see your photos or update. Now with all the latest updates, brands are free to promote their content to anyone who fits their profile of an ideal customer.

Whenever you want to use sponsored ads, make sure that the content you are using is not only engaging, but also appeals to your ideal customer demographic. In fact, even an existing post can be reformatted into a sponsored post. Whenever you notice that certain posts of yours are doing exceptionally well, you can later transform them into a sponsored post.

User-Submitted Content

Wouldn't it be rather wonderful if you could create content without having to do the necessary groundwork? Well, you can do this. The simplest way to gain content is by curating user-generated photos. If you already have an audience who is engaged with your brand, this becomes quite easy. You can always leverage your audience to create content for your brand. User-generated content is not as helpful to the brands, but it is quite engaging for users as well. Did you know that the cosmetics giant MAC uses user-generated content regularly? Whenever you use user-generated content, you are essentially providing validation to your followers. If you're wondering how you can get your followers to create content without coming across as being too pushy, then don't worry. It is pretty simple. Your followers are also interested in increasing the following on Instagram, just like you. So, by letting them know that you will be tagging them in your posts whenever you regram, it is a great incentive for your audience. GoPro does this quite frequently and even have a branded hashtag for it- #featuredphotographereveryweek.

Tracking The Right Metrics

If you want to improve the performance of your Instagram posts and optimize them, then it is essential to understand how your page, as well as the posts, are performing. Well, how do you do this? You can do this by tracking Instagram metrics like follower growth rate. Concentrating on the total number of followers that you have might seem vain, but the metric of follower growth rate is different from the number of followers you have. By keeping an eye on the growth rate of you following, you can analyze the effect the kind of content you post has on your followers. Another metric that you must always keep track of is the engagement rate. The number of likes or comments that every Instagram post earns influences the engagement rate. You can start curating content or creating content that is similar to the post with the highest engagement rate.

Apart from these two metrics, there's a third metric that you must watch out for, and that is the click-through rate. Before you can start tracking the click-through rate or CTR, you must have a business website. The CTR showcases the number of people who have clicked on the URL you have placed in the Instagram bio of your brand's profile. There's a direct correlation between the effectiveness of your marketing tactics on Instagram and the CTR. The higher the effectiveness of the marketing strategy, the higher the CTR be. You will learn more about Instagram metrics in the subsequent chapters.

Relate To Your Followers

Yes, it is quite essential to create content that will appeal to your target audience. In fact, spend some time and come up with the ideal description of your target audiences well. If you post content with your target audience alike, it is quite likely that your followers will increase. However, the content that you post must also be in sync with your brand's objective purpose.

For instance, let us assume that you offer financial consulting services. You spend some time and come up with the ideal buyer persona. Your buyer persona helped determine that your target audience loves sports cars and follow profiles that relate to sports cars. So, you might be thinking that you should start posting pictures of sports cars. Well, this might sound like a good idea in theory, but as a practical solution, it isn't that good. After all, your brand claims to be offering financial consulting services, yet your Instagram is full of pictures of sports cars. This doesn't sound like a good marketing strategy, does it? Therefore, it is quintessential to strike a balance between being able to relate to your customers while staying relevant to your brand. So, are you wondering what you can do? Well, since you know that your target audience like sports cars, you must come up with content that stays relevant to your brand while appealing to your target audience. You can create a post that includes a wonderful picture of a sports car along with a description that brings in a financial perspective to the same. Maybe you can add a caption that says they should probably hire your financial consulting services so that they can purchase the sports car that is shown in the picture.

Well, if you start following all the tips that are given in this section, you will certainly be able to increase the number of followers you have on Instagram. Don't be under any misconceptions that you will be able to increase your following overnight. It will take some time, patience, and consistent effort. The results will certainly be worth your while, so make an effort.

Chapter Eight
Creating High-Quality Content

It has been mentioned several times in this book that content matters a lot when it comes to Instagram and any other social networking platform. When it comes to marketing, content is king. If you are interested in increasing the popularity of your brand on Instagram, then you must start creating high-quality content, which will keep your audience hooked. Why is this important? Creating high-quality content is important for two reasons. The first one is that there is a lot of competition out there and if you want to stand apart from the rest, quality content is the key. The second reason is that audiences have become quite selective about the kind of content that they like and dislike. Apart from both these reasons, the Instagram algorithm has made it quite tough for brands to stand out. So, to create high-quality content, you will need a content creation strategy.

The Instagram algorithm is usually demonized by a lot of businesses and brands. To be fair, this algorithm isn't stopping anyone from growing, but it is merely changing the way in which you can grow. Producing high-quality content has become more important than it ever was. During the early days of Instagram, it was quite easy to grow your account without having to worry about all of these things. Well, all this has changed now. Gone are the days of sporadic posting and low-quality images. These days you must be able to churn out high-quality content and must do so consistently. Once the Instagram algorithm notices that your account is churning out content, which your audience likes, it improves the positioning of your content in front of a new audience.

The second reason is that it gives you a chance to monetize your Instagram account. A lot of businesses and brands tend to collaborate with Instagram influencers. If you're trying to position yourself as an Instagram influencer, then you need to have high-quality content. Only when you publish high-quality content will you be able to increase your engagement rate and grow your account. You will certainly lose your audience's interest if you provide them with poor quality content. In this section, you will learn about a few steps that you can take to come up with your own Instagram content strategy.

Content Planning

Before you can start creating content, there are two questions that you must answer.

- What kind of content will resonate with your brand?
- What kind of content will your audience be interested in?

If you are fully aware of what your brand stands for and the kind of content that your audience will like, you can start creating good content. So, you must not only find a niche for yourself on Instagram, but you must also stick to that niche. A common mistake that a lot of Instagrammers make is that they get sidetracked while posting content. They start posting content, which isn't clearly related to the niche they selected. In the long run, this will cost them, followers. For instance, if you want to post about desserts, then stick to that. You don't have to post anything about your outfit-of-the-day (OOTD) or selfies from your vacation. Remember that your followers are there for a reason: to see content related to desserts.

Once you've answered the two questions that have been mentioned above, you can start planning the content for your Instagram. The first step in this process is to make a list of all the content that you wish to follow in the upcoming week. Let us assume that you're a fashion blogger, then the content that you want to post for a week must include a couple of different things like outfit ideas, current fashion trends, mix and match ideas, flat lays, or even outfit shots. Now that you know what you have to do doing it becomes a lot easier. It also helps save time and effort.

Content Photos

You need to have high-quality photographs if you want to become a successful brand on Instagram. Low-quality pictures will get you nowhere. Well, don't worry about spending big bucks on professional cameras or equipment. You don't need a DSLR to generate great images. A lot of Instagram accounts are able to produce brilliant content using their smartphones. The only thing that matters when creating great photographs is the composition of the photograph. Think about the different angles from which you can take a photograph, the positioning of the object, the composition, and the lighting. By keeping these simple things in mind, you can start clicking professional quality photographs. Another tip that you can try is collecting as many photos as you possibly can in your next photoshoot. Think about changing the distance of the camera, the distance of the object, the positioning of the object, the composition of the picture, or even the angle. A couple of small variations here and there can surely make a difference.

For instance, let us assume that you are a food blogger. You might be interested in posting photographs from a wonderful meal you had to speak. Don't just click one or two pictures of that meal. Maybe you want to post something about the restaurant you had your meal at or the food you enjoyed a few weeks later. Instead of boring your audience by showing them the same photos over and over again, you can use the different pictures from the shoot.

Editing The Content

If you go through any of the popular accounts on Instagram, regardless of the industry they are related to, you will notice that they all have one thing in common: great aesthetics. They all have a consistent look that is easily recognizable, unique, and cohesive in all the posts. It might be a specific color scheme or an editing technique. Regardless of what they use, there is an overall theme of consistency. Carefully go through some Instagram newsfeeds of any influencers in your niche, and you will notice that their profiles look well thought out. You must spend some time and edit the content before it is ready for use. It will take some time, but it will certainly be worth your while. If you want to save some time, then you can edit all the content you wish to post in one go. Since you have anyway scheduled and planned the content for the upcoming week, why not just edit it all in one go?

Posting The Content

If you follow the first three steps, your content is primed and ready to be posted on your Instagram account. Well, your job isn't done yet. You not only need to be strategic about the content you want to post, but also about when you post. You must ensure that your Instagram profile has an appealing overall aesthetic. So, whenever you are planning your content, think about the way it will look on your profile. If you place too many similar-looking photos side-by-side, then they will get lost and, hence diluting the cohesiveness of your newsfeed. Once you are happy with your alignment of content, it is time to schedule your post and then post it.

Chapter Nine
Instagram Analytics

Do you spend some time and go through your numbers on Instagram? Maybe you keep track of all the comments or the likes that you get or might know the number of new followers you get on a monthly basis. But have you ever gone through the analytics on Instagram? If you haven't done this so far, then I highly recommend that you start doing so. By going through the analytics on Instagram, you'll not only understand how your profile is performing, but it will also give you insight into understanding the changes you must make for further growth. In this section, you are given information about Instagram analytics, the different analytics you must monitor, and the ways in which it affects your brand on Instagram.

So, why do analytics matter? There are over 25 million business profiles on Instagram, and over 200 million Instagram users visit these profiles every day. Therefore, it is quite clear that different brands, as well as businesses alike, are using this platform for advertising and marketing. Your audience is certainly present on Instagram, but how do you know if they are viewing your content if you aren't even aware of who views your profile or the ads, how your Instagram posts are performing, and the value that your account is generating. You are merely wasting all your efforts on this platform.

The failure to check your Instagram analytics regularly can lead to the following.

- Maybe you aren't targeting your ideal audience.
- You are either posting too frequently or infrequently.
- Ignoring comments or likes, which can reduce the chances of forming successful partnerships and collaborations.
- Not posting during the optimal hours of the day of the week.
- Not checking the profile frequently and missing out on any important collaborations.
- Creating content which doesn't appeal to your audience.
- Showing the right ads but to the wrong audience.
- Driving irrelevant traffic towards your website.

None of these things are desirable if you want to increase your followers on Instagram. If you want to avoid all of this, then you must check the data available on Instagram frequently. The data that you can gather from your analytics will help improve the way you use Instagram. After all, optimizing this platform will help increase the popularity of your brand.

Audience Analytics

Now that you've read through all the information in this book, you must be quite certain about who your target audience is. You might even have an ideal demographic in mind. Do you think your ideal demographic is in sync with the users who are viewing and interacting with your posts? Well, the good news is that there is an entire section of analytics dedicated to this topic. There are five main metrics that you must monitor in this section, and they are as follows.

Age group

One of the first demographics you must target is the age range. How old do you think your target audience is? Instagram makes it easy to answer this question. It divides your audience into different preset age ranges such as 13 to 17, 18 to 24, 25 to 34, 35 to 44, 45 to 55, 55 to 64, and above 65 years.

Top locations

It provides statistics about the five cities and countries wherein most of your audience resides.

Gender

As the name suggests, this provides statistics about the gender of your followers. This metric will help you understand the kind of content that appeals to a specific gender.

Follower activity

You can easily keep track of follower activity related to your profile on Instagram. The two metrics you can use are the follower hours and the follower days. The follower days provides statistics about the average time of the day during which most of your followers are active on Instagram. The follower days provide information about the days of the week during which your followers are the most active on Instagram.

Profile Analytics

These metrics can be readily accessed in the "My Profile" tab. It gives you insights on a weekly basis. You may have viewed these analytics in the past but might not have given it much thought. In this section, let us look at some of the important metrics you must start tracking.

Reach

This refers to the number of unique accounts that have viewed any of your posts.

Impressions

Refers to the number of times any of your Instagram posts have been viewed during a given timeframe.

Profile visit

Refers to the total number of views your profile has received on Instagram in a week.

Interactions

This refers to the number of times any action has been taken on your posts on Instagram.

Website clicks

It refers to the number of times the URL link posted in your bio was clicked.

Mentions

It tracks the statistics related to the times your account handle was mentioned by other users on Instagram.

Call or email clicks

If you placed a call or an email button on your profile page on Instagram, then this metric keeps track of times that button was clicked by other users.

Analytics of Posts

Now that you are aware of your target audience and metrics related to profile let us examine the metrics related to each of the posts on Instagram. By doing this, you can determine whether the message you are trying to deliver through your content resonates with the audience or not. The different metrics that you must track for analyzing the performance of your posts on Instagram are as follows.

Explore tab

This is a feature that allows existing users to explore content presented by accounts that they don't follow. If your account shows up on this tab, it means your content is doing pretty well. Instagram provides you with statistics related to the number of followers your account has gained via the Explore tab.

Interactions

Any action that was directly taken by the users in relation to a specific post on your profile is referred to as interaction. The action might be clicking on the hyperlink in your bio, visiting your profile, or even using the call button in your profile. Data related to all these items are tracked and maintained in this section.

Reach

The number of new accounts your post has reached.

Follows

The number of followers you gained on Instagram because of a specific post.

Impressions

It refers to the number of times a specific post was viewed.

Comments

As the name suggests, it helps keep track of the total number of comments your posts on Instagram receive.

Analytics of Stories

One of the most important aspects of Instagram these days is the Instagram Story section. Instagram Stories are steadily gaining popularity, and more and more brands are using it quite frequently. The Instagram Story feature is quite similar to the one available on Snapchat. This is a great opportunity for brands to easily and effectively interact and engage with their audience. The different metrics that you must track are as follows.

Reach

The number of accounts who have viewed your Instagram Stories.

Impressions

It refers to the number of times your Story was viewed on Instagram.

Exits

The number of times a user has closed the Story without making it to the end.

Replies

All the accounts that viewed only a particular portion of the Story instead of the entire Story.

Instagram analytics is a powerful tool that must not be overlooked. If you want to create a massive following for your brand on Instagram, then you must be aware of the kind of content that works and doesn't. By factoring all these analytics into your marketing strategy, you can easily optimize the content for your profile.

Chapter Ten
Data You Must Track

Well, in the previous chapter, you were given plenty of information about the different types of Instagram analytics you must be aware of. Going through all the data can be rather overwhelming, especially if you're just getting started. Before you think about analyzing the data, it is important to be aware of the specific things you're looking for or your goals. Maybe you have started using Instagram to drive traffic to your website. Perhaps you have started using Instagram to create brand awareness in your target audience. You must first understand your goals before you can start analyzing the data. The three common goals that a lot of brands who use Instagram have are: brand awareness, creating leads, and building a community.

Establishing Brand Awareness

If you want to carve a niche out for yourself or make a name for yourself, then you might be trying to establish brand awareness. Even if you are an established business who is launching a new product or offering a new service, you might also be interested in building awareness. Instagram is the best place to start building brand awareness. The sheer volume of users active on this platform makes it one of the best places to find your target audience. If you want to establish brand awareness, then here are some metrics that you must track.

Follower count

If you notice that your follower count is increasing, it means your brand awareness is too. An increase in your follower count essentially means that the content you're creating is working well, and your audience is resonating with your brand on Instagram. You can grow your followers by running ads, collaborating with others, hosting campaigns or contests, and even by engaging with your audience. You can follow the different tips that were given in the previous chapters in this book for increasing your number of followers on Instagram.

Impressions

It is quintessential for your audience to view your content if you want to increase brand awareness. It's not just your post, but the stories matter too. If you notice that the number of impressions you receive on a post is increasing, it means that your post is doing well, and the audience appreciates the content you're posting. On the other hand, if the number of impressions decreases, it means maybe you need to make changes to your content strategy.

Reach

The number of views that you get on your posts, account, and stories can be effectively measured with this statistic. Reach and impressions might sound quite similar, but they are quite different. Impressions refer to the number of times your content was viewed, whereas reach measures the number of times it was viewed by unique accounts. If you want to build your brand awareness, then you need to concentrate on increasing your reach.

Creating Leads

A lot of marketers use Instagram for generating leads or closing more sales. After all, what marketer wouldn't want to generate leads? There are various strategies that can be used for increasing your sales using Instagram. The best way to go about doing this is by creating targeted ads and coming up with special offers for your audience. However, how do you know when the latter doing well? There are three important metrics, which you must track, to understand whether your marketing strategy is performing well on Instagram or not.

Website clicks

As a marketer, your main objective would be to divert the traffic to your website or encourage them to make a purchase or maybe even fill out a form. The best way to go about doing this is by inserting the URL to your website in your posts, bio, and even stories. By tracking the number of individuals while clicking on the website link, will help ensure that your marketing campaign is working.

Email or call clicks

Another great way to track convergences is by keeping track of the phone calls and emails that you receive. Whenever there's an increase in these areas, it means that your strategy for the lead conversion is doing well.

Follower days or hours

You can certainly improve your Instagram strategy by concentrating on the days or the hours during which your audience is active on Instagram. By taking this into account, you can time your ads or targeted post on Instagram. When your audiences act on Instagram, it increases the chances of conversion. This, in turn, means that your return on investment from any marketing campaign on Instagram will be high.

Creating A Community

The best way in which you cannot only build a community, but also interact with them is by creating engaging and interesting content on Instagram. If building a community is your main goal, then there are certain metrics that you must constantly monitor as well as evaluate.

Comments

You cannot have a community without a conversation. What is a better way to start a conversation than by engaging in the comment section? It not only gives the audience a chance to engage with a brand, but it also gives the brand a chance to respond to its audience. Remember that you are trying to create a community for your brand on Instagram, and to do this, you must be socially active. Networking is key for attaining this objective. So, don't ever ignore any compliments and comments, and try to respond to them as promptly as you can.

Story replies

Instagram stories can also help in building a loyal community for your brand. It also helps you gauge how active your community is on Instagram. If you want to engage with your followers, then you must not only post to Instagram Stories, but you must also reply to any comments that you are tagged in on the stories. Track the different metrics related to the stories to determine the level of engagement with your audience.

Engagement

Another important metric that must rank is the engagement rate. If you want to build a community, then you must track the engagement rate on your post, profile, stories, and even the ads that you run. When the engagement rate is high, it means that you are building a community for yourself.

Analytical Tools To Use

Now that you are aware of all the different metrics that you must track, it is time to get started. You can certainly use Instagram Insights for tracking the necessary metrics, but that's not your only option. With the increase in the popularity of Instagram, several third-party analytical tools have started to crop up. Regardless of the metric, you wish to track; you will find an analytical tool to meet your requirements. The best analytical tools that you can use are as follows.

- Hootsuite
- Sprout social
- Socialrank
- Squarelovin

By using any of the tools mentioned in this section, you can start tracking all the necessary Instagram metrics. You don't have to worry about crunching any numbers or working out detailed analysis reports because these tools will do all the work for you. You merely need to start working with the results generated by the analytical tools.

Once you start tracking and analyzing metrics, you can come up with an effective Instagram marketing strategy. Not just that, it can also help make any necessary changes to your existing Instagram strategy. Don't ever ignore the metrics on Instagram and dedicate some time toward analyzing them. Your efforts will certainly pay off.

Chapter Eleven
Best Instagram Tools To Build Your Following

Snapseed

It is a brilliant application for editing photos. It gives you several options for fine-tuning any photograph before you post on Instagram. Unless you are fine with editing the entire photo at once, you need third-party applications like Snapseed. It allows you to tweak and edit details in photographs to make them look more appealing. This app also allows you to select a couple of filters and then save it as a template. By doing this, you will essentially be able to maintain your brand's aesthetic on Instagram. So, if you want a consistent look and want to save time, then Snapseed is a good option. The best part of this app? It is free!

VSCO

VSCO is one of the leading third-party apps for content creation, and it is a free app. During the initial stages, the photo editing tools offered by Instagram were considered to be revolutionary. Well, long gone are those days, and with this app, you can create wonderful and amazing photographs on the go. This app is a perfect combination of a social media network and photo editing tools. It offers a comprehensive editing suite that you can use to elevate the appeal of even those pictures you click on your smartphone. Apart from this, it also provides a wide variety of filters and gives you unlimited options for customizing your photographs.

Canva

It is a content creation tool, and just like the previous ones, even this one is a free application. You can start using this app for creating images that will stand out from the rest, regardless of whether you use it for your Instagram Stories or your newsfeed. It allows you to create multi-image posts or collages, superimpose text, and provide a variety of graphics that can help quickly transform the appeal of your posts. This tool comes in handy, especially while curating content that you want to post in your Stories. Also, if you wish to stick to a specific theme or color scheme, then try this app! This application is available on Android and iOS. You can also use this app directly on the web.

Afterlight

It is a paid application, and you can purchase it for about $2. It is available for iOS as well as Android. It is a brilliant photo-editing tool, which comes with dozens of default sets of filters, textures, and frames. By using this app, you can start creating and saving the combination of filters you wish to use. It also offers a typography tool. The simplicity of the app coupled with its user-friendly interface makes it a good option.

Later

When it comes to Instagram, you must not only create brilliant content, but also post it at the right time. Later is a content scheduling tool that you can use for optimizing your posting schedule. It is a third-party app, which enables you to publish content easily. The content scheduler offered by Later is not only simple to use but is easy to understand as well. Open the app, go to the publishing calendar, and drag in any media that you want from your library. Once you do this, a schedule window will open up. In this window, you are required to write a caption a post, any tags that you want to include, the location, and any relevant hashtags. This tool also gives you a list of any hashtags that you can use.

Iconosquare

It is not only a great analytics tool, but it also comes with an automatic scheduler. The scheduler provided by this app comes with several add-ons like social media calendar, an integrated media library for storing your content, and suggestions for the best time to post. The social media calendar essentially reminds you of all the days on which you are required to post so that you don't miss out on any opportunities. By opting to use this app, you get two services in one. Not only can you track all the metrics you want to analyze, but you can also schedule your content. Apart from this, it also has certain editing tools that you can use. You can edit the tools within this app, and then upload them into the content scheduler.

Sendible

If you don't like the idea of being constantly reminded about your posting schedule or hate receiving constant notifications, then this is a perfect option for you. It allows you to not just schedule your posts, but also automatically publishes a post directly on Instagram. You can even directly post videos to your Instagram account by using this app. Additionally, you can also funnel your content onto any other social media platforms your brand is active on such as Twitter, Facebook, and Tumblr.

Buffer

If you're looking for a tool that will act as a social network account manager, then don't look any further. Buffer will do the job for you, and it comes with several add-ons that are quite helpful. Once you set up the account on this app, you can directly schedule content that you would like to post on Instagram. Apart from this, you can also create a content queue so that the app can automatically post the relevant content at the right time. By using this app, you will certainly save yourself a lot of time and effort.

Never underestimate the need for scheduling posts or editing photos for your Instagram profile. It is something that a lot of people overlook, but you must not. If you want to increase your following and capitalize on Instagram, then you must pay close attention to the content you're sharing especially when scheduling posts on Instagram. There are various tools that you can use, but only some of them will meet your needs and requirements. So experiment with all the tools and see which of these you prefer. Most of these tools offer a free trial period. So, make the most of it. The best thing about using third party applications for creating and scheduling content is that it enables you to update your Instagram profile without much hassle.

Conclusion

I want to thank you once again for choosing this book. I hope it proved to be an informative and engaging read.

These days, the marketing priorities of brands are changing. Conventional marketing methods are still widely used, but online marketing has changed marketing efforts altogether. If you want your brand to have a robust online presence, then you aren't alone. All businesses, regardless of whether they are a small startup or a well-established brand in the industry, use Instagram as a part of their marketing strategy.

You can capitalize on Instagram's popularity for increasing your brand's online presence. It is quite common for brands to create an official business website and use the usual platforms like Twitter or Facebook. Almost all brands do this, but Instagram offers way more than either of these platforms. Instagram has over a billion active users, and if you want to reach your target audience, then it is the best platform. You must be well aware of all the nuances of Instagram if you want to use it optimally.

In this book, you were provided all the information you will need to create and optimize your brand's presence on Instagram. If you follow the steps mentioned in this book, you can certainly increase your brand's profitability and use Instagram more intentionally and strategically. So, increase your engagement rate, gain new followers, and create a loyal audience for your brand today! Now, all that's left for you to do is to get started as soon as you can!

Thank you and all the best!

Bonus Material:

Book: Social Media Marketing 2019

The Ultimate Guide to Boosting Your Business Through Social Media Marketing Efforts

“Sharing is the essence of social media” Zoe Sugg

Social Media Marketing - The Art of It

The art of social media marketing revolves around the idea of approaching or communicating with customers on social media platforms such as Facebook, LinkedIn, and Instagram. Today, businesses have turned to social media networks as a great place to meet and interact with their audiences. With the increased social media usage, more and more firms are rushing in to find their places on social media. It is for this reason that you will come across numerous websites providing guides on how to enhance your business’ social media presence. Generally, the art of social media marketing entails companies using social platforms such as Facebook to promote their brands. Depending on the social media network, marketing techniques and tactics would vary.

The following few lines provide a concise analysis of the basics of marketing brands over social networks such as Facebook, Instagram, and YouTube.

Marketing Your Business on Facebook

Facebook is one of the leading social media websites at the moment. Therefore, this makes it a valuable tool to sell your business in the online community. However, most companies fail while marketing their businesses over this platform. Here's why.

The mere fact that you have a running Facebook account for your business does not mean that you should post anything. NO! First, you have to do your homework. Marketing your business on Facebook should not resemble the marketing tactics that you use to sell your business over television or radio. Moreover, the marketing strategies that you use should differ from those that you use when marketing your brand over magazines. The first thing that an entrepreneur should understand is how Facebook operates. Undeniably, people consider Facebook as their ideal fun space. This is where they get to interact socially with their friends and relatives. This means that as a business, you need to interact with them on the same level. You should join the conversation that is going on around the community. A big mistake that most businesses make is selling aggressively over Facebook.

Imagine what people in a particular social group would say when they try to discuss something important that is affecting the community, and yet, you are there pitching your brand. Marketing on Facebook demands that a marketer should learn to differentiate when to use hard-selling strategies. This implies that tactics such as frequently posting about a brand should be avoided in certain conversations. The last thing that you need for your business is having people "unfollowing" you. This is a negative statement that shows that there is something wrong you are doing on Facebook.

Another important aspect of marketing your business on Facebook is that people crave to communicate in a friendly and more human tone. Honestly, we cannot deny the fact that we hate when companies reply to our queries through automated emails. It shows that these companies do not have time for us. Similarly, when communicating with customers on Facebook, they expect a human tone. Therefore, it is vital for a business owner to find the right voice that would communicate to customers out there.

Whenever I am browsing through my Facebook page, I often get peeved when I notice that the same ad that was running yesterday is still showing on my wall. Well, perhaps, this is the same feeling that thousands of customers have out there. As such, marketing on Facebook demands that one should post regularly. Unlike conventional media, social media is all about being up to date. This is what socialites expect from your Facebook business page.

It goes without saying that the greatest form of entertainment comes from watching videos and skimming through pictures over Facebook. Interestingly, thousands of people get caught up watching funny videos and end up wasting their time there. But, guess what? This is what it takes to lure customers to your Facebook business page. Good use of pictures and videos will undeniably get people to like and share your brand. Isn't this what you want? If yes, then you should make use of them to ensure that your audience is constantly entertained.

Probably you are wondering what kind of pictures you should post on your Facebook business page. I would say relevant photos. Say, you are selling clothing outfits. This implies that you should take advantage of the Facebook platform to post images of your new stock. Get your customers talking and sharing by posting these pictures all over your wall.

Your social media page will not be successful if you choose not to learn more about your clientele. Fortunately, you can easily make use of Facebook Insights. These are tools that aid you in better understanding the kind of people that continuously like the products and services you offer. Once you are well aware of the people you are dealing with, it would be easy to modify your posts to suit their needs and expectations. In the end, you would be sure that you are posting the most suitable material to individuals that would highly likely share your brand for the rest of the world to see and probably turn to it.

It never gets enough with Facebook. The funny thing that you should not forget is that it calls for your patience when marketing your brand through this platform. Building stable relationships is not easy. Take your time to engage sincerely with your customer base. Do your homework; research on what you think is best for your clients. This is what they expect from you. Remember, rival brands are doing it, so should you.

Marketing Your Business on YouTube

A newbie will deny the fact that promoting a business on YouTube could be a great way to grow a business. Well, it is highly likely that they would think about the hustle and bustle of recording videos and uploading them. One thing that they should realize is that visual content is more popular on YouTube as compared to other social media channels. Consequently, this makes it an essential marketing tool for your business.

The opportunities for businesses to exploit YouTube are always on the rise. It is because about 85% of online adults regularly visit YouTube. This makes it a great place to market your brand. But before that, there are essential aspects that any marketer promoting their brand on this platform should be aware of.

A key to succeeding on YouTube is optimization. One is required to optimize their videos for Google search as well as for clicks. Let me make this easy for you to understand. Marketing on YouTube requires that you make good use of keywords in your tags, description, and in your titles. Why? Obviously, YouTubers would want to find videos related to your brand with ease. To fulfill this requirement, it is imperative to optimize your videos.

One of the recommendations that I found from Google is that you should begin with keywords, and then this should be followed by branding. For instance, a user looking for a cooking show would use the keywords –"cooking show." This should then be followed by what they were looking, for e.g., "cake tutorial." The last thing should be the branding, e.g., "Kelly Brown." Knowing how to optimize your videos would make a massive difference in landing numerous clicks directed to your brand.

Marketers on YouTube often forget that description is also essential in winning over a vast customer base. So, after watching a good ad, you forget to entice your clients about other products that they might be interested in. Well, guess what? That is the end of the tunnel. People will simply click on other videos probably belonging to your rivals. The sad news is that if your opponents pitch their message better than you, you are bound to fail.

Consequently, think about the idea of including a call to action message. Tell your customers why they should watch another video before they leave. Entice them. Play with their minds and rest assured that you will have them glued to your YouTube page. Do not make assumptions that customers out there will follow you automatically. Trust me they won't. Give them information about how they can subscribe to your YouTube channel for the latest information regarding products and services that you offer. If your pitch is outstanding, rest assured that you will get numerous subscribers.

There is something important that I need to mention here. Often, I have received questions about the kind of videos that one should post. Undeniably, being creative is the key to enticing your clients. Therefore, it makes sense that you first mull over the type of videos that you would be posting. Here are some ideas that should help you.

Post tutorial videos. Your audience is always in search of how best to use your product. Therefore, an excellent trick to attract their attention would be to post videos demonstrating how specific tasks are performed or just how easy it is to use your product. Most successful online marketers will also recommend the idea of posting product demos. Let's be honest, you won't incur losses by merely using some products to shoot product demos for your customers.

People are often convinced to turn to your product when they come across customer testimonials. Therefore, a brilliant idea for convincing your target market about your product is by posting videos featuring testimonials from satisfied clients. Also, you can opt to introduce your business through your YouTube channel. Introduce who you are as a business and mention the products and services that you offer. Remember, don't forget about optimization. It will make an immense difference in getting your audience to land in the right place.

Marketing your business on Instagram

With the growing number of Instagram users, this platform also presents itself as an ideal place to sell your business. There are more than 700 million monthly subscribers on Instagram. Therefore, this means that your product or service could quickly get a wide market reach. Unfortunately, this does not come on a silver platter.

Just like any other social media channel, Instagram is also a community. It infers that it is up to you to prove to the community that you are a valuable member of the platform. Constant participation is thus required from you. Just posting videos and images is not enough. Join the community. Be part of the conversation. Respond to questions from the community and make relevant comments. Without a doubt, this will get them talking and thinking about how valuable your brand is. Why? Because it is a part of the social community.

There are numerous ways of marketing your product or service on Instagram. Nevertheless, your message should not be confusing. Your brand should not be mistaken for another brand or something else. As such, consistency is critical. Assume you are marketing your product on Facebook using a different image. If you use a different image on Instagram, you run the risk of confusing your followers. They will never be sure about the actual product or service that you are selling. It is recommended that your brand's profile picture should be similar across all social platforms. Most importantly, it should be professional.

Instagram followers are always on the lookout for feeds that would interest them. Accordingly, your marketing efforts on this platform should include a reason as to why people should follow your brand. Make them aware of the difference that you would make if at all they chose to follow you. I always recommend a short and exciting bio that does not have a "salesy" tone.

Buyers in the modern world are frequently turned off by hard-selling habits. After posting images and videos about your brand, do not yell to your audience. The last thing that you should do is to pitch illusory sentiments about how your product is good. Give your audience time to make their comments without feeling that they are being pushed to the wall. Just be creative and not pushy.

Business owners should take their time to understand that their brands are out there to build a lasting relationship with their customers. Doing this right is, therefore, the key to succeeding in winning over customers. Once they are ready to shop, rest assured that they will come for your brand as you had already connected with them. So, focus on posting quality videos and pictures that will surely tempt your customers to keep sharing.

Check out our Other *AMAZING* Titles:

1. Content Marketing:

Growth Strategies to Stay Ahead in the Changing World of Content Marketing and Maximize ROI

"Success is walking from failure to failure with no loss of enthusiasm." – Winston Churchill

If you spend much time online, particularly in internet marketing circles, you can't avoid hearing about the 'powers' of content marketing. To hear some people talk about it, you would think they'd found the fountain of youth and a vault full of money right beside it... but content on its own is just not enough. Yes, it's powerful because it can cut through the noise online and show your visitors that you can be trusted. But if you're going to build a relationship with those visitors, you've got to have a way to continue communicating with them regularly. You can't assume they'll remember to check your blog every week or that they'll buy from you unprompted.

Most content is distributed on platforms you do not own — Facebook, Twitter, content networks, search engines, and so on. Those platforms own the traffic, and if they change how they do business, you can lose your audience. That's why it's critical to start building a contact list that you own and can market to directly. This is where opt-in offers come into play. Whenever a new person visits your site, they should have the opportunity to join your mailing list or private community in exchange for some incentive. You need to get their email address or have them set up an account so that you can build up a profile for them over time, communicate with them directly, and make carefully targeted sales offers to them when the time is right.

Your opt-in offers do not need to be cripplingly complex. This is a critical aspect of a content marketing strategy, so let me be clear: done is better than perfect. Assets like this can always be more detailed, have a longer word-count, or be more testimonial-heavier, but once you have a good piece of information that's useful, polished and appealing, publish it. Every day that you do not have an active opt-in is a day that you are losing leads, and are wasting the resources you've put into creating your content so far. Ideally, you would give the subscriber a piece of premium content, but at the very least, a pop-up box that asks for their email address will do (use SumoMe.com to get that set up).

Here are some asset types for compelling opt-in offers:

•Industry report or white paper

- Case study
- Video series
- Webinar
- Demo
- Discount code
- Quiz or survey

- Cheat sheet
- How-to guide
- Industry or client profiles

Pick the type of asset most appropriate to your industry, and based on what your customers will value. Make sure that it's better information than they would usually find within your public content, and make it feel high-quality wherever possible so that they're impressed and want to see what comes next. The offer should also have a clear benefit for the subscriber: take care to communicate the value they are going to get as a result of giving you their information, and that you set their expectations accurately before they opt in. Make sure the asset is delivered to them immediately, via a thank-you page and/or a confirmation email.

Build an Onboarding Sequence

Getting someone's email address or having them create an account is a big win. This is a micro-commitment from them (which is the first step towards having them buy from you), as well as getting their permission to market to them. This is huge, and you want to capitalize on this opportunity. An email onboarding sequence creates a window for you to do that. Onboarding, also referred to as 'organizational socialization', is done through an automated sequence of emails by which subscribers are educated about your brand, engaged with your community, and indoctrinated with your values.

Here's a templated structure you can use for a general onboarding sequence. If someone has opted in to receive something, these are some general topics for the emails you might send them:

(We'll go into further depth on how to build your onboarding sequences later on in this book.)

The goal of this sequence is to establish yourself as an authority on the topic they opted in to hear about and to get them to take the next step with you. Whether it's booking a call, taking a demo, joining a webinar, or even just replying to an email, make sure you're positioning the subscriber to engage. This is mission-critical. People need to be led, so make sure you have something specific you are leading them towards. You never want someone to be unclear about what their next step should be. This is true at any point as the customer is moving through your ecosystem, but *particularly* at this stage when they've been exposed to your ideas and expertise, and it's time for them to make a purchasing decision.

Depending on the nature of your market, your offering, and the messaging that works best, common 'next steps' in a B2B business would be one of the following:

• Invite them to a free webinar. A lot of marketers do this extremely well — people like Frank Kern, Noah Kagan, and Ryan Levesque leverage webinars to engage people to great success all the time. This format works so well because it allows the marketer to give a lot of value up front, without requiring a large time investment from the prospect. Webinars are also a direct platform to sell from, as they basically create a captive audience: the prospect joins the webinar, learns lots of good stuff, and then (with the principle of reciprocity working quietly in the back of their mind) will sit through a sales pitch even if they don't have to. At this point, the prospect is primed: they think of you as an approachable authority who is speaking directly to their problems, and so you can offer them your solution while they are right there in a receptive frame of mind.

• Offer them a free demo. This works similar to the webinar model but works particularly well for SaaS (software as a service) businesses and companies that offer some kind of technical solution. We built a free demo offer into the onboarding email sequence for Wicked Reports, and they saw a significant uptick in both booked demos and sales. Having some prior education about the product, their prospects become very curious to see the tool in action in a few different scenarios, and are therefore willing to book in an hour to get to know Wicked Reports better. Most people learn well in a visual format, so seeing the tool in use is a powerful way to move them towards a conversion. Do you know the old saying "possession is nine-tenths of the law"? Well, an interactive demo is about as close as you can get to having the prospect 'possess' the product. If you can demonstrate your offer in action, they're going to be much more likely to take the next step you want.

• Invite them to a free call. This works particularly well for consultants and service businesses because often the offer is a little less tangible than what's being sold by other B2B businesses. Make it clear that it's an obligation-free call, and that they can spend as much time as they want to ask questions, picking apart your offer, and really getting a feel for whether you're the right fit for them. It's an opportunity for them to air any skepticism, get clarity about what they need, and get to know you. A very powerful part of the onboarding process is that they get sufficiently educated about your product or process so that they feel comfortable getting on the phone with you because they will then know what they're talking about. You never want someone to come into a conversation this blind, because the power balance is too much in your favor. In that situation, the prospect can feel that you hold all the cards and they don't have enough information to assess whether you're being straightforward with them. This makes people feel defensive, and wary of you trying to 'put it over them'. You want to make sure they have a locus of control in the interaction so that they're comfortable and more open to the conversation. Before getting on the phone with anyone, make sure they have as much information as they need, and let them know that you encourage a critical approach in your customers, that you only want to work with people who take their business seriously, and that you're not going to put a hard sell on them.

All the content that you produce up to this point should be driving the prospect towards having some kind of real-time interaction with you. Business is about people, and people won't do anything if trust and rapport is missing from an interaction. They need to relate to you as a person they can trust; a person who will be a positive influence in their business, and will ultimately help them fill whatever deep-seated need is driving them.

(And make no mistake — it's rarely a cut and dry desire to make more money that drives people. Some want status, others want recognition, others still want positive feedback… there's a whole neurochemical chain reaction going on when someone makes a buying decision, and while that's beyond the scope of this book, we'll be getting into a little bit of the behavioral psychology that should factor into your marketing later on.)

Carlos Ruiz Zafón, one of the most popular Spanish novelists of the modern age, says that we only accept as true what can be narrated.

Knowing, then, that people will only buy what you're selling when it's wrapped up in a story or narrative that resonates with them - you need to find a way to position your content in a way that does that. Your offer should be presented as a story they can see themselves taking an active part in, and you, yourself should be presented as a narrator they trust and find relatable.

Understanding that, you should always be driving them to some sort of interactive action. This is a critical aspect of high-converting content: there's always a clear call to action that moves them further through your funnel. The prospect is never left alone without a clear next step; they'll never wonder if you have some hidden ulterior motive — they know and trust you because you told them the story they needed to hear. This is why knowing deeply who your audience is, what offer they need to receive, and how to position your messaging, is the cornerstone of creating high-converting content.

Next, we're going to dive into the two most critical steps of all — making sales offers and following up with your prospects.

Make Sales Offers

The secret to creating content that converts is to create a conversion moment. Yes, despite all the progress that marketing has made, you still have to make sales offers if you want to convert your prospects. No marketing system in the world can extract a sale without first making a sales offer.

All businesses live and die by the number of sales they make. It doesn't matter how good your systems are, or if you have a great team, or you've got unrivalled SOPs… it doesn't even matter if you have hyper-focused marketing and a replicable lead acquisition funnel. If you don't make sales offers, it's all for nothing.

Of the dozens of B2B businesses I've worked with over the years, just one thing separates the success stories from the failures, and it's that the leaders of the company committed to sales. They committed to making the offer every time — they committed to ignoring their fear of rejection, their anxiety about pissing people off, and the voice in their head that said they couldn't do it. They committed, consistently made their offers, and came out on top because of it.

Sales offers come in all shapes and sizes, depending on the business. You might invite someone to book a paid consult with you, or you might offer them an ongoing service for which they pay you every month. You might offer them the purchase of a single unit, or the purchase of thousands of units. You might offer them paid access to a piece of software that will automate part of their business. Whatever it is, you need to explicitly offer to give them your product or service in return for a specific amount of money.

If you are afraid of making sales offers off the back of your content, or you 'sell from your heels' (making a half-hearted attempt at a sale that doesn't really showcase the benefits, or ask the prospect for an answer), your content will never convert a single customer. You will be wasting all your resources and in time, your business will fail.

- Being 'uncovered' as a fraud
- Being rejected
- Being found lacking in either their qualifications or what they're offering
- Being perceived as pushy, rude, or mercenary
- Being unable to deliver what they are offering

Usually, these fears are completely unfounded, and they're all rooted in the fundamental human need to be accepted by your tribe. It's horrible to think that someone you pitch would be offended by your offer, and then go and rip on you all over the internet… but with a content ecosystem that gradually entices people to your offer, and sharing information that benefits them and shows that you have their best interests in mind, you're not going to get that kind of treatment.

The great thing about the content ecosystem is that most of the people you will speak to will be pre-qualified as a potential buyer, so they're likely to respond positively to an offer. The best approach, in this case, is usually not a hard sell, but a simple mention of 'here's what I've got, here's what it will do for you, and here's how to get it.'

In fact, I've never had a client have a bad reaction from their customers when they make their sales offer at the end of a content funnel. I've never had a bad reaction for my own services, either. That doesn't mean bad reactions can't happen — selling is both art and science, and you *can* get it wrong, but if you are putting your customers first then you can feel confident that you'll usually get a good response.

If need be, practice your sales offers. Get a friend or colleague on the phone, or in however method you will be making pitches to customers, and practice on them. It's worth the awkwardness and will pay a huge ROI on the time and energy you spend on it. Ideally, your practice partner will actually fit your primary customer profile. Give them your onboarding material to read first, so that they come to the practice sales situation with all the same knowledge your real prospects will have. Go through the process of the onboarding event — whether it's a webinar, demo or call — and then transition into your sales offer.

Practice moving the conversation from the free content to the sales offer. Practice your positioning, and how you talk about the offer. Practice the language that works best to communicate all the benefits of the offer, and practice how to overcome objections by encouraging your partner to come up with as many as they can, based on what you've already discussed. Finally, find out from them what questions went unanswered for them during the process, what objections they kept to themselves, and what would have made them commit to the sale that you didn't address. Try to get a real-world interaction that will emulate the sales process for you, so that when you do it with real prospects, you're in familiar territory.

Never pass up the opportunity to make a sale. If you have someone on a call, or in some kind of interaction with you, do not put it off. Do not say to yourself *"I'll just send them an email that closes them after this"* or *'they'll tell me if they want to go ahead with something"*. No, you won't, and no, they won't. Unless you have explicitly promised not to sell them anything, always be selling.

(The only time you should ever promise not to sell during an interaction is when you need something from the prospect other than the sale, like early market feedback. Otherwise, avoid making promises that will prevent you from making money.)

Be as generous and fully present as you can be during the sales process. Answer every question honestly and with your full attention. Dig into their doubts, invite them to hit you with their best shot — make them understand that you *really* care about their situation and are helping them to find the right solution. Before they get off the call, get a yes or no answer from the prospect. Just ask: *"Are you ready to go ahead?"* No maybes, or let-me-think-about-its. Yes or no. If they push back on you, simply say that you want to get a specific answer from them so you know how to move forward with them. It might sound aggressive, but when positioned correctly, this is a powerful method to make sure that all the content you've produced so far actually does the job and makes people convert.

Want to read more? Check out our book on ***Content Marketing*** *on Amazon today!*

2. Business Promotion Techniques

A Marketer's Guide to Improving Your Business Visibility and Increasing Customer Engagement

"You can't use up creativity. The more you use, the more you have."

– Maya Angelou

Promotion is one of the important things you think about concerning your business. Effective promotion strategies are at the center of your business. Whether yours is a small, medium-sized or large business, you must have a promotion strategy that aligns with your long-term growth strategy. Flyers and posters have been used in many businesses over the years and prove to be effective promotional tools even today.

Flyers and posters are a good option for your business because they are scalable. They are very easy to create. Even with the simplest posters, you must still be creative in your design. Why is it that these mundane tools are very important for promotional purposes?

For many years, flyers and posters have been used because of how effective they are in delivering the advertiser's information to customers. As much as people are heavily reliant on social media today, flyers and posters still retain their role in business promotion. They are show stoppers and will always grab your attention.

Think about your recent encounter with flyers or posters, for example. You might not have intended to check them out, but when you came across them, you could not pass up the chance. The way they grab attention is one of the reasons why these age-old techniques are still in use today, and thriving.

Another reason why you should consider using posters and flyers is because you can design them to suit your budget. Startups with a limited budget can benefit from this technique in that you can create them without spending a lot. With basic graphics design skills, you can easily create some catchy flyers and distribute them to your audience wherever you feel suitable.

Importance of Posters and Flyers

Versatility is one of the benefits you get from using flyers and posters for your business. In terms of value for your money, it doesn't get any better than this. Listed below are some reasons why posters and flyers are still one of the best ideas you can consider for promoting your business today.

- Brand awareness

One of the first things many people do today whenever they need to find information about a product or service it to research online. This is a habitual decision-making process. Many people cannot explain why they prefer checking for product or brand information online because they have gotten used to this trend, it is almost natural.

However, you can tap into this and create awareness for your brand. While people fancy online searches, a localized solution sounds even better. People appreciate your business better when you can provide immediate solutions to their problems. Flyers are therefore, a good way to build a name for your business in the community.

- Affordability

There is always the argument in terms of cost-effectiveness, and in this regard, posters and flyers are a sure winner. You can design and print your own flyers and posters at home. Even if you hire an expert to do it for your business, it still would not cost you as much as you would spend on other promotional techniques.

- Simplicity

You can spend months working on some promotional strategies and tools. Flyers and posters, on the other hand, can be ready for distribution in a few hours from the moment you started printing them. Most people have them ready in a day or less, especially if the design is well-planned already.

Other than the ease of production, the simplicity in flyers and posters is another benefit your business will enjoy. You can choose to include as much or little information as you feel necessary in them. Therefore, you don't run the risk of confusing your audience, or overwhelming them with information. A few catchy words in the right font, and some good graphics, coupled with creative color selection will have your promotional content appealing to your audience.

- Introduce incentives

If you are thinking of incentivizing your business in some way, flyers and posters are a good way to go. People who have them will probably be talking about the 50% offer being offered at your store. They are good for peaking interest and could work well to help you create awareness for your business.

- Palpability

One of the main benefits of using flyers and posters is that they are palpable. Your audience can carry it with them wherever they go. This works well for you because your message can reach a lot more people than you had planned. If someone is traveling and they carry your posters with them, there's a good chance someone in their destination will get your message and think about it.

How many times have you received flyers at the mall, and ended up with them on your coffee table at home? A message that was dispatched through you ends up being received by everyone in your household, and all this is through one flyer.

While there are strong claims from individuals and businesses about the rise of promotional content on social media and its benefits, do not ignore what you can achieve with flyers and posters. They might seem outdated for the modern customer, but at times it is the old-fashioned techniques that still work best. Remember that you must be creative in your design to get the best results.

How to Design the Best Flyers and Posters

Flyers and posters are still winning, so many years since they were first used for promotional purposes. Even in the face of technology and social media where many traditional forms of marketing are struggling, flyers and posters are still leaving an impact. When you think of these tools, most people limit their ideas to the physical flyers and posters they come across in the neighborhood. This is a great idea. However, you can also create the same for online use, share them on social media, emails, or post them on your website. There are endless ways of using flyers and posters for promotional purposes, which makes them quite a spectacle in marketing and advertising today.

These tools have remained iconic in promotion over the years because of their dynamic graphic approach. For decades, companies have used flyers and posters to promote events, sales, or even invite people to a cause. In a world where your chances of coming across flyers and posters is as high as meeting a stranger, it is not easy to come up with designs that will attract your audience and keep them hooked. Bearing that in mind, let's look at some useful tips to help you design some amazing promotional content for your business.

- Be the audience

The first mistake that many people make when designing posters and flyers is to think about their own perspective. You have to change your vantage point. Put yourself in the audience. Assume you are the customer – what would you want to see? What message would attract you to the business? If you are unable to do this, it might help to think about one of your favorite businesses, for example. What is it that draws you to them? How do you find their posters?

If you can, brainstorm with someone and share your ideas with them. This is a good idea because you will learn so much from them. The design is not for you, it is for your customers. You have to be very careful when considering the kind of information you put in the flyers, and the mode of communication. Cartoon action figure designs are a good way to attract children, which means their parents will have no alternative but to bring them to your store.

- Call to action

Designs without a call to action are useless. A call to action is that one thing you want the customer to do once they see your poster or flyer. Do you need them to sign up, make a purchase or contact you? This is something so important yet you will come across many flyers and posters that don't have it. A call to action gives your design a purpose.

Assume you have been in the business for years, and you need to know more about your audience's views about your business, you would need honest reviews. Your flyers and posters should incorporate this message. Do not scream it out, however. Be subtle about it, but make it prominent.

While at it, be careful not to confuse your audience. We have seen many flyers and posters that contain more than one call to action. There's a common unwritten rule in web design that your website must load in less than three seconds. If someone has to wait longer than three seconds to load, they will probably move on to something else. The same applies to your flyer design. People should get the point in a few seconds, or they will be lost and miss the point altogether.

- Colors, themes, and fonts

Creativity in design will go a long way in helping you achieve your promotional objectives for your flyers and posters. You have thousands of color schemes, themes and font styles that you can use for your design. The problem here is that this variety can leave you spoilt for choice. This is the kind of nightmare that many designers have to deal with.

Given all the choices available, at times it is wise to go simple. If you are undecided, start with the basic options. Basic primary colors are a good place to begin. Once you have the work in process, you can tinker around with different hues, layouts, and design elements.

You can also use your business brand as a guiding principle to determine what the best color choice is for your flyers. Focus on the content flow. Using more than two fonts in your design will probably create chaos in your production. If you are design is targeting kids, primary colors are always a good option. If you are targeting a professional audience, you have to be bold in your design. White or black are always a good way to deliver that classy professional touch.

- Message clarity

Get to the point. Like the call to action, your message should be clear to the audience in a few seconds. To make this easier, use some visual cues to help the audience. Choose the right graphics, place the intended message in the right position. You want the message to be clear and unmissable. If you want the customer to contact you, they don't have to keep looking for your contact information. Put it in a section where they can see it.

While you work on this, remember value addition is important too. Indeed, you need the customer to get in touch. The question you should answer is why? Why should they contact you? Just dropping your contact information is not good enough. Show them what they benefit from contacting you and your inbox and phones will be blowing up.

- Maintain professionalism

Professionalism is not a preserve for the big businesses. As long as you are asking people to invest their time and resources in your business, they expect you to be professional about it too. Professionalism in flyer and poster design involves a lot of things. Start with the photos you choose, for example. Use high quality photos. Invest in a good camera, or hire an expert to handle production for you.

Today you can go online and use high quality stock photos to enhance your design. At the same time, remember that stock photos might not always be a good idea because some people feel they lack the personal touch or they fall short in originality. Whichever option you choose, always remember that a professional design is a great way to enhance your business profile.

- Creative distribution

It is pointless to design amazing flyers and posters when you cannot distribute them effectively. The design process doesn't end when you print your content, you must be creative in distribution too. There are lots of avenues you can use for this. Think about the audience because it will affect your budget too. If you have a large audience, your costs will be higher if you choose mail distribution. Instead, online distribution will cut costs, and even help you reach a wider audience.

If you choose to send the flyers through email, don't just upload the flyer and send. Reconsider the design. Test it on a temporary email to see how it displays on different browsers. Try it on your phone and tablet too. Whatever you do, make sure the final copy you send to your customers is perfect.

Tips for Effective Distribution

Your design is perfect, the message is clear, everything about your flyers and posters meets your promotional objectives. You have them printed and ready for distribution. This is the last step in bringing your customers closer to the business. Don't give up now, you're almost there. For all the input you have put into this project, it would be sad to fail at the last step.

Distribution is just as important as the design process. You have the message ready, you just need to get it to the right people. You have to be creative in the distribution process to ensure your flyers get to the right people. We have seen several cases where flyers are strewn all over the streets, but no one pays attention to them. This is no more than littering and is an environmental nuisance. You might as well find yourself in a fit with the law. Just as creative and precise as you have been during the design process, you must follow the same procedure in distribution.

The following are some useful distribution tips that will help you get your flyers to the right people:

- Send to mailboxes

You can personally send the flyers to customer mailboxes. This is good if you have a niche market and you know who your target audience is. If this is not the case, you could end up with a tedious delivery process, sending flyers to every mailbox in your neighborhood.

Rather than going through all that trouble, why don't you email them instead? email addresses? In one email, you can reach millions of inboxes in seconds. Better yet, share it on your social media platform and you will reach just as many people in a short time.

- Package inserts

Package inserts are a good way to send flyers. In many cases, you can do it blindly and hope to get some responses. Many times, you purchase your daily newspaper and find flyers inside. These have nothing to do with the newspaper, but they will still get your attention. Perhaps there's a new store that opened up in your neighborhood that is giving away insane discounts. You will probably check it out when you are running some errands, as will many other people. The flyers could also remind you of a purchase you have been putting off for a while, whereby you now end up completing your purchase as a result.

- Business partners

You don't have to go it all alone. You can consult other business partners around and ask them to display your flyers in their premises. This is a good idea if you have a good relationship with them already. They can display your flyers on their counters, and in return, you do the same for them when their time comes.

Talk to the management of the local hospitals, hotels, restaurants and any other public place where you are bound to get lots of human traffic. This kind of partnership is good and will go a long way in strengthening your ties with other local businesses, thereby expanding your network.

- Event distribution

Another good place for you to distribute flyers is at events. Luckily, there's never a shortage of events in most towns. As you look for events where you can distribute flyers, think about the audience too. Having flyers in the wrong place can lead to ridicule and make you the laughing stock. It's like going to an atheist event to distribute flyers for a christian fellowship program.

Some event managers can allow you to have a stand at their reception for your business. Here you can do more than just share your flyers, you can briefly discuss your business with the audience. Answer some questions, ask some of your own. The engagement will prop your promotional strategy. If you have some goodies to distribute, have them prepared and packed in neat presentable goodie bags alongside the flyers.

- Timely distribution

Timing is another important factor you must consider. Look at it this way, flyers are paper prints, other than those you distribute online. Paper prints generally do not have a long shelf life. If you are distributing them outdoors, their lifespan is considerably shorter thanks to the weather. In light of this, consider the weather before you start pinning them all over town. It would be unfortunate for you to pin all your flyers only for the rain to undo your work minutes after you are done.

Apart from the weather, think about the seasons too. If you are preparing flyers around Easter or Halloween, rest assured you are fighting for space with a lot of businesses. Your flyers might end up in a very crowded place they become insignificant and irrelevant. So, what should you do, give up? No. The holidays are a good time to send flyers out. You just need to change tact. Since most stores are busy, this would be a good time to talk to other store owners about displaying your flyers on their counters.

- The delivery method

Your preferred mode of delivery will also affect results. Are you handing out flyers directly to customers, delivering them door-to-door or putting them up in high traffic areas? Whichever method you prefer, it will affect your distribution plan in some way.

How many flyers do you have? How long do you plan to distribute them? Do you have permission to distribute flyers randomly? You have to consider the policies governing flyer distribution practices in your neighborhood before you begin.

- Build a reliable distribution team

Distributing flyers can be a gruesome affair if you are doing it on your own. Consider asking for help. You can reach out to family and friends, and depending on the size of your business, you might even hire a team of experts to assist. Whichever case, make sure your distribution team is highly motivated and well compensated to do the job. You need a team that is as enthusiastic about distributing the flyers as you are about your business. It would help to make sure they know more about your business too, so they can answer some questions if someone needs clarity.

Printed in Great Britain
by Amazon

54207944R00076